CONFIDENT WITNESS —
CHANGING WORLD

THE GOSPEL AND OUR CULTURE SERIES

A series to foster the missional encounter of the gospel
with North American culture

Craig Van Gelder

General Editor

• •

Volumes now available

Darrell L. Guder, et al., *Missional Church: A Vision for the
Sending of the Church in North America*

George R. Hunsberger and Craig Van Gelder, editors, *The Church
between Gospel and Culture: The Emerging Mission in North America*

George R. Hunsberger, *Bearing the Witness of the Spirit:
Lesslie Newbigin's Theology of Cultural Plurality*

Craig Van Gelder, editor, *Confident Witness — Changing World:
Rediscovering the Gospel in North America*

Forthcoming

Darrell L. Guder, *The Continuing Conversion of the Church*

CONFIDENT WITNESS — CHANGING WORLD

Rediscovering the Gospel in North America

Edited by

Craig Van Gelder

WILLIAM B. EERDMANS PUBLISHING COMPANY
GRAND RAPIDS, MICHIGAN / CAMBRIDGE, U.K.

255 Jefferson Ave. S.E., Grand Rapids, Michigan 49503 /
P.O. Box 163, Cambridge CB3 9PU U.K.

Printed in the United States of America

04 03 02 01 00 99   7 6 5 4 3 2 1

Library of Congress Cataloging-in-Publication Data

Confident witness, changing world : rediscovering the Gospel in
  North America / edited by Craig Van Gelder.
     p.   cm.
    Proceedings of a conference held in 1996.
    Includes bibliographical references.
    ISBN 0-8028-4655-6 (paper : alk. paper)
    1. Missions — North America. 2. Christianity and culture.
3. Missions — Theory. 4. Evangelistic work — North America.
5. North America — Religion — 20th century. I. Van Gelder, Craig.
BV2760.C53   1999
266'.0097 — dc21   99-12913
                CIP

Contents

II. Understanding the Church in the North American Mission Context

III. Understanding the Gospel in the North American Mission Context

Contents

Epilogue

Contributors

Stephen Bevans Stephen Bevans is a priest of the Roman Catholic Society of the Divine Word (SVD) and was a missionary to the Philippines from 1972 to 1981. He is currently Professor of Doctrinal Theology at Catholic Theological Union at Chicago and director of the Chicago Center for Global Ministries. Among his publications is *Models of Contextual Theology*.

George D. Beukema George D. Beukema served for many years as pastor at the Church of the Good News (Reformed Church in America), an urban, multicultural congregation on Chicago's north side. Dr. Beukema currently serves as Faculty Associate at the Chicago Metropolitan Center and as adjunct faculty at Western Theological Seminary, Holland, Michigan.

James Brownson James Brownson is academic dean and James and Jean Cook Professor of New Testament at Western Theological Seminary in Holland, Michigan. He recently has completed four years of service as moderator of his denomination's commission on theology, and is the author of *Speaking the Truth in Love,* published by Trinity Press International.

William R. Burrows William R. Burrows holds an STL from the Gregorian and a Ph.D. from the University of Chicago. He served as a missionary in Papua New Guinea for five years teaching theology, and for seven years assisted in an inner-city African-American parish in Chicago. Since 1989 he has been managing editor at Orbis Books.

Mary Lou Codman-Wilson Mary Lou Codman-Wilson received her Ph.D. from Garrett Northwestern in Psychological Anthropology. She has served as Adjunct Faculty in Cross-culture Theological Education at Garrett Seminary and as the editor of a cross-cultural magazine, *Bridges*. She is presently Associate Pastor of St. Andrew United Methodist Church in Carol Stream, Illinois.

Marva J. Dawn Marva Dawn is a theologian, musician, and educator with Christians Equipped for Ministry of Vancouver, Washington, and Adjunct Professor of Spiritual Theology at Regent College in Vancouver, British Columbia. She holds a Ph.D. in Christian Ethics and the Scriptures from the University of Notre Dame. Her books include *Is It a Lost Cause?: Having the Heart of God for the Church's Children, To Walk and Not Faint: A Month of Meditations from Isaiah 40, Keeping the Sabbath Wholly: Ceasing, Resting, Embracing, Feasting,* and *Reaching Out without Dumbing Down: A Theology of Worship for the Turn-of-the Century Culture.*

Dan Devadatta Dan Devadatta holds an M.Div. from Calvin Theological Seminary. He has served as a pastor in new church development in the Christian Reformed Church, and has developed a specialty in the area of intercultural ministry and diversity training. Since 1994 he has served as Director of Recruitment and Financial Aid at Calvin Seminary.

Paul C. Dinolfo Paul C. Dinolfo is the senior coordinator of the Work of Christ Community in East Lansing, Michigan. This is an ecumenical covenant community that includes Roman Catholics, Lutherans, Evangelical Protestants, and Eastern Orthodox. Begun in 1973 by a group of university students, the Work of Christ currently has 180 adult and 230 children members.

Isaac Fokuo Isaac Fokuo is an ordained minister in the Presbyterian Church in Ghana. He has served in various capacities, including pastor, Presbytery Executive, and Secretary for Interchurch and Ecumenical Relations of the Presbyterian Church of Ghana.

Robert Fortner   Robert Fortner is Professor of Communication Arts & Sciences at Calvin College in Grand Rapids, Michigan, where he has taught in the telecommunications program since 1989. He has published two books on international communications issues and is actively involved in teaching missionary organizations around the world to address issues of culture and media.

Douglas John Hall   Douglas John Hall is Professor Emeritus of Christian Theology at the Faculty of Religious Studies of McGill University, Montreal. He is the author of twenty-five books, including a trilogy on Christian Theology in a North American Context *(Thinking the Faith; Professing the Faith; Confessing the Faith)* and, most recently, a work on Christian Apologetics titled *Why Christian? For Those on the Edge of Faith.*

Walter C. Hobbs   Walter C. Hobbs served for several years as Director of Institutional Research and for thirty-two years as faculty (Higher Education) at the State University of New York at Buffalo before his retirement in 1993. He holds a Ph.D. in sociology, a J.D. (law), and an honorary LL.D. (Houghton College, N.Y., 1988).

Jon M. Huegli   Jon M. Huegli is a Director of Church Consultants Group, located in Ann Arbor, Michigan. For twenty-five years he has consulted with local church leaders, district officers, and national church officers in North America, the Pacific Rim, and Western and Eastern Europe. His consulting work focuses on issues of organizational structure, leadership development, and change.

Stanley K. Inouye   Stan Inouye is President and Founder of Iwa. He has served as an ethnic ministry consultant to many churches, denominations, and ministry organizations. He has been an adjunct instructor at Fuller Theological Seminary, has held national and international positions with Campus Crusade for Christ, and has directed the Asian American Christian Fellowship (AACF).

Christopher B. Kaiser   Christopher B. Kaiser is Professor of Historical and Systemic Theology at Western Theological Seminary in Holland, Michigan, where he has taught since 1976. He has a Ph.D. in Astro-Geophysics from the University of Colorado and a Ph.D. in

Theology from the University of Edinburgh. His published works include *The Doctrine of God, Creation and the History of Science,* and *Creational Theology and the History of Physical Science.*

Mary Jo Leddy Mary Jo Leddy is the Director of Romero House Community for Refugees in Toronto, and adjunct professor at Regis College, University of Toronto. She holds a Ph.D. from the University of Toronto in the philosophy of religion. She has authored many books and articles and is a frequent radio and TV commentator on human rights and religious concerns.

Patricia Lloyd-Sidle Patricia Lloyd-Sidle is an ordained pastor in the Presbyterian Church (USA), and has served various congregations including two in Uruguay. At present she is the Coordinator of Global Awareness and Involvement in the Worldwide Ministries Division of the PC (USA), where her responsibilities include oversight of global people-to-people programs.

Richard Mouw Richard Mouw is a philosopher, scholar, and author who has taught for many years in the area of social philosophy and ethics. He joined the faculty of Fuller Theological Seminary in 1985 as Professor of Christian Philosophy and Ethics; since 1993 he has served as the president of that seminary. His most recent books include *The God Who Commands, Uncommon Decency,* and *Consulting the Faithful.*

Alan J. Roxburgh Alan Roxburgh has served since 1994 as pastor of West Vancouver Baptist Church in West Vancouver, British Columbia. He holds a Th.M. in philosophical theology and a D.Min. from Northern Baptist Seminary in urban missiology. Previously Alan directed the Center for Mission and Evangelism at McMaster Divinity College in Toronto after serving as an inner-city pastor for nine years. He has published *Reaching a New Generation* and *The Missionary Congregation: Leadership and Liminality.*

Clinton Stockwell Clinton Stockwell is a faculty member for the Chicago Metropolitan Center, an urban internship program for college students, where he teaches The Metropolitan Seminar, an introduction to the city. He has a Ph.D. in urban history from the University of Illinois at Chicago.

Contributors

Craig Van Gelder Craig Van Gelder holds a Ph.D. in Missions from Southwest Baptist Theological Seminary and a Ph.D. in Urban Studies from the University of Texas, Arlington. He has worked as a church consultant for many years, and taught at Calvin Theological Seminary for ten years as Professor of Domestic Missiology. Presently he is Professor of Congregational Mission at Luther Seminary in St. Paul, Minnesota.

Lee Wyatt Lee Wyatt is a Presbyterian pastor serving St. Andrew Presbyterian Church in Longview, Texas. He holds a Master of Theological Studies degree in Biblical Studies from Columbia Theological Seminary in Decatur, Georgia, and an M.Div. from Louisville Presbyterian Theological Seminary.

Introduction

"This gospel and culture discussion is interesting, but can you translate this for us into more practical terms?" This is a rather common question in conversations within the Gospel and Our Culture Network. It has surfaced regularly over the past decade as pastors and educators together have sought to understand the church's role in our North American mission context. The challenge is real. How do you make the gospel come alive and help the church become relevant as you seek to critique the whole of our culture within which the gospel and church are located? The task is complex. On the one hand, there is always a tendency to slip into a philosophical analysis of Western culture that is too complicated for people working on the front lines of ministry to use in relating to their work. On the other hand, there is a tendency for those working on the front lines of ministry to look for workable programs and methods without always thinking carefully about the cultural assumptions embedded in such approaches.

In 1996, The Gospel and Our Culture Network conducted a major conference titled "Confident Witness — Changing World: Rediscovering the Gospel in North America."[1] The format of the conference included a series of plenary addresses and workshops pre-

1. Funding support for this conference was provided through a grant from The Pew Charitable Trusts. Persons serving on the conference planning team included: Ben Beaird, Judy Bos, Dan Devadatta, Pete Hammond, Walter Hobbs, George Hunsberger, Patricia Lloyd-Sidle, Mary Mott, David Risseeuw, Alan Roxburgh, Jean Stromberg, Craig Van Gelder, Lee Wyatt, and Scott Young.

sented by persons who, though academically trained, were all skilled practitioners in doing ministry on the front lines. The purpose was to "translate" the gospel and culture discussion into terms that would make this conversation more readily available to pastors and church leaders. While the conference itself was successful in this regard, it was felt that much of this work could serve a broader audience if these materials were available in the form of a book. This volume represents that work.

This volume, *Confident Witness — Changing World: Rediscovering the Gospel in North America,* is the fourth in a series published by Eerdmans that has grown out of the work of the Gospel and Our Culture Network. The essays in the first volume, *The Church between Gospel and Culture: The Emerging Mission in North America,* provide the reader with a discerning analysis of the issues facing the church in North America today. The interrelationships of culture, gospel, and church are explored at length, where biblical, theological, historical, and contemporary reflections inform the discussion. The second volume, *Missional Church: A Vision for the Sending of the Church in North America,* is a more focused biblical and theological work addressing the missionary nature of the church as it lives out its life within our present North American context. The third volume is a monograph by George R. Hunsberger, *Bearing the Witness of the Spirit: Lesslie Newbigin's Theology of Cultural Plurality,* which serves as an interpretive framework for understanding Newbigin's writings as they relate to the issues of gospel, church, and culture. In many ways this present volume, though intended to stand alone as a useful resource, serves as a companion reader to these other works, especially the first. In particular, it provides practical examples on how the church can live out specific application of the analysis and theses presented in the first two volumes.

Themes Developed in This Volume

The present volume is divided into five sections. Each section is introduced by a plenary address given at the 1996 conference, and is followed by a series of three articles written by persons who made workshop presentations at the conference. The materials in each section work as a unit in providing the reader with both analysis and application in addressing specific issues. The first section addresses our changed context. We are now living in a changed social location, what might be described as both postmodern and post-Christian. The articles in this section help the reader understand this changed cultural context from the perspective of Christian faith.

The second section addresses the changed position of the church in light of this changed context. Congregations today are becoming increasingly marginalized from the broader culture, but instead of seeing this as a loss to be grieved, these articles offer insights for seeing the location of the church on the margins as an opportunity for gospel and faith to become both more real and more relevant. The third section addresses our understanding of the gospel in light of our changed context and a marginalized church in this context. If faith is to become more real and the church more relevant, then it is critical that we hear the gospel again on its own terms. These articles offer a number of perspectives for hearing the gospel as good news in our postmodern, post-Christian culture.

The fourth section addresses how the gospel as good news in this changed context translates into applied ministry in the life of the church. Growing out of the personal experiences of the authors, these articles illustrate new forms of giving confident witness and fresh approaches to demonstrating Christian faithfulness. The fifth and final section addresses the issue of what the church needs to become as it continues to live into the fullness of our changed North American context. While the images of what the church will look like are still forming, these articles make it clear that the journey we are traveling toward the future is filled with both challenges and rewards. As an epilogue to the entire work, the reader is provided with a closing address given by Mary Jo Leddy at the 1996 conference. In it, she offers a helpful summary of many of the themes developed in the other essays presented in this volume, especially the theme of the church learning to live as a parallel community within the broader culture.

Using This Volume for Ministry

There are a number of ways in which this volume might be used in the church to assist leaders in doing ministry. These include:

1. *Studying Individual Articles* — Church leaders will find it helpful to use individual articles from this volume as a springboard for group discussion in a Sunday School class or training event.
2. *Studying Sections of Articles* — Church leaders will find it useful to focus on all the articles in one section as a block of material for study, discussion, and application of a congregation's work in this area of ministry.
3. *Companion Reader* — Church educators will find it helpful to have students read various articles and/or sections of this volume as a companion to the first two publications by GOCN *The Church between Gospel and Culture: The Emerging Mission in North America* and *Missional Church: A Vision for the Sending of the Church in North America.*
4. *Text on Applied Ministry* — Church educators will find this volume useful to assign as a text for courses that deal with applied ministry.

The challenge before all of us is real — "How are we to live faithfully as the church offering confident witness in a changing world?" The conversation carried on within the Gospel and Our Culture Network has attempted to provide helpful resources for answering this question. It is our prayer that this present volume will be of great usefulness to congregations and church leaders in helping them carry on this conversation within their own ministries.

SECTION I

Understanding the North American Context as Mission Field

Today North America needs to be treated as a mission field in the same way that we in the West have approached much of the rest of the world for the past several centuries. Critical to making this shift in perspective is to develop the skills and tools necessary to function as missionaries in this context. This section provides the reader with an overview of the challenges involved in going through this change in perspective, along with some practical helps in learning to read, diagnose, and exegete our postmodern and post-Christian cultural context.

"The North American Christian community today is in a missionary location." Thus begins the article by Richard Mouw. His thesis is clear — the cultural context of North America has been going through fundamental changes over the past few decades. These changes now require congregations to think increasingly of their location in their community in missionary terms, and to utilize missionary tools for developing ministry for these communities. These tools include: developing skills in diagnosing the community being served by a congregation; using a missionary methodology to reach people in that community; and developing missionary sensitivities and vision among the members in approaching persons in their community.

Our present North American culture is increasingly producing within all of us a fragmentation of values, views, and behaviors. It is hard to know who we are when we are forced to live in so many worlds at once. But the gospel calls us to wholeness in relating to all of life in an integrated manner. In the second article in this section, Chris Kaiser provides readers with a helpful perspective on understanding the postmodern fragmentation that impacts all of us. He then draws on biblical foundations and the work of sociologist Peter Berger to offer some tools and approaches for Christians to learn in order to live as whole persons, where they are able to translate gospel faithfulness into practical living.

Most persons today are familiar with the concept that we are now living in an "information age." However, many of us have not reflected on the ways in which this information comes to us. Bob Fortner, in the third article in this section, helps us unpack what stands behind this concept of the information age in relation to the rise of digital culture, with its electronic formatting and dissemination of information. With skill and clarity, he introduces the reader to the full range of media that are working to reshape us within this digital culture. With the same skill and clarity, he offers some helpful suggestions for thinking through ways in which the gospel can and should function in relation to these media.

Movies are a powerful tool for shaping people's perceptions of reality in our image-driven culture. In the final article in this section, Craig Van Gelder provides a framework for reading postmodern culture through the medium of movies. He does this by first introducing the character of postmodern culture. This is followed by an overview of the rise of cinema and the movie industry, which shows how movies have been used to present/represent particular worldviews — most recently a postmodern one. He provides examples of recent movies that help enable us to read postmodern culture through this medium, and he closes with suggestions on how the gospel can be proclaimed as good news to persons shaped by this new postmodern culture.

The Missionary Location of the North American Churches

RICHARD J. MOUW

The North America Christian community today is in a missionary location. This is not an original thesis with me; it is elaborated, for instance, with intellectual and theological depth by the authors of the essays in *The Church between Gospel and Culture: The Emerging Mission in North America,* edited by George Hunsberger and Craig Van Gelder.[1] The essays in that volume expound Lesslie Newbigin's important call for the missionary encounter of the gospel with Western culture, addressing especially how we are to contextualize that call here in North America.[2] My purpose in this essay is not to rehearse their formulations, but rather to explore some of the implications entailed in that shift of our awareness. I see three elements that are particularly critical to our rethinking: we need to take seriously the fact of our missionary location; we need to develop a missionary methodology in this context; and we need to cultivate missionary sensitivities while operating with a missionary vision in North America.

---

1. George R. Hunsberger and Craig Van Gelder, *The Church between Gospel and Culture* (Grand Rapids: Eerdmans, 1996).
2. Lesslie Newbigin, *Foolishness to the Greeks: The Gospel and Western Culture* (Grand Rapids: Eerdmans, 1986).

Taking Seriously Our Missionary Location

This shift in perspective will require ever more serious reflection on the missionary context in which we find ourselves. Certainly, we are now more explicitly wrestling with themes and issues that in the past were almost exclusively the work of missionaries who went to other countries and cultures. In recent decades, for example, the "world religions" have found a foothold, and even a home, in North America. The number of mosques in our cities, to refer only to Islam, has grown in fantastic terms in the last decade or so. But in addition to the arrival of world religions, we are also experiencing an equally important phenomenon, namely, what has been termed the "reenchantment" of Western culture. In the nineteenth century, people like Max Weber and Auguste Comte argued that we had finally succeeded in disenchanting Western culture. By that, they meant that the emergence of a scientific worldview had finally, for all practical purposes, succeeded in exorcising our world of all the angels, demons, occult powers, and deities that had held the fascination of earlier ages.

But in recent decades there are signs that we have begun to experience the reenchantment of our culture. Angels are all over the place these days. Occult practices have become very prominent. Folk magic and astrology pervade our context, and not just among the socially marginal communities where such beliefs have always existed as a type of subculture. Such beliefs are popular even among the cultural elites. It is not unusual these days to find university professors who practice pre-Christian goddess religions, therapists who employ shamanic techniques, or computer programmers who consult their astrological charts. Practices of this sort make it important for us to reevaluate our situation: ours is a missionary location.

There are also old and long-ignored reasons for thinking of ourselves as being in a missionary context. David Bosch rightly argued that we must abandon the distinction, a heritage of the old "Christendom" model, which held that when we go to other cultures we do missions, and when we engage our own culture we do evangelism.[3] Wilbert Shenk has argued recently that the missionary posture is the

3. David J. Bosch, *Transforming Mission: Paradigm Shifts in Theology of Mission* (Maryknoll, N.Y.: Orbis Books, 1991), pp. 9-11.

normal mode of presence for the church in all times and all places.[4] Missionaries know that the complex questions relating Christianity and culture are not adequately addressed by Niebuhr's fivefold "Christ and culture" typology.[5] The sacred grove, the totem, oppressive patriarchal structures, child sacrifice: such issues require a very concrete response that takes full account of the nuances, tensions, and ambiguities of trying to clarify and address cultural issues to make clear the gospel of Jesus Christ. There is evidence that many of the missionaries got it right, more often than not, in terms of unpacking the complexities of how the gospel relates to culture. In many ways, these persons were inspired by God in their work. We have much to learn from them, specifically as we think about how to be God's people in our own North American context.

There are obstacles, however, that must be overcome in trying to take our missionary location seriously. Let me address two such obstacles. One is that many people in today's Christian community are too fond of the culture that makes up our missionary location. The other is that many people in the Christian community are too disdainful of this culture.

The fondness that many Christians have for the dominant patterns of North American culture, and especially the expressions of popular culture, is well documented by scholars who have offered profound critiques of the Christendom model, of American civil religion, and of cultural Christianity as we've experienced it here in North America.[6] But we need also to think about the disdain that many Christian people have had for popular culture in North America. There has been an adamant refusal on the part of many theologians and other Christian leaders to think charitably, or even empathetically, about popular culture. Thus there has been a real gap between the cultural elites in the Christian community and the ordinary folk, a gap that has often kept leaders from communicating

4. Wilbert Shenk, "The Culture of Modernity as a Missionary Challenge," in Hunsberger and Van Gelder, *The Church between Gospel and Culture,* pp. 69-78.

5. H. Richard Niebuhr, *Christ and Culture* (New York: Harper and Row, 1951).

6. E.g., Colleen McDannell, *Material Christianity: Religion and Popular Culture in America* (New Haven, Conn.: Yale University Press, 1995), pp. 1-17 *et passim.*

adequately with people in their accustomed social and spiritual context.

Colleen McDannell's *Material Christianity: Religion and Popular Culture in America*[7] is a fascinating study, not only because Professor McDannell has an instinct for telling cultural images, but especially for her insight on how we are to understand popular religious culture in North America. She is convinced that approaches to popular culture, and especially religious culture, systematically distort the reality they are studying because they characteristically fail to attend carefully to the meanings that those expressions of culture actually have for the people who use those artifacts. Her observations are confirmed by a look at much of the commentary offered by intellectuals regarding the so-called "Christian Right." Every couple of years some journalist attending the Christian Booksellers Association writes an article about all the strange things on display there. This commentary often provides clear evidence for what McDannell sees as the widespread — and, she is convinced, much too simple-minded — conviction on the part of intellectuals "that the material dimension of Christianity results from ignorance, superficial commercialism, status competition, and the desire of institutional churches and 'The Culture Industry' to manipulate people."[8]

Similar attitudes hold, I would argue, not just toward religious popular culture in particular, but toward popular culture in general, among many of our Christian leaders. The cultural elites in the Christian community have often been guilty of the same kind of carelessness which two recent anthropologists, George Marcus and Michael Fisher, have ascribed to their own colleagues in cultural anthropology: "they are careless precisely about that which would be sacred to the anthropologists in considering other cultures — indigenous commentaries. For the most part, anthropologists have taken the job of reflecting back upon ourselves much less seriously than that of probing other cultures."[9]

I believe that a similar carelessness is observable in the intellectual leadership of the Christian community as well. Many of us have

7. See n. 6 for bibliographic information.
8. McDannell, *Material Christianity*, pp. 271-72.
9. George E. Marcus and Michael M. J. Fisher, *Anthropology as Cultural Critique* (Chicago: University of Chicago Press, 1986), p. 111.

failed to take seriously the job of reflecting back upon ourselves as a Christian community in North America. Or to the extent that we have done so, we have gone about it somewhat carelessly compared to the probing we have made of other cultures. Our cross-cultural reflections on North American culture have, in fact, been rather limited, and often guided by biased sensitivities. This will not do in the light of our missionary location as a North American church. It is important for us to think carefully about how we can correct this situation, especially with reference to the broad patterns of indigenous popular culture in North America.

Using a Missionary Methodology

My second point is that we are in need of developing a methodology for our mission work in North America. As I look for biblical resources for missionary methodology, I am very impressed with the way in which the Apostle Paul made his case on Mars Hill. The basics of the story in Acts 17 are familiar. Paul meets a group of Greek philosophers, Stoics and Epicureans, who invite him to present his perspective on reality. "Men of Athens!" he begins, "I see that in every way you are very religious. For as I walked around and looked carefully at your objects of worship, I even found an altar with this inscription, 'TO AN UNKNOWN GOD.' Now what you worship as something unknown I am going to proclaim to you" (verse 23). He proceeds to quote some of their poets: "For in him we live and move and have our being," and "We are God's offspring" (verse 28).

   This approach allows the apostle to establish some type of philosophical bond with them, before introducing the unique elements of the Christian gospel: the incarnation and atoning work of Jesus Christ, the coming judgment, and the resurrection of the body. And he clearly got through to them with these more "offensive" elements of the message: "When they heard about the resurrection of the dead, some of them sneered" (verse 32), the writer says, observing that only a few believed on the basis of what Paul said there.

   I am aware of objections that some have offered to the approach Paul took. One such objection is that Paul was theologically misguided. The pagan philosophers, the argument goes, were right to sneer at what he had to say. Paul shouldn't have assumed that you can establish a common ground. He shouldn't have looked for shared elements in their respective worldviews. He should simply have confronted them directly with a message that stands in radical opposition to the views of these Greek philosophers.

A second kind of objection suggests that Paul used an approach that was methodologically misguided. It is not surprising, according to this view, that few believed: Paul moved too quickly to the unique themes of the Christian message. He should have established more solidarity, more commonality with them. He went too fast into a thoroughgoing, confrontational-type message.

I want to take the position that Paul got it just right. I think he presents to us a profoundly biblical and practical missionary methodological model. He did four things, as I see it. First of all, he had studied the Athenian perspective on reality. He knew their writings and was conversant with their poetry. Second, he had discerned an underlining spiritual motif, observing that, "I see that in every way you are very religious." Third, he looked for positive points of contact within their worldview, noting that even their own poets had said, "For in him we live and move and have our being," and that "We are God's offspring." And finally, he invited them to find their fulfillment in the person and work of Jesus Christ.

This is the kind of approach evident in the work of many great missionaries and in the writings of many great missionary thinkers. For example, Bishop Stephen Neill, in *Christian Faith and Other Faiths,* concludes his discussion of Hinduism in this way: "The Christian must not be surprised if, between now and the end of this century, the work of Christian witness in India becomes more difficult than it has been for a century. He must be prepared to face the possibility that the greater part of his work must be from within Hinduism, in putting questions to the Hindu and helping him to understand himself better. . . . All the time he will be attempting to help the Hindu to see the radical unsatisfactoriness of all the answers that have been given to his questions, and so to point him to the One in Whom those questions can receive their all-sufficient answer, the Lord Jesus Christ."[10]

This observation, a profound description of a missionary meth-

---

10. Stephen Neill, *Christian Faith and Other Faiths* (London: Oxford University Press, 1961), p. 98.

odology and attitude, ought to be generalized. I have tried my own hand at this on occasion, attempting to apply this methodology to things I observe in my cultural surroundings. Several years ago, I wrote a book that began with this anecdote: "On one snowy afternoon in a West Michigan shopping mall, during the Christmas season I received a very profound theological message from Perry Como."[11] I was at a Sears store, searching up and down the aisles somewhat desperately for inspiration for Christmas gifts. I was only vaguely aware that Christmas music was being piped in over the loudspeaker system and that Perry Como was singing carols.

All of a sudden I heard a line that brought me to a halt: "The hopes and fears of all the years are met in Thee tonight." I stopped and looked around the store, and thought, "In what sense and in what way are the hopes and fears of all the years met in this store tonight by the babe who was born in Bethlehem? What about the child looking longingly at the bicycle. Is that hope met in the coming of Jesus Christ? How about the woman who is trying to look cheerful, even though she is desperately worried that her husband will come home tonight drunk again from this year's Christmas party, and beat her up like he did last year? Or what about the man who is thinking of trying on a jacket, but knows that he has been eating too many Christmas cookies and is a little afraid that the size he always wears won't button correctly?" I think that we need to reflect carefully and think deeply about the ways in which the hopes and fears that we encounter in shopping malls are met in the babe who was born in Bethlehem.

There is a more profound example of such missionary reflection and thinking in Don Richardson's best-seller, *Peace Child*.[12] The Richardsons were sent as missionaries to the Sawi people in Netherlands, New Guinea. In the particular tribal setting where they found themselves, they were the first people representing the Western world that these folks had ever experienced. But in presenting the gospel to the Sawi people, the Richardsons ran into an important philosophical obstacle: the Sawi people celebrated treachery. That is, they celebrated those of their own tribal group who successfully befriended a

11. Richard J. Mouw, *Distorted Truth: What Every Christian Needs to Know about the Battle for the Mind* (San Francisco: Harper and Row, 1989), p. 1.

12. Don Richardson, *Peace Child* (Glendale, Calif.: Gospel Light Publications, 1974).

person of another tribe in order ultimately to betray and kill that person — those who were able, as they put it, to "fatten him with friendship for an unsuspecting slaughter," just as you would fatten up the pig for a special feast.[13]

The Richardsons discovered this element of the Sawi culture when they told the gospel story to the Sawi people and were astonished to hear the Sawi people acclaim Judas as the hero of the story: "That was a true pig-fattener!"[14] The Richardsons began to wonder whether it was even possible to communicate the good news to the Sawi culture. But they prayed, waited, and observed their hosts, and in due time a solution to the dilemma came from within the Sawi culture itself. One morning they awoke to find preparations occurring for something they had never seen before. The people said that they were going to engage in the rare exchange of "the peace child." In the Sawi culture, if one tribe wanted to make peace with another tribe, they would choose a healthy boy baby to be brought up by the other tribe. As long as each of the boys lived, the tribes remained at peace. Assuring the continued life of the peace child was held to be a sacred duty for all. But in a situation where infant mortality rates were very high, the resultant peace was always a fragile one.

Here the Richardsons found an entree to preach the gospel story of the God who gave his Son, who died and rose and lives forever, and whose promise is peace. Isaiah's message came alive in a new way here: a child has been born to us whose very name is Prince of Peace. Jesus is the great peace child, and of the increase of his peace there will be no end.

Clearly this speaks volumes about the value of a missionary methodology that observes the customs, looks for deeper motifs, rejects those that stand in radical opposition to the gospel, and patiently waits until some kind of opening for the gospel appears. Such an opening is required so one can speak words that are genuinely words of good news to a people who do not yet believe.

It is precisely this kind of work that needs to be done in relation to our own North American culture.

13. *Peace Child*, p. 179.
14. *Peace Child*, p. 178.

Developing Missionary Sensitivities and Vision

This leads to the third point I want to address, namely, our need to cultivate missionary sensibilities for the culture in which we live. The wonderful Vatican II document *Gaudium et Spes* articulates a place to begin: "The joy and hope, the grief and anguish of the men of our time, especially of those who are poor or afflicted in any way, are the joy and hope, the grief and anguish of the followers of Christ as well. Nothing that is genuinely human fails to find an echo in their hearts."[15] As we attempt to communicate the gospel to people in a specific cultural context, we need to discern that which is genuinely human and cultivate a genuine empathy for that which is human.

In *The New York Review of Books* several years ago, John H. Elliott, Regius Professor of Modern History and a Fellow at Oriel College Oxford, reviewed several historical studies of colonialism, arguing that contemporary writers who critique early missionary activity, especially those exhibiting a postmodern mentality, frequently distort the motives of the evangelizers. He cited the example of the sixteenth-century Spanish friars who were, as Elliott put it, "clearly struggling to discover resemblances, not differences, in their pursuit of the not unworthy objective of establishing the common humanity of the human race."[16] Looking for commonalities rather than differences in the hope of establishing the common humanity of the human race is the essence of the mission enterprise. It involves entering into the experience of others. It involves cultivating empathy, which literally means, "feeling within" — having the same kinds of feelings within that they have and that they experience.

We need a missionary empathy as we approach North American people who are immersed in the hopes and fears of North American culture, an empathic approach that looks for commonalities rather than differences. Developing missionary sensitivities requires a certain teachability, for two reasons: first, to have our own cultural packaging of the Christian gospel corrected; and second, to have our un-

---

15. Austin P. Flannery, ed., *Documents of Vatican II* (Grand Rapids: Eerdmans, 1975), p. 903.

16. J. H. Elliott, "Going Baroque," in *New York Review of Books* 41 (17) (October 20, 1994), p. 31.

derstanding of that gospel amplified by the encounter with other cultures, including other non-Christian cultures.

The Christian gospel was addressed to a rich variety of human cultural situations. It speaks to these situations out of its own many-faceted storehouse of divine truth. I have long been fascinated by an observation made by the nineteenth-century Dutch theologian, Herman Bavinck, on the subject of the image of God. Bavinck suggested that in addition to the ways in which each human individual is created in the image of God there is also what he calls the "collective possession" of the divine image.[17] The Lord distributes different aspects of the divine likeness to different cultural groups. Each group receives, as it were, a different assignment for developing some aspect or another of the divine image. And only in the eschatological gathering-in of the peoples of the earth, when many tribes and tongues and nations will be displayed in their honor and glory in the new Jerusalem, will we see the many-splendored *imago Dei* in its fullness.

The missionary enterprise is not only the broadcasting of a message, it is also the gathering of fresh insights into the gospel. Often these are insights we would not have received had we not interacted with a different cultural context. Such interaction often provides us with new insights into the rich and mysterious splendor of God's creating and redeeming purposes among the peoples of the earth. These insights help us appreciate even more the Church of Jesus Christ which God is drawing together from every tribe and tongue and people and nation on earth. This gathering motif has been an important element in the missionary task.

The Richardsons, when they discuss their work with the Peace Child people at the end of their book, talk about the need for missionaries to discover redemptive analogies in a specific culture. A number of us at Fuller Seminary have been in dialogue with some evangelical Christians who are very well placed in the Hollywood entertainment industry, and we have discussed at length the notion of redemptive analogies, as exemplified in the "peace child" encounter. The discussion has centered around Christian movies that don't deal with explicitly Christian themes, but which deal with redemptive analogies. A member of the group, a producer friend, thinks that one of the most

17. Herman Bavinck, *Our Reasonable Faith* (Grand Rapids: Baker, 1956), pp. 206-7.

profoundly Christian movies of recent years is "The Fugitive," the story of a doctor falsely accused of murder and the lawman who pursues him. Everywhere the fugitive runs, he brings healing and reconciliation, and ultimately his enemy is transformed into his friend. That is something like the idea of a redemptive analogy translated into the culture of Hollywood. When the Richardsons discovered the "peace child" theme, they welcomed it as evidence that the Spirit of God had long been at work in the Sawi culture, preparing them for the reception of the gospel of Jesus Christ.

Missionary vision might be defined as an insightful awareness of how the Spirit of God is already at work in a culture before we go there. The critical question is: How do we apply this to our contemporary situation in North America? Even more specifically, how do we apply this to those manifestations of popular culture in North America that many of us have been inclined to treat with a disdainful attitude?

Several years ago I went to a Rolling Stones concert at the invitation of a couple of pastors who were leading a group of men in reflecting on how the gospel relates to youth culture. They called knowing that I had access to a box in the Rose Bowl, where the concert was being held, and offered to pay for it, asking me in return to come along and help them engage in theological reflection on the Rolling Stones concert. So I went. I later mentioned my attendance at this event at one or two Fuller functions, and got a letter from an alumnus of Fuller Seminary who was very angry with me. "I am ashamed that the president of a large evangelical seminary could admit publicly, without embarrassment, that he attended a Rolling Stones concert, especially one entitled the 'Voodoo Lounge' tour," he fumed. I responded with a missionary rationale: If we were sent to proclaim the gospel to an unreached tribe we would study their customs, we would go to their sacred groves, we would observe their rituals and ceremonies, and we would probe for deeper motifs that we could address with the gospel. Why not approach a Rolling Stones concert with at least as much care as a rite in a non-Christian tribal culture?

We sat that night in a box high up in the Rose Bowl looking down on 80,000 people who were energetically, sometimes even frantically, joining in the festivities led by Mick Jagger. It was a tremendous technological show, a multimedia show filled with lights, images, and sound. As we looked down on that crowd of 80,000 people, one of the pastors turned to me and said, "Mouw, there are more people here tonight in this stadium than will be in all the churches in the Pasadena area on Sunday morning. If you had a chance to say something to them, what would you say?" At that point I was in the same state that the Richardsons were when they heard the Sawi people delight in the treachery of Judas. I had no idea of what my point of contact might be.

But something happened that changed my own perception of the situation. Jagger began to lead his group in their well-known song "Can't Get No Satisfaction." As Mick Jagger led, the whole crowd of 80,000 people joined in the chant, "I can't get no satisfaction, I can't get no satisfaction, 'cause I try and I try and I try and I try, I can't get no, I can't get no . . ." — and the chant went on.

As I listened to the chant, I remembered the time a couple of years earlier when I was on the same conference program with Ken Medema, a wonderful and creative musician who composes on the spot, and responds to a speaker's address by creating an appropriate piece of music. After I was done speaking, Ken played a piece in which with his right hand he did honky-tonk music, very loud honky-tonk music. But with his left hand, he played the tune to Psalm 42 that every person of Dutch descent, at one time at least, would have known. He played the Psalm loud and strong as a melody underneath the honky-tonk music. Suddenly, there at the Rolling Stones concert, I heard that tune. "As the hart about to falter, in its trembling agony. . . ." "Can't get no satisfaction." ". . . panteth for the brooks of water, so my soul doth thirst for Thee." "Can't get no satisfaction." I felt like calling out, "Mick Jagger, meet Saint Augustine! 'Our hearts are restless till they rest in Thee.'"

We have a missionary task to the tens of thousands who gather in the Rose Bowl to sing with Mick Jagger. We need to exegete that culture in the same way that missionaries have been so good at doing with the diverse tribal cultures of previously unreached people. And we need to exegete not only the cultural themes of the Rolling Stones, but also of Dennis Rodman, Madonna, David Letterman, Rosanne, Seinfeld, and "Tales from the Crypt." We need to comprehend that the Spirit of the Living God is at work in these cultural expressions, preparing the hearts of men and women to receive the gospel of Jesus Christ. We have to find, in a good missionary fashion, those motifs and themes that connect with the truths of the gospel. We need to

14

learn how to proclaim, "That which you worship as unknown, I now proclaim to you." This is missionary vision at its best.

But I want to make clear, as a final point, that missionary vision is not static: it is dynamic. It is not "having" a vision so much as engaging in a dynamic envisioning of the presence of the Spirit of God in the world. As a philosopher I have taught a number of courses on the idea of worldview. I still think that this provides us with a provocative and helpful way of thinking Christianly about the world. But I am also very impressed these days with the need for thinking not only of having a worldview, but also of engaging in world-viewing.

Missionary visioning, the willingness to see reality through the eyes of Jesus, has always been fundamental to the Christian movement. As people who love the Lord Jesus Christ, we desperately need as North American people to view our culture from a missionary perspective. No one ought to take me to be saying that we should no longer send people to other cultures. We must continue to do this because there are millions of people who have not yet heard or who have not yet responded to the gospel of Jesus Christ. We need to do this with all of the insight, sensitivity, and theological savvy that has been developed over the years of profound missionary activity. But we also need desperately to take those very skills of missionary empathy and vision and apply them to our North American missionary location. So as we turn on our television sets, as we look at the desperate poverty in our cities, as we think of the issues of abuse, as we reflect upon what it means for human beings to be dying of AIDS, we need to be able to see what Jesus sees, to hear what Jesus hears, to touch what Jesus touches, and to go where Jesus goes.

Wearing Different Hats: Christian Living in a Fragmented World

CHRISTOPHER B. KAISER

Lesslie Newbigin has called our attention to the modern dichotomy between a public world of facts and a private world of values, feelings, and beliefs. For many modern people, religion has been relegated to the private world of personal faith and values (e.g., Schleiermacher, Ritschl, Bultmann) as the public world has become increasingly secularized.[1]

The general picture, however, of separate public and private worlds is an oversimplification. I have found this simplification helpful in calling my attention to blind spots in my own life. But once I seek to move beyond that realization, to find my way as a Christian in the modern world, I find that the general picture needs to be refined in several ways. Here I shall expand on the work of Peter Berger[2] to outline some needed modifications and share some thoughts about attempting to recover wholeness.

---

1. Lesslie Newbigin, *Foolishness to the Greeks: The Gospel and Western Culture* (Grand Rapids: Eerdmans, 1986), pp. 17-20, 44-50 passim.

2. I have adapted Berger's ideas and will not try to document them all. For the interested reader, I recommend Peter Berger, Brigitte Berger, and Hansfried Kellner, *The Homeless Mind: Modernization and Consciousness* (New York: Random House, 1973). There is also a good summary in chapter two of Peter Berger, *A Rumor of Angels: Modern Society and the Rediscovery of the Supernatural* (Garden City, N.Y.: Doubleday, 1969).

Fragmentation of the Life-World and Intrapersonal Pluralism

From a sociological point of view, the public world is not a monolithic entity, but rather is fragmented into distinct subworlds, or enclaves. As a result of our vocational and avocational specializations, only some of these enclaves are accessible to a given individual, while others appear to be alien. Note, for example, the alien appearance of specialized sciences or of military life to those of us who are not initiated into their respective languages and styles.

Each of these subworlds, or enclaves, has its own values as well as its own facts. In Peter and Brigitte Berger's terms, each enclave has its own worldview with its own plausibility structures that realize and sustain that worldview.[3] For example, as soon as you walk into a medical clinic, you have to report to a receptionist and fill out certain forms. A set of facts and values is articulated through this procedure even if it is not stated explicitly. You may be an avid baseball fan or a proponent of church growth. But what is "factual" in the present situation is your medical history and current medications. You may be the consultant who trained the receptionist to use a computer or the police officer who just gave her a ticket. But now you listen to her giving instructions, take seriously what she says is important, and corroborate all of the information you gave the last time you were in the clinic. The sign-in clipboard, the location of the receptionist behind a sliding window, and the form of the questionnaire together construct a world of facts and values quite different from any other you know.

When entering most worldview enclaves, an individual will experience a high degree of anonymity, along with a seeming indifference to his or her personal background, which may result in a restructuring of one's personal identity. In any given enclave, the basis for relationships is located within a limited range of personal interactions. For example, a conversation with the teller at the drive-through bank is normally limited to a need for cash and an ability to gain access to the appropriate accounts. A visit to the service station is based on a need for gas and occasional snack food. In situations such as these, interpersonal relationships in the public world are experienced in primarily functional terms and are lacking in depth.

3. *The Homeless Mind*, pp. 15-16.

The private world, however, is not a monolithic entity any more than the public world is. It too is fragmented. It is segmented into enclaves like families, ethnic cultures, youth cultures, churches, and clubs. Each of these subworlds has its own facts as well as its own values. Each has plausibility structures that sustain those facts and values. But these private enclaves differ from the enclaves of the public world in that they allow greater personal expression and recognition of individual identity. Being a daddy, a motorcycle rider, or an antique collector will probably express my personal identity more deeply than my being a customer or the consumer of prepackaged services.

One's personal world, or life-world (*Lebenswelt* in German), is a composite of all our subworlds, those both public and private. We wear different hats as we move from one enclave to another, from one group of associates to another, from one set of facts and values to another. If we have a religious faith, it is largely confined to one or two of these subworlds, such as the church and/or our family life. It is unlikely that our faith will function as an overarching canopy that embraces all of life.[4]

Before proceeding further, it should be recognized that the sociological perspective being followed here has to compete with other current perspectives such as psychological types (e.g., Myers-Briggs), theological worlds,[5] and gender differences. It could be argued that one's psychological type and/or gender are more important to one's experience of life than the structure of a life-world. However, these competing paradigms generally assume that the relevant categories of life are equally applicable to all times and in all cultures. Personality types and gender differences are certainly present in all cultures, but their meaning and value are largely determined by specific social-cultural contexts.

For example, berserkers, who in Nordic society were honored as mighty warriors, would probably be classed as manic-depressives in industrialized societies, and their experiences of life would differ accordingly. And Madonna's experience of life as the material girl is rather different from Miriam's (Exodus 15; Numbers 12), even

---

4. Peter Berger, *The Sacred Canopy: Elements of a Sociological Theory of Religion* (Garden City, N.Y.: Doubleday, 1967).

5. Paul W. Jones, *Theological Worlds: Understanding the Alternative Rhythms of Christian Belief* (Nashville: Abingdon Press), pp. 42-43.

though there are similarities in the way their gender created opportunities and obstacles for them both. The underlying psychology and biology in these two examples may be the same, but the social context determines their value and conditions the individual's sense of self-worth. In other words, social systems can coopt personality type and gender. Therefore, the sociological perspective is necessary for our understanding of the modern condition even though it may need to be supplemented by other analyses.

Personal Goals and Pragmatic Means

Most people function in the public world in accordance with specific personal goals. Those goals generally have their origin in one's private life and are nourished by the plausibility structures of family, ethnicity, and faith. Most of us work at our jobs in order to care for our families and pay for leisure activities. The intensity of such personal desires can have the effect of sanctifying public enclaves that would otherwise seem alien. Even a train station can seem a warm and friendly place if we are there to meet someone we love. So there is a degree of moral unity to the life-world, at least as far as ends are concerned.

The means, however, by which those ends are pursued in the public world are generally based on the plausibility structures embedded in the public enclaves. Very likely they do not reflect the values of the person in question. You go to the supermarket in order to feed and clothe your family — a deeply personal commitment. However, your mode of transportation, your strategies of product selection, and your means of paying the bill are chosen on strictly pragmatic grounds (e.g., speed, economy, and convenience) rather than on the basis of your personal aesthetic, moral, or religious values. In fact, our personal values are more likely to be expressed in situations where the very opposite values are sustained (quality time, generosity, and cooperation).

Note that the pluralism we experience in our lives is an intrapersonal, functional pluralism. This type of pluralism is not the same as the interpersonal, worldview-pluralism of biblical times (e.g., Acts 16:19-21), or that found even today in relatively traditional cultures, such as India. Our public values of economy and convenience are much the same as those of modern people from other ethnic and religious backgrounds. But they are radically different from the private values we espouse in our respective families and churches.

Naturally, intrapersonal pluralism places a strain on our lives, and this pressure must be kept from getting out of hand. There are at least four tools we utilize in order to avoid complete relativism and psychological disorientation, what the Bergers referred to as the "homeless mind."[6] These are: the reification of an everyday world; common beliefs; mediating commodities; and bridging institutions. These secular mechanisms must be examined before we can explore a Christian alternative.

Reification of the Everyday World

The only sphere of life that is common to all members of a society is what they experience as the everyday world. In our modern culture, the everyday world consists primarily of commodity markets (stores and catalogs), banking, timekeeping, communication systems, transportation, and basic food services. For most people, this subset of the public world is their "real world." It embodies values of exchange of both material and information that are common to people of all subcultures in our society, and which are becoming increasingly common to all cultures around the world. As a recent news headline stated, "Money, not morals, governs relations between Europe and Asia."[7]

Apparently, the inner dynamics of this everyday world resist adaptation to the facts and values of any of the other enclaves of the life-world, whether public or private. Political reform is one avenue of adaptation. Consumer boycotts are another. The stoutness of resistance to such approaches is painfully evident in both cases. Idealism and reform-mindedness are encouraged to a point, but there is usually a reaction when ideals are pressed too far.

Paradoxically, the fragmentation of the life-world into various enclaves is accompanied by a homogenization of diverse cultures and

6. *The Homeless Mind.*
7. News headline, *Associated Press,* 4 March 1996. The subheading reads, "Eager to get a cut of Asian growth, the European Union set aside worries about worker safety or human rights.

subcultures at the everyday level. We can patronize any of a variety of specialized markets, banks, or restaurants in our hometowns, but they look and work pretty much the same as the markets, banks, and restaurants in other parts of the country.[8] Martial arts are also interchangeable from state to state, as are most health foods. You can even travel around the world using your Visa Card and eating at McDonald's (or at Szechuan Chinese restaurants, if you prefer). If pluralism and diversity are among our values, it appears that the modern world has taken away with the left hand what it has given with the right.

Common Beliefs in the Everyday World

A second way in which we avoid complete relativism is through maintaining a set of common beliefs. These beliefs are affirmations about our common life by which people act and interact in public. They are not necessarily philosophical ideas or theological dogmas. Many of us act on beliefs (e.g., individualism or materialism) about which we may be critical or even hostile.

Some of the shared beliefs that Americans hold most fervently are those of commonsense realism (that there is a common world of objective facts), pragmatism (what works best is what is right for the situation at hand), individualism and personal freedom (dissociation of personal identity from social roles), and the individual's control (ideally) of his/her life.[9]

These beliefs are clearly not applicable to all areas of one's life. Pragmatism does not work well in love-making or child-rearing. Ethnic identity can overrule individual freedom. But these common beliefs are ideally suited to the everyday world of commodity markets, banking, and transportation, where they are widely shared.

The net effect of this inconsistency is to insulate everyday, economic life from the interference that might come from the demands of peripheral enclaves such as ethnic cultures and prophetic religion. In fact, the desire for rapid, unhindered economic growth

8. Richard Barnet, *Global Dreams: Imperial Corporations and the New World Order* (New York: Simon & Schuster, 1994).

9. A similar list of beliefs is reviewed in Cora DuBois, "The Dominant Value Profile of American Culture," in *American Anthropologist* 57: 1232-39.

was the major impetus toward the fragmentation of the life-world into relatively autonomous enclaves in the eighteenth and nineteenth centuries.[10]

Mediating Commodities

Another way in which we avoid complete relativism is through the purchase and use of mediating commodities. These are products and media that function as bridges between the public and private worlds for individuals and groups.

Such mediating commodities are designed and produced in enclaves of the public arena, but they are imported into our churches, homes, and clubs, where they serve our private needs even though they continue to function in accordance with the logic of industry. In many cases, they are referred to as "systems" (e.g., prefabricated "office systems" in our homes and "sound systems" in our churches). Often private institutions feel their integrity is threatened by such imports and attempt to limit their influence by "stoppage"[11] (e.g., no clocks in the sanctuary; keep the TV off during mealtime).

Automobiles are the most visible mediating commodities between our public and private worlds. Cars are produced and distributed in the public sphere and operate in accordance with the laws of industrial chemistry and mechanics. But they are integrated into the home through attached garages and serve to carry us back out into the public world of streets, offices, banks, and malls. In our cars, we are surrounded with our personal artifacts (coffee mugs, tapes, etc.) and even religious paraphernalia, while we negotiate the publicly constructed world of speed limits and potholes. The automobile is a kind of portable home, an amphibious machine that transports us into an alien environment and back.

10. Martin E. Marty, *The Modern Schism: Three Paths to the Secular* (New York: Harper & Row, 1969).

11. These phenomena are treated as "carry-over" and "stoppage" in Berger et al., *The Homeless Mind*, pp.16-17.

Bridging Institutions

Since the privatization of religion in the nineteenth century, government and the public school system have helped to unify our society at the institutional level. Government is the major public arena in which most individuals and groups can voice their personal beliefs. On the other hand, the requirements of economics, business pressures, and military exigencies often outweigh the voices of individuals and groups ("special interests"), particularly at the national level. There is much ambiguity and conflict here.

The public school system provides a public arena for many of our youth, and often helps them emerge from the private sphere of home, church, and youth culture into the public (real) world. Today public schools are adopting many of the values of the business world (mission statements, objectives, outcomes, etc.). Still there is room for behaviors such as parental involvement, debate about textbooks and T-shirts on religious and moral grounds, and a tolerance for distinctive forms of dress and behavioral "styles" (black, white, Hispanic, etc.).[12]

Since politics and public education function at the intersection of the public and private spheres of our culture, they are inevitably the most conflicted and unstable areas of our society. Until recently, the American way of life has been able to assume a strong popular commitment to both of these institutions. But our present crisis of confidence may indicate a sharper polarization of public and private than ever before, making the need for new strategies even more pressing.

Options for Personal Integration

If the above analysis is anywhere near correct, the achievement of wholeness in modern life will be much more difficult than we are usually led to believe. The world we have constructed is overwhelmingly massive, and our freedom is severely limited. I would like to suggest several strategies to help persons address this fragmentation.

12. I take the idea of ethnic "styles" from Thomas Kochman, *Black and White Styles in Conflict* (Chicago: University of Chicago Press, 1981).

First, in seeking to heal the fragmentation described above, a good step would be simply to review the many different aspects of your life-world (the different aspects of life as you experience it) and to look for an overall pattern. The pattern may take the form of a particular image like a five- (or six- or seven-) pointed star or a staircase. Several different patterns or images may be possible. It will help to seek new ones from time to time in order to become more comprehensive. Reflection on the successive stages of your life can also reveal diversity and continuity. Different stages may reflect different aspects of your life; earlier stages may represent aspects that you have neglected or forgotten.

Second, Christ needs to be invited to live as Lord and Savior in this context. In this regard, I have found familiar biblical texts to be sources of insight and integration, such as: "The fear of the Lord is the beginning of knowledge" (Proverbs 1:7); and "He himself is before all things, and in him all things hold together" (Colossians 1:17). It may help to think of Jesus in very human terms, in terms of his earthly life. Sometimes it may be better to think of him as the cosmic Logos or the Wisdom of God. In any case, I would try to imagine what it would mean for Christ to encompass the pattern of my life-world, to re-vision my life-world as being somehow centered in Christ.

Finally, on the basis of these patterns and images, you may have insights for restructuring some of the enclaves of your life (your home, garden, car, office, and business) in such a way as to give objectivity to your self-understanding and bear testimony to the role of Christ. Rearranging things may not make them more accessible or convenient. But it does posit an alternative, more integrated world as the reality within which you live.

Toward Holistic Ministry

In trying to relate to others, it is important to remember that we ourselves are affected by modern fragmentation and are still in process of seeking integration. The unity of life is not found in our personal life-patterns, but in Christ and in God's pluriform Spirit (Isaiah 11:2; Revelation 1:4-5). So it is important to affirm the God-given roles and gifts that may operate in a variety of enclaves, particularly in those that seem unfamiliar or alien to us.

For Christians it will be important to recognize and value the gifts of non-Christians. A good example here is John Calvin's affirmation of the gifts of pagan writers, particularly scientists, based on his belief that God's Spirit is the fountain of all truth.[13] For professional ministers it will be important to affirm the work and gifts of lay people, particularly as they function in their own enclaves (not just for what they contribute to the work of the church). A good example is the wisdom of a priestly sage named Jesus ben Sirach, who, in the deuterocanonical book of Ecclesiasticus (Sirach 38:1-15), affirmed the healing skills of physicians as gifts of God.[14]

By seeking a pattern of unity in the fragments of our lives, both public and private, we can begin to construct a canopy that will embrace all of our complex life-world. By affirming all of modern life's many enclaves, both religious and secular, we can bear witness to a Lord who is above all and over all (Romans 9:5; 10:12) and fills all things (Ephesians 4:10).

13. John Calvin, *Institutes of the Christian Religion,* II.ii.15-16. For a theological interpretation of the sciences in terms of the historic "creationist tradition" see Christopher Kaiser, "Humanity as the Exegete of Creation with Reference to the Work of Natural Sciences," in *Horizons in Biblical Theology* 14: 112-29; "The Creationist Tradition in the History of Science," in *Perspectives on Science and Christian Faith* 45: 80-89; and "Scientific Work and Its Theological Dimensions: Toward a Theology of Natural Science," in *Facets of Faith and Science,* 4 vols., ed. Jitse Van der Meer (Lanham, Md.: University Press of America), vol. 1, pp. 223-46.

14. For a theological interpretation of the secular vocations in general, see Christopher Kaiser, "Holistic Ministry in a Technological Society," in *Reformed Review* 41: 175-88; and Lee Hardy, *The Fabric of This World: Inquiries into Calling, Career Choice, and the Design of Human Work* (Grand Rapids: Eerdmans, 1990).

The Gospel in a Digital Age

ROBERT S. FORTNER

Two issues of *Time* magazine, both published in April 1996, together provide an opening for understanding the implications of the digital age. One carried an article titled "The Gospel Truth?" It reported that a book called *The Acts of Jesus* would soon appear, with claims that "close historical analysis of the gospels exposes most of them as unauthentic; and that, by inference, most Christians' picture of Christ may be radically misguided."[1] The second issue, which appeared two weeks later, carried an article "Fly Till I Die." It was about Jessica Dubroff's ill-fated attempt to become the youngest person to fly across the country. In it Richard Stengel wrote, "Reared by separated parents whose fuzzy New Age philosophy was that children should follow their bliss, Jessica was encouraged to pursue an adult ambition that ill fitted her."[2]

What's wrong with this picture? On the one hand, *Time* carries multiple stories that give voice to gospel debunkers and iconoclasts — those who would see the most significant of all binding moral elements crumble under the supposedly "democratic" judgment of scholars. On the other, *Time* indignantly criticizes those who choose to violate these same biblically based moral norms in favor of some fuzzy philosophy that led to the death of a child and, through her, to the death of innocence itself.

1. David Van Biema, "The Gospel Truth?" *Time,* April 8, 1996, pp. 52-59.
2. Richard Stengel, "Fly Till I Die," *Time,* April 22, 1996, 35-38. See also Elizabeth Gleick, "Every Kid a Star," *Time,* April 22, 1996, pp. 39-40.

That *Time* apparently sees no disjointedness in such reporting — which undermines religion while lamenting the dissolution of values in nearly a single breath — is symptomatic of the digital culture that America has now entered. Digital culture is not merely the replacement of one system of transmission by another. It is also the replacement of a multi-stranded but continuous line of culture (what can be described as an analog culture) with one comprised of discrete bits (digitally coded ones and zeros, if you will). In this new culture, the only relationship between any two bits is their proximity to each other — something that often occurs randomly.

The differences between the two ages we now inhabit (the electronic age and the digital age) can be characterized as follows:

The Electronic Age	**The Digital Age**
Continuous (analog)	Discontinuous (separated bits; bits time-division multiplexed — combined into a stream)
Enabling demagoguery	Enabling and legitimizing "persona"
Providing an iconography	Promoting iconoclasm
Passive entertainment	Interactive edutainment
Promoting populism	Enabling anarchy
Defined by rebelliousness	Defined by "virtualness"
Defining people by lifestyle	Defining people by technological sophistication
Anti-authoritarian at base	Authority irrelevant
Pro-symbolic	Irreverence to the symbolic

There is not space here to explain each of these columns in detail, but some additional commentary is warranted. In the *electronic age* radio, television, and film provided a significant power base for the aspirations of such figures as Adolf Hitler, Benito Mussolini, Father Charles Coughlin, Huey Long, Joseph McCarthy, G. Gordon Liddy, and Rush Limbaugh, all populists — and, arguably, all demagogues. Each of these personalities began their media-based campaigns by adopting an anti-authoritarian posture, although some became the worst type of authoritarians themselves. Each of them used symbolic rhetoric to promote their cause, from the *Volk* and anti-Semitism of Hitler, to the witch-hunting of McCarthy's Un-American

Activities committee, and the anti-FBI/ATF harangues of G. Gordon Liddy.

In the *digital age* the capacity and speed of the developing electronic infrastructure is so extensive that demagogues such as those listed above, in fact, become marginalized. The logic of the digital age is that people make choices from an immense variety of possibilities. They use interactive cable to define their own television programming. They choose which news groups and listservs to join on the Internet. They construct their own newspapers from wire service copy or electronic versions of various daily papers on the World Wide Web. Proponents of the digital age claim that debates about pornography are irrelevant due to the choice factor operating in this rich information environment. Every user becomes his or her own editor, and thus authority becomes irrelevant. Readily accessible information and personal-opinion anarchy become the name of the game.

This shift, which I believe is as significant as the shift from oral to writing culture about 3,000 B.C., or the shift from print to electric culture in the mid-nineteenth century, has profound implications for the propagation of the gospel. Postmodernists have argued that this emerging digital age has fragmented the "self," leading to confusion as to who we are. Kenneth Gergen argues that people now suffer from "multiphrenia," a condition of multiple selves brought on by the encouragement of "pastiche personalities" cobbled together from both past and present in an age of media saturation.[3] Michael Strangelove has argued, on the so-called "information highway" itself, that the rise of an alternative "cyberculture" changes the geography of existence and thus the "nature of the self."[4] David Nicholson seems to lament that while we keep hearing that computers have changed our lives, "almost no one seems to be asking what all this portends for what it means to be human."[5] Ashley Dunn writes, in the *New York Times Cybertimes,* that even our notions of paranoia have had to be changed in the digital age. No longer is "big brother" a

3. Kenneth Gergen, *The Saturated Self: Dilemmas of Identity in Contemporary Life* (New York: Basic Books, 1991).

4. Michael Strangelove, "Cyberspace and the Changing Landscape of the Self," Http://dept.english.upenss.edu/~sgarfink/eng9/strangelove.html (circa 1994).

5. David Nicholson, "The Pitfalls of a Brave New Cyberworld," *The Washington Post National Weekly Edition,* October 9-15, 1995, p. 25.

threat because "the world has become a fragmented place, lacking the clear and comforting division of us and Big Brother that for so long offered a comforting, if simplistic, explanation for why the world was so screwed up. . . . 'They' are still watching, but this time, 'they' is potentially everyone."[6]

How should the church respond to this new, quickly developing age? Does the church even have a theology of "self" that enables it to respond adequately to the destruction or transmogrification of self into a virtual, evanescent reality? If an adequate definition exists within Christian theology to respond to this situation, I have not seen it.

This is not really surprising. The church has been behind the curve in responding to cultural change in this century from the very beginning. It struggled to respond to the development of film at the turn of the century; it embraced radio enthusiastically, but naively, several decades later; for the most part, it ignored television until the violence and sex quotient rose high enough to get its attention; and it has had little to say about the computer at all.

Theology has not completely ignored culture during this period. H. Richard Niebuhr's contribution to a Christian perspective on culture is probably the best known.[7] Most other authors who have tackled the issue of culture from a Christian foundation have not been theologians; they have been poets, educators, historians, and artists.[8] Doreen Rosman even wrote in 1984 that, "A study entitled *Evangelicals and Culture* [the title of her book] must of necessity begin with reference to Matthew Arnold's *Culture and Anarchy,* a work which, through its scathing denunciation of mid-nineteenth-century nonconformity, has done much to establish the legend of evangelical philistinism."[9] This is hardly a propitious starting point to engage a

6. Ashley Dunn, "Tracking Crumbs of Data That Threaten to Define Us," *The New York Times Cybertimes,* May 12, 1996.

7. H. Richard Niebuhr, *Christ and Culture* (New York: Harper, 1951).

8. See, e.g. Herbert Butterfield, *Christianity in European History: The Riddell Memorial Lectures 1951* (London: Collins, 1952); T. S. Eliot, *The Idea of a Christian Society* (London: Faber and Faber, 1982); John Cowper Powys, *The Meaning of Culture* (New York: W. W. Norton & Company, Inc., 1929); Frank E. Gaebelein, *The Christian, the Arts, and Truth* (Portland, Ore.: Multnomah Press, 1978); and Nicholas Wolterstorff, *Art in Action: Toward a Christian Aesthetic* (Grand Rapids: Eerdmans, 1980).

9. Doreen Rosman, *Evangelicals and Culture* (London: Croon Helm, 1984), p. 1.

postmodern culture. What is interesting to note is that none of these authors speaks directly to the issue of "self" and its centrality to evangelicalism premised on "knowing Christ as personal savior" or Paul's claims about man being "justified by faith apart from obeying the law" (Romans 3:28).

Christian theology's lack of sustained theological critique of culture is unfortunate because individuals, institutions, and corporations continue to develop and apply new technologies within a cultural tradition that has placed high value on their potential contributions. For example, the cultural ethos in both the United States and Canada have embraced communications technologies that contribute to solving problems of distance, geography, and topography in the effort to knit their societies into single national states.[10] These technologies have also responded to the *cultural ethos* that encouraged their development to achieve political ends, such as democratization and equality; and economic goals, such as national markets which have increased standards of living. They have likewise responded within what Jacques Ellul called *la technique,* a mode of thinking that values "efficiency" above all else, what we might call a *technological ethos.*[11] And they have responded to an instrumental *moral ethos* that was market driven, a *laissez-faire* approach that views the penetration of markets as a social responsibility or a justice issue. This allowed them to justify commercial as opposed to public service broadcasting.

Like the print, electric, and electronic technologies that preceded them, digital technologies developed within this same cultural framework and responded to the same cultural values. It would be unfair, therefore, to suggest that the culture that is being created in the wake of the developing interactive 500-channel TV system, direct broadcasting satellite developments, the Internet, or even the convergence of these technologies into a single integrated system, is introducing or causing change that is somehow ahistorical or acultural. Acknowledging this cultural continuity, however, does not diminish the reality that the digital culture now under construction is a vastly

10. James W. Carey, *Communication as Culture: Essays on Media and Society* (Boston: Unwin Hyman, 1989), chs. 5 and 6; also Robert S. Fortner, "The Canadian Search for Identity, 1846-1914," Parts I-IV, in *The Canadian Journal of Communication* 6 and 7, 1979, 1980.

11. Jacques Ellul, *The Technological Society* (New York: Vintage Books, 1964), p. 20.

different one from what the norm was before. It is different from, while being rooted within, the sequences of culture that have developed in response to new technological changes.

Make no mistake: the arrival of the digital age has profound implications for culture, self-identity, and the gospel. Sherry Turkle says, for instance, that "Technology catalyzes changes not only in what we do but in how we think. It changes people's awareness of themselves, of one another, of their relationship with the world." Computers "enter into the development of personality, of identity, and even of sexuality."[12] In a later book, Turkle refers to Kenneth Gergen's discussion of the "saturated self" as it is dealt with in a WELL discussion group and the fondness that members of the group had for the concept of a "multiplicitous being." But, she says, "Without any principle of coherence, the self spins off in all directions. Multiplicity is not viable if it means shifting among personalities that cannot communicate. Multiplicity is not acceptable if it means being confused to the point of immobility. How can we be multiple and coherent at the same time?"[13]

Stephen L. Talbott argues that the corollary of the mechanism of the Internet, which stands outside the framework of "social immersion," with its personal frictions, antagonisms, and frustrations, "is the scattered self."[14] And Michael Sullivan-Trainor, reflecting on the culture change in our definitions of self, returns the discussion to the relationship between technology and culture. "Technology can act as a platform for and reflector of cultural change. It is rarely the change itself. As a tool, it must yield to the attitudes and needs of the majority of users. It also can, when controlled by a few, help shape the attitudes of the majority in much the way television has influenced our culture."[15]

There are several points to understand here. First, it would be unfair to blame the development of digital technology for all its nega-

12. Sherry Turkle, *The Second Self: Computers and the Human Spirit* (New York: Simon and Schuster, 1984), pp. 13-15.

13. Sherry Turkle, *Life on the Screen: Identity in the Age of the Internet* (New York: Simon and Schuster, 1995), pp. 257-58.

14. Stephen L. Talbott, *The Future Does Not Compute: Transcending the Machines in Our Midst* (Sebastopol, Calif.: O'Reilly & Associates, Inc., 1995), p. 8.

15. Michael Sullivan-Trainor, *Detour: The Truth about the Information Superhighway* (San Mateo, Calif.: IDG Books Worldwide, Inc., 1994), p. 230.

tive consequences, or to give it credit for all the constructive ones. But second, because this technology is rooted in our cultural values, it would also be unfair to see it as merely another insignificant alteration in the cultural landscape. We are undergoing profound changes — in those very cultural values that served as the foundation for the development of this technology. The nature of communication, relationship, value-formation, and self-identity are all being redefined in our consciousness in profoundly new ways.

We are participating in that redefinition just as we are being socialized into acquiescing to it, or are being forced into accepting some of its more disturbing qualities, such as redefinitions of privacy, appropriate surveillance, and connection to others.[16] As Clifford Stoll puts it, "Then there's the myth that computer networks will bring diversity, culture and novelty into our classrooms and homes. . . . Yet I suspect these interactions are mostly shallow and ephemeral. . . . There's no *there* there. . . . Superficial network interactions don't carry the same risks as face-to-face conversations do. At the same time, they lack depth, commitment, and ordinary etiquette."[17] Daniel Burstein and David Kline see both sides of the equation. On the one hand, they say, "technological change comes to the world only *on the world's terms,* constrained within the limits of human nature and our political economy." On the other hand, they continue, the digital revolution "will generate its own unique values, economic and social relationships, political institutions, belief systems, ideas, truths, biases, dogmas."[18]

There are other implications in this developing culture. One is the fact that the culture is heavily biased toward, and controlled by, those in the intellectual and financial elites of the society. Michael Sullivan-Trainor puts it simply: "The Internet . . . is primarily accessible to the technically gifted."[19] Theodore Roszak asks, "When was the last time you saw 'information' associated with the needs of the distressed and victimized? This is not the image or the reality that the

16. Robert S. Fortner, "Privacy Is Not Enough: Personhood and High Technology," *The Conrad Grebel Review* 7 (Spring 1989): 159-77.

17. Clifford Stoll, *Silicon Snake Oil: Second Thoughts on the Information Highway* (New York: Doubleday, 1995), pp. 21-24.

18. Daniel Burstein and David Kline, *Road Warriors: Dreams and Nightmares along the Information Highway* (New York: Dutton, 1995), pp. 6-8.

19. Sullivan-Trainor, *Detour,* p. 3.

computer industry wants to cultivate. From its viewpoint, information is upscale merchandise priced to the budget of top-dollar professionals and executive decision makers."[20]

Another implication of these changes is that they are not merely the result of technological change *per se,* but are also the result of the particular capabilities that are part and parcel of these technologies. In the mid-nineteenth century, the telegraph broke the relationship between transportation and communication. The telegraph was the first means of communication that allowed discourse to occur apart from the physical means of transportation. The result was a vastly increased speed of communication and the development of communication as a means to control transportation itself. It was used, for instance, to make train travel safer in an age of single-track transcontinental lines.[21]

Digital technologies have likewise severed the link between communication and information. These technologies allow information to become a pure commodity even as communication becomes a means of promoting inclusion and relationship apart from the movement of information. In other words, while people in communication may also pass along information in a conversation, information may just as easily be transferred, bought, sold, accessed, searched, and dealt with in whole or in part, independent of any type of developing relationship. People access information according to what they can, or are willing, to pay for. They buy just as much as they need; they eschew context if they don't wish to pay for it, and no one has the right to demand — as happens in communication — that they use it properly, or completely, or within the confines of its original meaning.

In this context, information may be put to particular uses by in-

---

20. Theodore Roszak, *The Cult of Information: A Neo-Luddite Treatise on High-Tech, Artificial Intelligence, and the True Art of Thinking,* Second Edition (Berkeley: University of California Press, 1994), p. 175. See also Robert S. Fortner, "Excommunication in the Information Society," *Critical Studies in Mass Communication* 12 (1995): 133-54.

21. See Daniel Czitrom, *Media and the American Mind: From Morse to McLuhan* (Chapel Hill, N.C.: University of North Carolina Press, 1982); Neil Postman, *Technopoly: The Surrender of Culture to Technology* (New York: Alfred A. Knopf, 1992); and Allan R. Pred, *Urban Growth and the Circulation of Information: The U.S. System of Cities 1790-1840* (Cambridge, Mass.: Harvard University Press, 1973).

dividual users. This is even assumed in the American cultural tradition to be a basic right, or good. The point here is not to condemn the practice, but to note its occurrence and the significance of the change. We must not minimize this new development in the cultural flow, lest we fail to notice its significance. This is the issue that Talbott wrestles with in response to a "friendly critic." In part of that struggle, he says, "those institutions being adapted to the computer will almost certainly continue to be drained of their remaining human dimensions."[22] This is obviously something to take note of from the perspective of the gospel.

What is the impact of splitting communication from information? In a nutshell it is this: the logic of the digital age replaces the logic of the analog age. The analog age was an age of continuity that was based in relationship. This age extended back into prehistory and continued to develop in spite of the discontinuities visited upon it by the technologies of writing, print, electricity, and electronics. Even television and radio stations have been forced into relationship-building, promoting themselves and their programming to audiences as being local, or most watched, or aired by personalities you can trust.

The logic of the digital age, however, has a different set of characteristics that are fundamentally discontinuous and non-relationship driven. These characteristics sometimes mirror the older cultural norms, but they are fundamentally at odds with them. Three characteristics, in particular, are important to note.

One primary characteristic, a hallmark of the digital culture, is interactivity. Interactivity is not merely another word for communication. Interactivity implies the ability of a user to manipulate a technical system by making choices. In a video game, the player's moves have consequences as he or she interacts with the game. TV, however, is passive. Using the World Wide Web or a gopher to search for text documents is also interactive. The user enters search terms, words, or concepts (depending on the system used) to access what he or she is interested in seeing on his or her own machine. Information is retrieved on demand in largely asynchronous time, that is, the user pulls it down when he or she wants, from a remote machine, without having to interact with another human being.

22. Talbott, *The Future Does Not Compute,* pp. 20-22.

The information that people retrieve meets their own definition of need, or desire, or prejudice. And this system is, by definition, off-limits to external controls or limits. Choice implies absolute, self-defined activity. Community needs or values are irrelevant. Users also carry out their search activities by treating resources as made up of discrete bits. This discontinuity of source is unlike the treatment accorded a newspaper, for instance, which arrives whole on your doorstep, even if you are only interested in the sports section; or a book, which you purchase as a unit even if you're only interested in a single chapter. In the digital age you only get what you choose to get.

A second characteristic of the digital age is multiplication. In this culture, the more channels the better. TV channels are predicted to rise to 500, then 1,000, to allow individual homes to create customized streams of programming, selecting programs across individual channels at will, regardless of the continuity that programmers may attempt to impose on their individual streams. Digital systems also allow people to touch up photographs by digitizing and manipulating them, or even morphing them into images quite unlike the original. These systems allow people to produce their own newsletters, desktop videos, and personalized Web pages. All of this heightens the long-standing debate about authentic art and introduces new ethical issues around an information flow that is so replete with editors that the term itself loses meaning.

The third characteristic of digital logic is its accompanying use of mass storage and networked systems. Computers become faster and more powerful by the month. Computers that in the early 1980s contained 20 megabytes of capacity now routinely have 6 Gigabyte hard drives. Computers that had 512k RAM now have 32 megabytes. Stand-alone PCs are increasingly attached to networks and the Internet. Companies have begun to create Intranets for distribution of information in-house. The digital logic is connectivity, speed, and mass storage.

In this respect the computer is similar to the telephone. The logic of universal service for the telephone was that the value of each instrument, and hence the value of having an instrument in your home, was increased by the number of other instruments with which you could connect. The more telephones the better. Hence an expectation that Ma Bell, in the days of near monopoly, would charge everyone the same amount to connect their telephone, whether they had to run five feet or five miles of wire to get to your house. With the computer, the more information that can be accessed the better. It's the same logic. There's some advantage to accessing 360k worth of data on a 5.25-inch floppy disk, but phenomenally more advantage to accessing 6 Gigabytes of data on a hard disk, or thousands of access points and an unfathomable number of Gigabytes on the World Wide Web. And if everyone's on-line with an e-mail address, then there is even further value added. That's the logic of the digital age.

People understand this logic, even if they don't want to admit it. That's the reason for the struggle between the major players in the information age: Microsoft, Intel, Apple, MCI, AT&T, Compaq, CapCities/ABC, Disney, Adobe, Corel, Ameritech, RCA, TCI, IBM, etc. Increasingly they compete with one another to push their way into American homes: satellite companies versus cable versus telephone service providers; CD ROM manufacturers versus on-line services; one software product, or operating system, or computer manufacturer, or search engine, or browser, versus another. There's big money to be made, hundreds of billions of dollars by the turn of the century, all based on connectivity and access to information.

As this digital age develops, the culture responds. The value of a multiplicity of narratives enabled by desktop publishing, Web access, or interactive TV is offset by the consequent discontinuity of narratives within the culture. What holds a culture together when it is not communities that decide its values, whether these communities are defined geographically, religiously, ethnically, or whatever? The alternative is for each person to do what is right in his or her own eyes. The empowerment that comes from controlling information and having the ability to communicate rapidly with others can also lead to narcissism — a sense of mastery, of one's own self being the center of things. Even the degree of personal control promoted as a value in this digital culture is at odds with the logic of networking. Now we are increasingly obligated to respond to others' e-mail or spam, or wade through inane comments on listservs, as we become overwhelmed with the irrelevance of data that can be retrieved by a search engine on any conceivable topic. As Clifford Stoll puts it, "What the Internet hucksters don't tell you is that the Internet is an ocean of unedited data, without any pretense of completeness.

Lacking editors, reviewers or critics, the Internet has become a wasteland of unfiltered data."[23]

At this point, we can begin to identify some of the implications that the digital age has for communication of the gospel. For one, the gospel becomes just one narrative (or four separate narratives) among many other narratives. The continuity of the *Bible* itself is now up for grabs in an age of searchable CD ROMs, or *Bible* versions on the Internet.

Another implication is that we have to consider the demands of scripture. God's claims on humankind are absolute, holy, continuous, and non-accommodating. God is sovereign, and his claims are un-compromising. We may not serve both God and mammon. Yet these claims will have to be made relevant in a culture that is discontinuous, independent, and individually defined — in other words, in a culture of anarchy where authority is irrelevant.

A third implication for gospel communication relates to its wholeness, or oneness. The gospel appeals to the instinct that longs for meaning in the human heart as it connects with the soul, which is by definition an individual possession. Now, it will have to learn to make connection with the heart and soul in an age of multiple selves, in the multiphrenia of the digital age.

How can Christians reasonably respond to such dynamics? How can they bring the gospel to this digital age? This is no easy task, to be sure. But there are certain aspects of this digital age to which we may reasonably respond. There seem to me to be four essential require-ments that might serve as starting points for developing an adequate strategy. First, Christianity must develop a theology of self. It must be one that defines the dimensions of this concept, establishes its value based in humankind's ontological status of being the *imago Dei,* and bases its evangelistic strategies on that value. Second, Christians must respond to the tendencies within this developing digital culture to de-value noncommodified information. They must establish the value of the common weal, of community, of connectedness, and of relation-ship. The fellowship of believers and the body of Christ must take on new salience in Christian thinking and serve as the basis for valuing information available to all, thinking of it in a manner similar to that accorded to citizenship. Third, Christians must take the lead in de-

23. Stoll, *Silicon Snake Oil,* p. 57.

manding that social justice prevail in decisions made about determining levels and points of access to information. The poor should not be forgotten in the rush to commodify information by those in economic power. Fourth, and most important of all, Christians must demand that the culture take account of the centrality and necessity of the gospel narrative as an inclusive and crucial dynamic. The culture must be invited into rediscovering its debt to the gospel.

These are the crucial issues. The changes taking place in the digital age are so crucial that even secular authors have begun to write about the importance of its spiritual implications. Mark Slouka laments the tendencies within the "cyberspace revolution" to "erase the world as we had known it. It was of the same spirit as Christianity [to deny the world], but bigger. Colder."[24] Sherry Turkle warned in 1984 that as a result of the computer "our sense of identity becomes increasingly focused on the soul and the spirit in the human machine."[25] The most poignant reminder I have seen, however, comes from David Nicholson. "It's too late, of course, to turn back and retreat to pre-digital times. But it isn't too late to think about what kind of future we want to live in and how we might affect things from here on out. . . . The more technology invades our lives, the more it obscures the real issues — the fact that our lives are really about love and work and death, about creating and maintaining relationships that sustain us, about finding meaningful vocations, and about living with the knowledge that, alone among all creatures, we know one day we're going to die. Technology may affect the material conditions of our lives, but it hasn't done much yet for our souls."[26]

That is the province, the task, and the joy of the gospel.

24. Mark Slouka, *War of the Worlds: Cyberspace and the High-Tech Assault on Reality* (New York: Basic Books, 1995), p. 22.

25. Turkle, *Life on the Screen,* pp. 312-13.

26. Nicholson, "The Pitfalls of a Brave New Cyberworld."

Reading Postmodern Culture through the Medium of Movies

CRAIG VAN GELDER

We all know the psychic powers of the televised image. But we need to capitalize on it, make it work for us, instead of us work-ing for it. To me, my thing is — a video image is much more powerful and useful than actual events. Like, back when I used to go out, I was walking down the street. This guy came barrel-ing out of a bar. He fell right in front of me and he had a knife right in his back, . . . well, I have no reference to it now. I can't refer back to it. I can't press rewind. I can't put it on pause. I can't put it on slow mo and see all the details. And the color-ation was all wrong. It didn't look like blood. The hue was off and I couldn't adjust the hue. There I was standing for real, but it just wasn't right. I didn't even see the knife impact the body. I mean, I missed that part.

TV Man in *Slacker*, 1991[1]

So speaks TV Man in Richard Linklater's 1991 cult film, *Slacker*, a satire on the culture of Generation X. For TV Man, the image on the screen is more real than experiencing actual life, and besides, you can get the coloration right and see all the details from various angles as

1. Richard Linklater, *Slacker*, an Orion Release, 1991.

you replay the image over and over. For this reason, TV Man now resides permanently in a room filled with television screens and VCRs, where he can create and control his images of reality. TV Man serves as a metaphor for the postmodern condition.

For the emerging generation, the camera is the new eye of the soul, imprinting on the human psyche a code of images and scripts for interpreting life. As Norman Denzin notes in *Images of Postmodern Society*, "The search for meaning of the postmodern moment is a study of looking. It can be no other way. This is a visual, cinematic age. The collage and the mixed-media-tele/audio text are the iconic markers of this moment."[2]

Ours is a postmodern age, one that is increasingly being shaped by images on the screen. Central to this influence of images is the role of movies. Understanding the medium of movies, and the messages contained in this unique discourse, offers important and helpful insights into understanding the postmodern condition. This article provides the reader with an introduction to reading postmodern culture through this medium.

The presentation is developed in five sections. First, a brief description of what we have come to know as the postmodern condition provides the reader with some reference points in understanding our current culture. Second, a short history of cinema and the development of the movie industry provide perspective on the transition in recent decades into the postmodern condition. Third, the malleable nature of the medium of movies as an art form is discussed in relation to various theories that have been offered for interpreting movies. Fourth, a number of cinematic examples demonstrate ways in which some recent movies reflect and/or present characteristics of the postmodern condition. And finally, some reflections will be offered on how the gospel might be proclaimed as good news to persons who represent the newly emerging postmodern self within the postmodern condition.

2. Norman K. Denzin, *Images of Postmodern Society: Social Theory and Contemporary Cinema* (Newberry Park, Calif.: Sage Publications Ltd., 1991), p. viii.

What Is the Postmodern Condition?

The word *postmodern* is gaining increasing public usage and a substantial literature is now available to describe this new condition.[3] However, as recently as the late1980s, this concept was still limited primarily to the domain of philosophers and social theorists. While it now has a more popularized usage, little progress has been made in clearing up the ambiguities associated with it. These ambiguities appear to be inherent in the cultural conditions that are increasingly being described as the "postmodern condition." Something of these ambiguities is evident in the definition provided in the recent work by Denzin:[4]

> Postmodernism is defined by the following terms: a nostalgia, conservative longing for the past, coupled with an erasure of the boundaries between past and the present; an intense preoccupation with the real and its representations; a pornography of the visual; the commodification of sexuality and desire; a consumer culture which objectifies a set of masculine cultural ideals; intense emotional experiences shaped by anxiety, alienation, ressentiment, and a detachment from others.

While by no means exhaustive of the themes found in the current discussion of the postmodern, this definition indicates something of the diversity of its character. It also indicates something of the complexity of the transition that is taking place within our culture. Although people today may not be able to articulate a coherent definition of what they understand as the postmodern condition, they are clearly aware that something fundamental has shifted in our culture.

Various theories have been suggested in trying to bring some clarity to this shift. Most theorists work from the premise that the key

---

3. Persons not familiar with this literature might find it helpful to read the following — from the perspective of the social sciences, Steven Best and Douglas Kellner, *Postmodern Theory: Critical Interrogations* (New York: The Guilford Press, 1991), or Robert Hollinger, *Postmodernism and the Social Sciences* (Thousand Oaks, Calif.: Sage Publications, 1994); and from a Christian perspective, J. Richard Middleton, *Truth Is Stranger than It Used to Be: Biblical Faith in a Postmodern Age* (Downers Grove, Ill.: InterVarsity Press, 1995), or Stanley J. Grenz, *A Primer on Postmodernism* (Grand Rapids: Eerdmans, 1996).

4. Denzin, *Images of Postmodern Society,* p. vii.

threshold of change took place somewhere in the late 1960s to early 1970s, although many recognize that there are precursors to the postmodern dating back into the nineteenth and early twentieth centuries. Frederic Jameson suggests that the postmodern shift is rooted primarily in the recent transition in our economy to a globalized, consumer capitalism. Jean-François Lyotard suggests that the shift is tied to the recognition of "difference" as the basic reality of life in the face of the collapse of metanarratives that once provided explanations of the social order in terms of uniformity, the essential, and objectivity. Gilles Deleuze and Flex Guattari place the postmodern shift in the dethroning of reason along with the rise of feeling and desire as the basis for human choice. Michel Foucault suggests that the unmasking of the Enlightenment notion of objectivity is the key turning point, as he demonstrates the inherent power embedded in all conceptual frameworks, theories, and worldviews. Jean Baudrillard places the transition within the emergence of an image culture of simulation, where signs have become disconnected from the reality they are supposed to represent.[5]

These notions — a changed economic order, difference, desire, power, and simulation — all provide clues to understanding that the world we now live in is a different social location from that occupied by persons only a few generations ago. While the "modern world" is still very much with us, the "postmodern condition" now thoroughly invades its space. It is helpful to note how a number of the common traits identifiable within this condition are interrelated with the rise of an image culture in our cinematic age.

Living in the "Here and Now"

The postmodern condition is identified with the collapse of the boundary between being here versus being there. The focus of our image-oriented world places all reality within immediate proximity. We see this in our ability to transcend both time and space as we go

---

5. A fuller discussion of these theorists is provided in Craig Van Gelder, "Mission in the Emerging Postmodern Condition," in George R. Hunsberger and Craig Van Gelder, eds., *The Church between Gospel and Culture: The Emerging Mission in North America* (Grand Rapids: Eerdmans, 1996), pp. 127-34.

"around the world in 30 minutes" with news coverage that is up to the minute. The postmodern condition is also identified with the collapse of the boundary between the past and the present. We see this especially in architecture, where historical styles are eclectically woven into a new collage of meaning; but also in film, in movies like *Batman* (1989) where the past and present merge, as cities of the 1920s and 1990s are woven together into a new urban form.

Living with "Perspectival Understanding"

The postmodern condition is identified with a relativity that comes from seeing something from multiple perspectives. This perspectival and relative character of viewing is illustrated in our ability to judge the "truth of the matter" as we watch four different camera angles replay the previous catch of the football to see if the receiver really did keep his feet in bounds, all of which can be manipulated through slow motion and freeze frame. The eye of the camera places us in the position of making a personal judgment based on a variety of perspectives.

Living with "Constructed Meanings"

The postmodern condition is identified with what is known as the social construction of reality. This consists of truth claims (with a small "t") that depend on the angle of one's perspective, or the angle of the camera chosen. The multiple conspiracy theories related to the assassination of J. F. Kennedy all work from the same source materials of written testimony and recorded audio and video tapes. But they often come to quite contrary conclusions depending on how one constructs the evidence (e.g., Oliver Stone's *JFK*, 1991). While multiple theories based on the same evidence are nothing new, it is the malleability, in particular, of audio and film texts which heightens the impact of constructed meanings on our interpretation of history and/or reality.

Living with "Endless Choices"

The postmodern condition is identified with the continued expansion of choices that are made available to us. We can now go to the video store and choose from thousands of titles that are readily available for us to rent. We can also sit in front of our TVs and constantly reconstruct our present-tense world as we flip through the hundred-plus channels on our cable system. Endless choices, however, while increasing our personal freedom, tend to fragment any shared meanings as they lessen our shared social experiences.

These traits of the postmodern condition, interrelated as they are with the rise of our cinematic image culture, suggest the importance of understanding this culture through one of its more important mediums — the movies. Although consisting of much more than movies, as seen especially in the pervasive influence of TV and video, movies nevertheless make up an essential part of the formation of the image culture that is now part of the postmodern condition. In understanding movies, it is helpful to know something of their historical development.

A Short History of the Cinema

We have lived now with motion pictures for a century. The first "Cinéomatographe" was produced in 1895 by the French brothers, August and Louis Lumière. The technology was developing in the U.S. about that same time, and by the turn of the century a new industry was beginning to take shape. While the construction of any scheme of periodization is always fraught with difficulty, especially in the face of the deconstructive tendencies of postmodernism, it is possible to discern some basic themes of development and change within the film industry during this century. The following discussion draws primarily on the recent work of William D. Romanowski, *Pop Culture Wars.*[6] Using his material, I am suggesting four periods as a way of interpreting important changes that have taken place within the movie industry.

---

6. William D. Romanowski, *Pop Culture Wars: Religion & the Role of Entertainment in American Life* (Downers Grove, Ill.: InterVarsity Press, 1996), esp. chs. 6-11.

Silent Pictures for Working-Class Immigrants, 1900-1920s

During the first several decades of this century, the fledgling film industry produced silent pictures. For the most part, these early films were directed at a working-class constituency, made up mainly of recent immigrants who flocked to the movies to better understand the American way of life into which they expected to be assimilated. These movies were fairly straightforward stories that developed along a linear plot-line: a presentation of the characters, an introduction of a difficulty or crisis, and the solving of the problem, usually developed within a romantic love story while typically offering some type of moral lesson. A classic from this period, representing the development of the full-length feature film, is the work of D. W. Griffith, *The Birth of a Nation* (1915). His use of close-ups, long shots, traveling shots, pans, and cross-cutting demonstrated the possibilities of this new medium as an art form.[7]

Increasingly, many of these movies began to reflect issues inherent within the dynamic urban culture of the growing cities of the nation. The old morality of the elite was commonly critiqued as repressive and out of touch with the times. Out of concern for the welfare of the community, the Board of Censorship of Motion Pictures was formed in 1909, with its name changed to the National Board of Review in 1915. The Board's membership and its work clearly reflected the middle-class, Protestant community. Its intent was "to establish standards for the moral and social improvements of movies that were universally accepted."[8] While the Board accepted movies as primarily an art form protected by First Amendment rights, an interesting development took place in 1915. That year, the Supreme Court ruled in an Ohio case, where *The Birth of a Nation* had been protested on racial bias grounds, that movies were primarily a business, not art or speech, and therefore were not to be given First Amendment free-speech protection. This led to increased efforts by the middle-class, Protestant establishment to define moral boundaries for this growing industry.

7. William V. Costanzo, *Reading the Movies* (Urbana, Ill.: National Council of Teachers of English, 1992), p. 51.
8. Romanowski, *Pop Culture Wars,* pp. 134-35.

Craig Van Gelder

The Rise of the Studio System, 1920s-1950s

By the 1920s, significant changes were taking place in the film industry. The production of films was largely taken over by a handful of recent Jewish immigrants, who chose to relocate the industry to the growing town of Hollywood. These entrepreneurs developed what came to be known as the studio system, which consisted of the large studios of Universal, Paramount, MGM, and Warner Brothers developing vertical control within the industry through owning all phases of production, distribution, and the showing of films. What emerged within these studios, was a "star system" where leading actors/actresses came under long-term contracts with a studio. These systems became even more powerful after 1927 when the introduction of the "talking" movie further expanded the popularity of cinema among the public.

Increasingly the content of movies explored the new morality of urban life. Representative of this development was Cecil B. DeMille, who exploited a "basic duality in his audiences — on the one hand their tremendous eagerness to see what they considered sinful and taboo, and on the other, the fact that they could enjoy sin only if they were able to preserve their own sense of righteous respectability."[9] This duality heightened the intent of both Catholic and Protestant reformers to provide clear guidelines on movie content. Reflecting these concerns, the industry developed a voluntary Motion Picture Production Code. The basic intent of the Code was to preserve the "synthesis of the general principles of Judeo-Christian morality and the ideals of American middle-class culture."[10] The end result was to lock much of Hollywood filmmaking into a stylistic straightjacket, while doing little to calm the concerns of the reformers.

The Code lasted well into the post-WWII period, when significant changes began to undermine its viability. Not diminished during this time, however, was the sheer production of films. Over 7,600 feature films were produced between 1930 and 1945, although the vast majority were made for the B movie market, being bundled with more substantial feature films offered by a particular studio. Only a few

9. Arthur Knight, *The Liveliest Art: A Panoramic History of the Movies* (New York: New American Library/Mentor Books, 1957), p. 115.
10. Romanowski, *Pop Culture Wars,* p. 152.

46

films from this period have come forward as classics, some of the most significant being *Gone with the Wind* (1939), *The Wizard of Oz* (1939), and *Citizen Kane* (1941).

New Directions in the Movie Industry, 1950s-1960s

There is a certain irony in the fact that it was Jewish immigrant outsiders who came to control a film industry that became the guardian of middle-class values and the American way of life. However, the self-imposed, voluntary Production Code, while keeping films morally safe, also tended to keep them artistically immature. This began to change in the 1950s following the Supreme Court's decision of 1948, which found studios in violation of antitrust laws. The major studios were forced to divest themselves of their theater chains, giving rise to the expansion of independent producers. The Court also reversed itself on the free-speech status of movies, viewing them no longer as "a business pure and simple," but as constitutionally protected art.[11]

Another influence that began to reshape cinema was the influx of European "art" movies that often presented sexual themes in a more explicit manner. Since they fell outside the purview of the Production Code, they were unregulated and gained increased public support through the rise of "art theaters." But the biggest change to impact the movie industry in the 1950s was the introduction of TV, which quickly led to substantial declines in movie attendance. Movie revenues as a percentage of entertainment expenditures declined from 12 percent in 1950 to 3 percent in 1970.

As the studio system broke up and studios began to lose their domain, they attempted to maintain market share by introducing new technologies. The 1950s saw the introduction of innovations such as 3-D movies, Technicolor, Cinerama, CinemaScope, and, most importantly, the "blockbuster" film.[12] The latter was an effort by a studio to dominate the movie market through producing a smash hit. While some blockbusters were successful monetarily (*The Robe*, 1953; *The Ten Commandments*, 1956; *Ben Hur*, 1959), many others were fi-

11. Romanowski, *Pop Culture Wars*, p. 169.
12. Costanzo, *Reading the Movies*, p. 55.

nancial failures (*Spartacus*, 1960; *Cleopatra*, 1963; *The Greatest Story Ever Told*, 1965). As the well-being of studios became increasingly dependent on achieving a hit, several became insolvent in their failure to do so. The blockbuster pattern remains to this day as a driving force in the industry.

By the mid-1960s, it was becoming evident that the Production Code was no longer providing adequate guidelines for movie content. The Supreme Court's decision in 1968 to give local authorities the right to protect children from obscene materials hastened the adoption of a Motion Picture Rating System that classified movies by age categories according to the suitability of content. One key development in light of this was the production of many films that previously would have been impossible to make under the Code, many of which have come to be viewed as important cinematic works of art (e.g., *The Godfather*, 1972; *Nashville*, 1975; *One Flew over the Cuckoo's Nest*, 1975; and *Platoon*, 1986).

Transitions into the Postmodern Condition in Movies, 1960s and Following

The period of the late 1960s and early 1970s was a tumultuous one in which a plethora of movements worked to challenge the prevailing worldview of middle-class values, the American Dream, and the intrinsic authority of institutions. The medium of movies, which had once served to reinforce this worldview, became increasingly used by a new generation of directors to challenge its basic tenets. In this transition, the core audience for movies shifted from families to youth. The youth market was made up of the baby-boom generation that was now coming of age in the form of the counterculture. Before long the target demographic for many movies was the nineteen-year-old male who was attracted to the formula of the visual, sensual, violent, and horrific.

What resulted was the formation of a New Hollywood, one that was no longer restricted by the Production Code, and one where film could now be pursued as art on its own terms. These terms included both changes in technology and new directions in content, and they were pursued by a new generation of smaller, independent studios, exemplified especially by American International Pictures (AIP).

This studio became the training ground for a host of talented directors who pioneered youth-oriented genres such as beach and surfing, horror, teen comedies, rock 'n' roll, and countercultural films.[13] Art and entertainment became commingled into the medium without distinction. In particular, it was the emergence of the social protest movie that alerted the larger public that the medium of movies was in transition toward a different worldview in terms of content. Two movies that typify this genre and its importance in reshaping the role of movies in society were Mike Nichols's *The Graduate* (1968) and Dennis Hopper's *Easy Rider* (1969).

Another major transition into the postmodern was stylistic, with the incorporation of the subjective perspective introduced earlier in European art films. The emphasis shifted toward "an exploration of the nature and sources of the character's psychological state. Characters are often confused, ambivalent, alienated; their goals and desires uncertain; and their actions inconsistent and often followed by self-doubt."[14] In order to portray such, directors exploited the malleability of the medium through the techniques of dream sequences, fantasies, flashbacks, and hallucinations, with the technology of freeze frames, slow motion, and jump cuts. What once had been a typical movie narrative with a clear story line and predictable characters was now a subjective and tentative presentation of life's disarray.

These transitions were more fully pursued during the 1970s with the addition of an increasing emphasis on special effects, especially in the genres of the disaster film (e.g., *Poseidon Adventure*, 1972; *The Towering Inferno*, 1974; *Jaws*, 1975) and the adventure film (e.g., the *Star Wars* series — 1977, 1980, 1983; or the *Indiana Jones* series — 1981, 1984, 1989). Increasingly, technological developments made

---

13. Romanowski (pp. 237-38) points this out through the work of Roger Corman, who was "AIP's most prolific and influential director, producer and sreenwriter" for many years. The "Cormanesque formula became a staple in contemporary filmmaking: action, sex, humor, and a 'slight social statement.'" His formula reflected the experimental and protest mood of the 1960s and 1970s, and its influence can be seen on a whole generation of new directors he worked with and helped mentor, including Francis Ford Coppola (*The Godfather,* 1972), Jonathan Demme (*One Flew over the Cuckoo's Nest,* 1975), Peter Bogdanovich (*The Last Picture Show,* 1971), Martin Scorsese (*Raging Bull,* 1980), Jonathan Kaplan (*The Accused,* 1988), and Ron Howard (*Night Shift,* 1982).

14. Romanowski, *Pop Culture Wars,* p. 232.

special effects standard fare for any movie that intended to become a blockbuster. The same pattern continues to the present, as seen in the continued use of bigger and more dramatic images of disaster (*Independence Day,* 1996) or adventure (*Jurassic Park,* 1993).

The postmodern turn in movies intersects with all of these transitions. It includes shifts within the content of movie narratives, differences of approach and perspective by various directors, developments in the technology of movie making, and continued changes in the general cultural milieu. It is the very malleability of movies that has made them such a natural medium for expressing the postmodern condition.

The Malleability of the Medium of Movies

Film represents a unique type of language, a language that appeals to the eye and ear in addition to the mind. It contains literary elements such as plot, theme, and character development, but it also has unique cinematic properties such as framing, lighting, sound, and editing. Over the past several decades, film has increasingly come to be seen as "a symbol system, much like language, which encodes the values of society, reflecting and reforming our most essential cultural beliefs."[15] It is not a neutral medium that simply entertains. Movies help us reflect on the world as they hold it up to our view, and they help shape the very way we see the world. There are "countless ways in which (films) have trained us to observe the world. Without the model of movies, much of our mental editing, focusing, and filtering would be unthinkable."[16]

Film has helped give rise to what can be defined as the "postmodern self," the self that is oriented primarily toward the visual, a visual that has increasingly been shaped by film images. Christian Metz interprets this in terms of Lacan's "mirror image" stage of a person's identity formation. Especially through film, an individual is taught to be viewer, one whose identity becomes shaped through perception of film images. The postmodern self is first of all a voyeur, one who assumes the privileged, and somewhat passive, position of

15. Costanzo, *Reading the Movies,* p. ix.
16. Costanzo, *Reading the Movies,* p. 1.

being able to observe and perceive.[17] In addition, "the postmodern self has become a sign of itself, a double dramaturgical reflection anchored in media representations on the one side, and everyday life on the other."[18] The influence of film in shaping the postmodern self is significant. A study conducted by Costanzo with her college students found that they watched an average of twenty-two movies a month, a figure that has grown substantially with the rise of cable TV and VCRs.[19]

It is the unique properties of the medium of movies which make them so powerful as an art form. On the one hand, there is in film the ever-present narrative text that provides the viewer with a story. This represents the "what" of film, and, as discussed above, has continued to undergo significant developments in the transition into the postmodern. On the other hand, there is the reality of film itself which represents the discourse, or medium, by which the story is conveyed.[20] As noted by Eisenstein over fifty years ago, it is the "synthetic" character of film, its malleability, that makes it such a powerful art form for shaping and presenting a view of reality.[21]

It is this malleability of the medium that raises certain issues in relation to the production of films. These issues are interwoven into the discussion and debates on film theory which began to surface early in this century, but which have become especially pronounced since the transition into the postmodern condition in the 1960s and 1970s. A brief review of these issues is helpful to gain some perspective in learning to read postmodern culture through the medium of movies. There are four that need to be addressed.

17. Christian Metz, *The Imaginary Signifier: Psychoanalysis and the Cinema,* original 1977, trans. Celia Britton et al. (Bloomington: Indiana University Press, 1982).

18. Denzin, *Images of Postmodern Society,* p. viii.

19. Costanzo, *Reading the Movies,* p. 3.

20. Costanzo, p. 14, as based on the work of Seymour Chatman, *Story and Discourse: Narrative Structure in Fiction and Film* (Ithaca, N.Y.: Cornell University Press, 1978).

21. Sergei Eisenstein, *Film Sense,* trans. Jay Leyda (New York: Harcourt Brace and Meridian, 1957).

Art Versus Entertainment

As noted in the discussion of the historical development of movies, this issue caused no little controversy for many years. If movies are an art form, then they should receive the same protection of free speech as guaranteed to other forms of art by the First Amendment. However, if movies are primarily entertainment, then they are subject to regulations tied to the production, commodification, packaging, and distribution practices of the marketplace. What confuses this issue in public discussion about movies is that for many years they were treated primarily as commercial entertainment products, thus raising expectations for public censorship of content. Also complicating this issue is the fact that movies have always found their popularity primarily among the masses rather than the elite, as is the case for many other art forms. This raises the suspicion that movies are more entertainment than art. The debate that continues to recur in public policy discussions about "cleaning up the movies" reflects the ambiguity of this issue of whether movies are primarily art or entertainment. In reality they need to be seen as both.

Representation Versus Interpretation

The powerful recording properties of film, similar to those of still photography, have caused some to stress that the purpose of film is to present a realistic depiction of the world. These theoretical "realists," as illustrated in the work of Siegfried Kracauer *The Theory of Film* (1960), stand in contrast to those who stress that the very character of film allows for the image to manipulate and interpret reality in unique ways. These theoretical "formalists," as illustrated in the work of Rudolf Arnheim, *Film As Art* (1966), note that the power of film is related to its very limitations. The properties of being two-dimensional and fixed-frame, and being subject to cut-action and editing, allows film to be used to present a unique interpretation of the world.[22] The postmodern turn in our culture, of course, lends its bias toward the latter view of film, especially with its tendency to privilege the inner life of emotion and the subjective.[23]

22. Costanzo, *Reading the Movies,* p. 65.
23. Costanzo, *Reading the Movies,* p. 23.

Author Versus Viewer

Directors have always left their personal imprint on their films. What has become an issue within the transition to the postmodern is whether film is to be understood primarily from the perspective of the director's intent, or from the perspective of the audience's interpretation of the presentation. This discussion has developed around the concept of "auteur," which refers to the director as the author on his or her film. Most agree that directors create something unique when it comes to producing a film, even when a film is based on an existing literary work (as up to 65 percent of all films are).[24] The technical aspects of the debate about an author's intent versus a reader's response are deeply embedded in the postmodern characteristics of perspectival understanding and the relativity of truth. Needless to say, in a subjective, image-driven, postmodern culture, the powerful character of film as a medium to present a more holistic version of reality tends to bias interpretation toward the viewer regardless of the intent of the director or author.

Structured Code Versus Ambiguous Code

Another postmodern debate has raged over the issue of structuralism as introduced through the work of Ferdinand de Saussure in language studies. De Saussure's contention was that all language has a system of discernible codes, or signs, which can be objectified. The deconstruction approach of Jacques Derrida in attacking the assumptions of structuralism, along with the work of other poststructural theorists, served as a doorway of transition into the postmodern discussion. The whole issue of coherence versus deconstructive tendencies within any particular film has become part of the postmodern debate. The details of this discussion go beyond the purpose of the present article, but in relating this discussion to movies it is important to note that some theorists have tried to discern a standardized code within film. For the most part, the limits of discerning such a code have been noted. As Christian Metz observes in his *Film Language,* the codes for film in both shooting and editing are far less precise than the syntax

24. Costanzo, *Reading the Movies,* p. 13.

and grammar of most languages — "Film is a rich message with a poor code."[25] The very malleability of the medium inherently means that film codes will constantly be undergoing development and change, even within films by the same director.

These issues make it clear that the medium of movies is complex, and attempting to interpret them is fraught with difficulty. Interpretations usually reflect one's theoretical perspective. However, it is possible to engage in the task of interpretation, as long as we recognize that like movies themselves, this process is as much an art as it is a science.

Interpreting Movies in Relation to the Postmodern Condition

In learning to read postmodern culture through film, there are at least three dimensions of the medium that need to be considered.[26] These are presented below along with a brief explanation of their relationship to the production of a film.

Dimension #1: The Narrative of a Movie

As noted earlier, this dimension relates both to the "what" of a movie, its story/text, and the "how" of a movie, its presentation/discourse. Critical to understanding any movie is to understand the director as "auteur," as the creator of a particular way of telling and presenting a story/text. The presentation of the story through the discourse of the medium of movies needs to be understood in terms of the presentation of various shots, which function much like a sentence and/or paragraph in a written work. The key is to note how shots are set up and edited. As Sergei Eisenstein observed years ago, the goal of editing is to develop a "montage," or a composition of related shots.[27]

25. Christian Metz, *Film Language: A Semiotics of the Cinema,* original 1968, trans. Michael Taylor (New York: Oxford University Press, 1974), p. 69.

26. This grid is adapted from the work of Philip Rosen, ed., *Narrative, Apparatus, Ideology: A Film Theory Reader* (New York: Columbia University Press, 1986).

27. Sergei M. Eisenstein, *Film Form: Essays in Film Theory,* edited and translated by Jay Leyda (New York: Harcourt, Brace & World, 1949).

"To Eisenstein, the essence of montage is conflict, a dialectic in which A collides with B to form something entirely new."[28] The complexity of setting up shots is evident in such techniques as: an establishing shot, reverse-angle, insert, reaction, match cut, jump cut, and cross cutting. The complexity of editing shots is evident in the utilization of fade-ins, fade-outs, dissolves, wipes, enlargements, repeats (freeze frames), and skips.[29]

Dimension #2: The Apparatus of a Movie

Movies represent a particular technological usage, one which is, as we have noted above, quite malleable. The technologies used in the development of a movie include: the film, shutter speed, lenses, framing (shots/angles), lighting, motion/movement, sound, a soundtrack, and special effects. All of these variables go into the development of a scene, what might be thought of as the space constituting each particular frame of a shot. This represents what is referred to as the "mise-en-scène," all the elements that go into a single shot of film. As theorized by André Bazin, the frames of film in cinema have the ability "to stop the flow of time and hold it in abeyance, in an eternal present tense."[30]

Dimension #3: The Ideology of a Movie

Every movie is embedded within a cultural milieu. This point is related to the central thesis of this article, that we are able to gain some insight into our contemporary postmodern culture by reading it through the medium of movies. Movies reflect their time and place. They are inherently rooted in ideological views and historically reflect the social history of their context. An example of this can be seen in a film written and directed by Oliver Stone — *Platoon*. Following a tour of service in Viet Nam, Stone wrote the

28. Costanzo, *Reading the Movies,* p. 64.
29. Costanzo, *Reading the Movies,* pp. 47-48.
30. André Bazin, *What Is Cinema?* (essays 1958-63), trans. Hugh Gray (Berkeley: University of California Press, 1967); as summarized in Costanzo, p. 65.

manuscript for this movie in 1970. However, the country was not yet ready to reflect on the war from a critical perspective. This would not occur until over a decade later, as movies like the *Deer Hunter* (1978) and *Apocalypse Now* (1979) were made. But even these movies tended to avoid the "stark, brutal, ground-level realities which [Stone] and others had known as soldiers."[31] It was in 1986, in the context of a national debate over U.S. involvement in Central America and President Reagan's complicity in such, that the time was right for *Platoon* to be made. The "stunning success" of the movie indicated the willingness of the country to take a more introspective look at the complicity of the United States in waging a war against the peoples of Viet Nam. Its success soon led to other movies stressing similar themes (e.g., *Full Metal Jacket*, 1987; *Good Morning, Vietnam*, 1988; and *Casualties of War*, 1989).[32]

It is now time to turn to a few examples of movies that reflect and/or present characteristics of the postmodern condition. Our method will be to introduce the movie and discuss it relative to one or more of the three perspectives noted above — its narrative, the apparatus used, and/or its ideology. The movies selected are intended to be illustrative and suggestive of the postmodern condition. Readers are encouraged to spend some time watching these movies to test the interpretations offered, and then try their own skills in evaluating other movies produced during the past several decades.

Blue Velvet (1986): The Quintessential Postmodern Movie

David Lynch's production is considered by many to be the "quintessential postmodern movie."[33] It introduces the viewer to a collage of postmodern themes, such as commingling past and present, sexual fantasy and exploitation, violence without moral direction or judgment, the power of gazing/viewing in shaping the voyeur's identity, and exposing the darker side within the best of any human motive. It

31. "A Filmmaker's Credo: Some Thoughts on Politics, History, and the Movies," in *The Humanist* 56 (5) (1996): 3.
32. Romanowski, p. 250.
33. Denzin, *Images of Postmodern Society,* p. 65.

is cast in a small town where Jeffery and Sandy are seen as teenage sweethearts on one level, with Jeffery stepping into a darker underworld of drugs, sex, and violence on another level.

Lynch's use of light and darkness, his contrasts of colors, and his commingling of the two worlds within the same social reality are all incorporated to play out a recoding of "the positions of male and female within an oppressive postmodern family scene."[34] As Sandy expresses at one point, "It is a strange world, isn't it?" Lynch's own commentary on the film notes that it "is a trip beneath the surface of a small American town, but it's also a probe into the subconscious or a place where you face things that you don't normally face."[35] These things include rotting, cut-off ears, sexual violence, brutality, insanity, homosexuality, the degradation of women, sado-masochistic rituals, drug use, and alcohol abuse. In the midst of facing his own darker side in all this, public and private boundaries collapse as Jeffery crosses into and out of a peaceful, suburban existence with Sandy as if the other world did not exist. The movie's postmodern subversion is to invite (force) the viewer to explore (own) the realities of his/her own darker side.

Sex, Lies, and Videotape (1989): A Film's Look at Film

The 1980s were about yuppies trying to work out their personal identity in a me-oriented world that stressed style over substance. In this endless search for identity, sex is disconnected from both personal commitment and relational intimacy. The movie *Sex, Lies, and Videotape* (1989) explores these themes at some length using the voyeuristic character of video as the means to unpack issues of personal identity. It is a movie about video therapy as the central character Graham, who is sexually impotent, is found mediating his world through the video-cam. For over nine years he has been inducing women to talk with him on tape about their sexuality, and to even undress for him at some point in the process. Graham's friend John is having an affair

---

34. Denzin, *Images of Postmodern Society,* p. 67.
35. David Chute, "Out to Lynch," in *Film Comment* 22 (Sept./Oct. 1986): 32-35.

with Cynthia, his wife's sister. Ann, the wife, challenges Graham at one point to own up to his own problems.[36]

Ann: "Why do you tape women?"

Graham: "Why should I tell you why? You don't know who I am. I can't just recount all the points in my life up to this moment. I have no idea who I am. Why explain myself to you?"

Ann: "Your problems."

Graham: "Problems. I look around this town and I feel and see John and Cynthia and I feel comparatively healthy."

Ann: "You've got a problem."

Graham: "Right. I've got a lot of problems. They belong to me."

Ann (now holding the camera on Graham): "You think they're yours. They're not. Everyone who walks into your life is affected. I'm leaving my husband because of you. You've had an effect on my life."

Graham wants to stay behind the camera as voyeur and hide the problem of his own impotency, but Ann forces him to face the fact that as much as one tries there is no place to hide from the reality of human relationships. The movie is about "video therapy," with the message that if we only learn to confess, things will work out. And there is much to confess — lies, deception, truth, self-denial, and sexual infidelities.[37] The movie's postmodern subversion is to use the eye of the camera to unmask the insecurities of life as we struggle to understand ourselves and one another.

JFK (1991): Perspectival Understanding and Constructed Meanings

Earlier, the work of Oliver Stone was introduced through his movie *Platoon.* Following the remarkable success of that movie, Stone moved into "the JFK business."[38] His early childhood was dramatically

36. Denzin, *Images of Postmodern Society,* pp. 109, 111.
37. Denzin, *Images of Postmodern Society,* p. 110.
38. *The Humanist.*

shaped by an unmasking of some lies that had been perpetrated within his family history. This led to his becoming intrigued with the power of disinformation to control social realities. This theme is evident in *Platoon*, but took on a heightened focus with his making of *JFK*. Stone was heavily criticized for what many felt was a reconstruction of historical fact in his presentation of a conspiracy theory in the assassination of Kennedy. Stone, in making his own defense, noted:[39]

> Had JFK been examined intelligently by its critics, they would have discovered that the body of thought presented in the movie wasn't original and certainly wasn't invented by me; it was a compendium of facts and findings which have been made by people who have been challenging the Warren Report and conducting their own citizen investigations into the murder since the 1960s. What was unique about my film was the style in which it was made; even so, it shocked the political establishment, incurring their wrath in a way I had never imagined possible. After all, this was old material to me, but for some reason it seemed new and radical to others.

What Stone did was take familiar materials and turn them into high-impact images in the form of a movie. Because of the historical character of the event of the assassination, and the representative power of film to present images that appear to portray history, *JFK* took on a life of its own. In it Stone demonstrates the power of the medium of film to construct alternative meanings. The conspiratorial theme has continued to serve as a genre for Stone in such films as *Natural Born Killers* (1994) and *Nixon* (1995). The intent of the former was to attack the medium of television for its trivialization and sensationalizing of events. The intent of the latter was to unmask the darker side of the American political establishment. The postmodern subversion in much of Stone's work is the demonstration that reality and truth are often not what they seem to be, and many times are, in fact, the opposite of what is portrayed.

39. *The Humanist.*

Slacker (1991): Randomness, Chaos, and Conspiracy

A vignette from this movie was used to introduce this article. The movie consists of a whole series of personal experiences of unconnected characters whose lives randomly meet on the streets of Austin, Texas. The movie was literally "made up" as it went along, with the actors often designing the next day's shootings the evening before. The theme of the movie is that there is no coherent theme to life. This coherent theme of incoherence is developed through the movie's presenting several scores of vignettes, all independent and without connection to each other in content or characters. They are woven together through random meetings flowing out of the events of everyday life. This randomness and chaos is captured well in the opening scene as a character catches a taxi from the bus station and spins his philosophy of life.

> Every thought you have creates its own reality. It's like every choice or decision you make, the thing you choose not to do fractions off and becomes its own reality, you know, it just goes off from there forever. . . . All the other directions, just because you think about them, become separate realities. But we'll never see it because we're kind of trapped in this one reality restriction type of thing.

The structure of the entire movie follows this randomness of reality being constructed by chance encounters. If there is any sense of a common theme in this movie it is probably best captured by the notion of conspiracy. A significant number of the vignettes portray various conspiracy theories about the assassination of JFK or the control of information by the government. Although the movie is an obvious parody on the aimlessness of Generation X, it is nevertheless a powerful cinematic portrayal of the emptiness and meaninglessness of life once the façade is stripped away. Its postmodern subversion is the stark presentation of a full-blown nihilism that was first theorized a century ago by Nietzsche.

Sleepless in Seattle (1994): Narrative? —
Any Old Movie Will Do

Coming out in the summer of 1993, this movie faced an uphill battle for box office attention in the midst of such blockbusters as *Jurassic Park*. However, this movie caught the public's attention as a romantic comedy. Several things are interesting in evaluating this movie from the perspective of the postmodern condition. One is that the movie raises all the great philosophical questions of life (suffering, death, aloneness), but proceeds to answer them without referring to the God-categories. It is a movie about a postmodern secular spirituality that offers experiences without answers. A classic example of this is seen in Jonah's waking up from a nightmare after his mother has passed away, and being comforted by his father, Sam.

> Jonah: "I miss her. What do you think happens to someone after they die?"
>
> Sam: "I don't know."
>
> Jonah: "Like, do you believe in heaven?"
>
> Sam: "I never did believe anything about the whole idea of an afterlife, but now I don't know, because I have these dreams about your mom. And we have long talks about you, about how you're doing. So, what is that? That's sort of an afterlife, isn't it?"
>
> Jonah: "I'm starting to forget her."

The only comfort that a secular spirituality can offer for immortality is memories, but memories fade over time.

Another interesting postmodern theme introduced in this movie is the use of an older movie, *An Affair to Remember* (1957), as the controlling narrative for the development of the story line. This older movie's story line becomes the recurring referent for the various characters to interpret their reality and construct personal meaning. The message is clear — the loss of metanarratives in the postmodern condition means that any old movie will do as a narrative for constructing meaning. The postmodern subversion of this movie is its enchanting story of love and human relationships on one level in the midst of a roaring nihilism that rages just below the surface.

How is it that Christians should respond to movies such as those

61

noted above? How can they help us understand the culture in which we live and carry out our responsibility of proclaiming the gospel as good news?

The Gospel as Good News to the Postmodern Self

What is critical to recognize is that most people today are in a different social location from persons of only a few decades ago. The extent of the shift is most evident among youth today, but its effects are by no means limited to them. Persons of all ages now find themselves shaped by characteristics of the postmodern condition. What should be the posture of Christians in facing this shift?

First, it is important to recognize that not everything within the postmodern condition necessarily presents a problem to Christian faith or the gospel. The emphasis on holism within the postmodern is closer to the biblical worldview than much of the atomistic ideology of the Enlightenment and modernity. A focus on earthkeeping and on stewardship of natural resources within the postmodern also finds points of convergence with Christian thinking. And the postmodern resurfacing of spirituality as a viable and necessary dimension of human existence provides a very effective bridge for communicating the gospel as good news to persons shaped by the postmodern condition.

Second, it is important to recognize that the gospel always meets people where they are, while calling them into a new space of living in the redemptive reality of God's kingdom reign. It is critical to find points of contact within the worldview of the other person in trying to present the gospel as good news. For too long, much of the Christian movement has spent its energies trying to shore up a churched culture that shared some form of Christian values. This often placed Christians in a defensive posture in relating to persons outside the faith. In the postmodern condition, the role of the church in society has been marginalized, as discussed at length in other articles in this volume. But it is from this posture that fresh attempts to bridge to the postmodern worldview can be made. This is why the medium of movies provides such a powerful tool for both analyzing the culture and for finding points of contact.

Third, it is critical to understand the limits of the postmodern self as a way of understanding the human condition. It is important for Christians to "live into" the space that postmodern persons occupy and to experience something of the angst that these persons feel in the midst of randomness, chaos, and nihilism. Being created in the image of God provides all persons with aspirations that go beyond these limits. But unless we can feel the brokenness of other people, it is unlikely that we will be able to present the gospel to them as good news. The medium of movies offers all of us a profound way to enter into the angst of the postmodern condition and to increase our capacity for empathy with postmodern people as we seek to invite them into God's redemptive reign.

Summary

The medium of movies provides a power tool for understanding the postmodern condition and for developing capacity in presenting a gospel that can relate to persons shaped by this condition. As we engage this task, we also need to become more discerning of the extent to which we ourselves have been shaped by this same culture. For those who are discerning, movies can function much like a mirror to help us see ourselves and our own shortcomings in relation to the call that God has placed on our lives. They can also remind us of the marginality that is often required of those who choose to sing the songs of Zion in a foreign land.

SECTION II

Understanding the Church in the North American Mission Context

If the church takes seriously the fact that North America is now a mission field, this has tremendous implications for congregations. One of the most important implications is that many of the assumptions that have guided the development of the church over the past several centuries are now in need of critique and redefinition (e.g., denominations, individualism, and success). Another implication is that the church will increasingly need to recognize that its own location in the present culture is no longer at the center, but at the margins. Being on the margins, however, can provide fresh opportunities for thinking about offering confident witness as the church. This section of articles provides the reader with insight into this shift in the church's location.

The scope of this change is dramatic, although it has taken different turns in Canada and the United States. In the former, a pervasive nominalism now invades the church. In the United States, the privatization of the faith continues to disarm the church from having a voice in relating to our culture. These changes are discussed in the article by Douglas John Hall. He invites readers not to linger too long over the carnage of a Christendom that is now collapsing, but instead to engage boldly in the task of untangling ourselves from the vestiges of such a Christendom. His thesis is that our new position of "diaspora" is more consistent with the very nature of the gospel and the character of the church as a people of Jesus. Living in diaspora, however, is not to be equated with resigned passivity. It is to be seen as a fresh opportunity to rethink the faith theologically in order for the church to be in mission to its culture.

At one time the urban landscape was dominated by church steeples; today it is skyscrapers. This transition is used by Clinton Stockwell, in the second article in this section, to illustrate the tremendous changes that have taken place in this century in the place and role of the church in society. He uses an analysis of power and "the powers" to unmask some of the oppressive urban structures that now shape our culture. The reader is provided with a "tour" of the streets of Chicago, and some of its local level church leaders, as a way of gaining perspective on developing strategies for effective Christian witness by a church that is now on the margins of society. Today, even if religious congregations no longer build impressive cathedrals, their life together is still vital in urban communities.

The church always lives in a cultural context, and must always find relevant ways of relating to its context. In doing so, the church is always subject to the problems of syncretism. While Christians in the West have been quick to note church syncretisms in other parts of the world, they have not been as quick to reflect on their own. In the third article in this section, Wally Hobbs provides helpful insights into thinking about syncretism as a problem in North American congregations. Using the three areas of modern science, individualism, and organization, he unpacks some of the ways the gospel has been syncretistically trivialized within our culture.

Living as a faithful community on the margins of society is not necessarily easy. Nor is the gospel an easy message to preach within congregations that have grown used to living in a declared "truce" with our changed culture. Dan Devadatta offers, in the last article in this section, an example of how such a message can be preached. By drawing on the content of Peter's first letter, he points out what this new mission situation entails. Foundational to the task is understanding that we are still God's people, even if our circumstances have changed. Dan offers some practical suggestions for living as a parallel people in this new location by learning to live courageously, redemptively, and wholly.

Metamorphosis: From Christendom to Diaspora

DOUGLAS JOHN HALL

My thesis is this: In so far as our outlook is really based on today, and looking towards tomorrow, the present situation of Christians can be characterized as that of a *diaspora;* and this signifies a "must" from which we may and must draw conclusions about out behavior as Christians.

When we say that we [must] make a cool, dispassionate reckoning with the fact that the Church is a *diaspora,* we mean . . . the very opposite of resignation and defeatism. If we once have the courage to give up our defense of the old facades which have nothing or very little behind them; if we cease to maintain, in public, the pretense of a universal Christendom; if we stop straining every nerve to get *everybody* baptized, to get *everybody* married in church and onto our registers (even when success means only, at bottom, a victory for tradition, custom and ancestry, not for true faith and interior conviction); if, by letting all this go, we visibly relieve Christianity of the burdensome impression that it accepts responsibility for everything that goes on under this Christian top-dressing, the impression that Christianity is . . . a sort of Everyman's Religious Varnish, a folk-religion (at the same level as that of folk-costumes) — *then* we can be free for real missionary adventure and apostolic self-confidence. . . .

We have still not fully wakened from our dream of a homogeneous Christian West. It often leads us to react furiously and in a false context when something happens to shake us out of the dream; we often seek, again in a false context and with inappropriate means, to realize this dream-ideal, and so apply ourselves to the wrong point altogether.[1]

None of what I have just written is my own. It represents very accurately, however, the point of view I wish to express in this brief article. If I tell you who was the author of this quotation, you may be somewhat surprised. For these are thoughts that emanate from one whom many regard as the greatest Roman Catholic theologian of our century, Karl Rahner. They appear in his work titled *Mission and Grace,* published in the early 1960s. They constitute part of Rahner's forthright prescription for the exercise in radical self-knowledge that the Christian church must undergo if it is to engage in any mission based on reality and on grace, and is not just a perpetuation of the expansionism that, for most of its history, Christendom mistook for mission.

In the spirit of Rahner's assessment, but operating a little later in time and in the context of another continent, I want to develop here three consecutive observations. The first is *metamorphosis* — the Christian movement today is undergoing an immense transformation. The second is *intentionality* — we are not called to resist this transformation but to understand it, embrace it, and try to give it meaningful direction. The third is *theology* — we can only implement such an intention if we become more serious about our own distinctive spiritual and intellectual foundations, and the way they both separate us from our culture and enable us to engage our culture in contrast to merely reflecting it.

Metamorphosis: The Changing Form of the Body of Christ in the World

The alteration in the *morphe* or shape of Christianity that is occurring in our historical period is a momentous one. It is not to be compared with other historical transitions through which the Chris-

1. Karl Rahner, S.J., *Mission and Grace,* vol. 1, trans. Cecily Hastings (London, Melbourne, and New York: Sheed and Ward, 1963), pp. 1-55.

tian religion has passed, such as the Great Schism between East and West, or the breakdown of the medieval synthesis of faith and reason, or even the Reformation of the sixteenth century. There is only one previous transformation of the *morphe* of Christianity that adequately matches, in reverse order, this metamorphosis. This is the fourth-century transition of the Christian movement from the voluntary, minority, scattered, and often persecuted *communio viatorum* of the pre-establishment period, to the imperial church begun under Constantine and elevated to the status of exclusively legal cultus under Theodosius the Great.

To that beginning sixteen centuries ago, there now corresponds an ending. Once again the worldly form and vocation of the Christian movement is being fundamentally altered. Once again, as during its first three centuries, the Christian community is being required to live outside the protective walls of power and privilege. Once again, the church finds itself being pushed to the sociological periphery, where its message and mission must authenticate themselves quite apart from any external props and pressures, rewards and punishments. This is a hard and shocking thing for most Christians in the West, for a millennium and a half of living in the imperial household has profoundly conditioned all of us to expect that kind of preeminence as our birthright. We tend to forget the price we had to pay for our proximity to power.

The effective disestablishment of Christianity, of course, represents a long historical process. We are not speaking here of just decades. The humiliation of Christendom has been under way now for at least two centuries, and it may continue to occur for another century or more. But its reality, the basic character as disestablishment, can no longer be doubted by thoughtful people. Ever since the Renaissance, but more conspicuously since the Enlightenment of the eighteenth century, Christianity has experienced a steady erosion in the face of the great tide of autonomous rationality and the burgeoning secularity of the West. To this has been added, more recently, the graphic reality of religious pluralism. Nineteenth-century Christians could still sing blithely about conquering the world for Christ. Today we are conscious that our triumph-songs are overheard by others, namely by those who are no longer abstract statistics, but rather are persons with names and faces. These others are now our neighbors and coworkers, as well as the playmates of our children.

As anyone familiar with patterns of great historical transition would expect, the metamorphosis of Christendom is far from being globally uniform. Its progress and intensity vary from place to place. In many ways, those Christians in regions such as eastern Europe, where hostile regimes abruptly terminated the privileged status of the church during much of this century, have had a certain advantage. In such contexts, serious Christians could no longer pretend that nothing had changed. They had to become truthful. They had to become inventive. And they had to learn to think the faith, for they knew that they must be able to "give a reason for the hope that was in them" (1 Peter 3:15).

In our own part of the world, on the other hand, where the process of disestablishment has been more gradual and ambiguous, there are special problems that have to be faced by responsible Christians. Here, complacency and self-deception on the part of Christian denominations and congregations are the greatest dangers. In the absence of conspicuous evidence of Christendom's malaise, some of us are able to continue to play at being the official religion of the dominant culture for a very long time. We do so by exaggerating our supposed successes and rationalizing our losses and failures as either a lack of faith or a function of inadequate leadership.

For the same reason, we tend to be less open, with some of us being entirely closed, to the more honest assessments of the religious situation that are a prerequisite to any genuine renewal. Locked into a culturally determined logic of progress, success, and positive-thinking, Christian bodies in North America regularly resist imaginative and viable proposals for the future of the church because they do not correspond to the great expectations that have been fashioned by centuries of ecclesiastical triumphalism. These expectations are being compounded, in our context, by the pressures of the marketplace. To those who are attracted to church growth and the megachurch, Karl Rahner's vision of the future church as a diaspora of little flocks here and there seems paltry and defeatist. So long as established patterns of institutional Christianity still work, even if they work only under exceptional circumstances, many will continue to be enticed by them. And they will continue to be blind to alternatives that may be more realistic and more faithful.

There are of course reasons why a type of Christian establishment has endured in North America, and especially in the United

States. Unlike the legal establishments of the Old World, which our forebears rejected, ours has been a cultural establishment. This is the identification of Christian faith with the aspirations of modernity in its New World expressions. European ecclesiastical establishments were created to legitimate and sustain the authority structures of premodern societies — the monarchies, class systems, and power bases of the classical and medieval periods. Christian establishment in North America has functioned more nebulously to undergird our official values, hopes, and moralities — what we like to call our way of life. The disintegration of the Christian establishment in Europe, which emerged earlier and more dramatically than ours, is bound up with the failure of the medieval synthesis, the *corpus christianum,* the monarchies, the class structures, and the power bases in which it was embedded.

In North America, the American Dream which Christianity was expected to sanction and uphold has also foundered visibly in our time, along with its "paler Canadian version" (James Laxer). But the very failure of the New World Dream has in some sense enhanced the public role of religion. For large numbers of our fellow citizens are unable to face the decline of their culture, and many look to the churches to help them repress their social doubt and identity crisis. Ironically, the perspective of a biblical and Reformation faith now works against many of these persons. Now these churches are expected to reinforce the social vision of success, happiness, and progress long after it has ceased concretely to inform most other institutions of the society, even government. Now one goes to church in order to be able to believe in America again!

There are many churches that are apparently quite willing to supply that demand. One of the great ironies of our time is that many of the churches that became most successful in this role of culture religion during the past two or three decades are those denominations and sectarian groups that formerly prided themselves on their strict separation from the world. Today, they have become so important in the scheme of things public that all who seek civic office must court their favor. Meanwhile, most of the old, mainline denominations that once formed the backbone of the Christian establishment on this continent now find themselves depleted and increasingly, almost arrogantly, ignored by the centers of power.

This, I would say, is to their advantage, if not exactly to their

71

credit. The Christians in the United States and Canada who should really be worried today are those who are being counted on for their support of the very policies that are killing the humanitarian gain we have been able to mount on this continent. The sidelining of the mainline churches, on the contrary, could possibly be the beginning of something very interesting. But unfortunately, apart from minorities within all of these once-mainline denominations, this change in position is not being perceived as an opportunity for ministry. Most of us are still, as Rahner observed, "dreaming Christendom dreams."[2] We envy the seeming success of the Christian Right, and we are made despondent by our reductions.

This despondency, this failure of nerve, this vocational confusion are all manifest in the high incidence of burnout among clergy. This is a consequence, in large measure, of bad theology! If the only criteria of authenticity that church folk know are drawn from sixteen centuries of theological triumphalism and ecclesiastical bravado, then almost anything that we can achieve in the churches today must seem inadequate. What we must begin to question, however, is not our performance so much as the theological standards (or the lack of them) by which our performance is determined and assessed. If we are ever going to be able to open ourselves to the diaspora that Karl Rahner and others consider the necessary shape of our Christian future, then we must develop a better theology of the church. We need one that will allow us to contemplate that form of the Christian movement with an expectancy that is, in Rahner's words, "the very opposite of resignation and defeatism."[3] We must see the hand of God in our changed circumstances, and so regard this metamorphosis through which we are passing not so much as the end of something, but as the beginning of something new.

Intentionality: On Being Stewards of Change

Basically there are only three alternatives for Christians caught in the tempestuous waters of the metamorphosis now taking place. They may resist the change, either openly or by a process of repressive de-

2. Rahner, *Mission and Grace*, pp. 1-55.
3. Rahner, *Mission and Grace*, pp. 1-55.

nial, and attempt to put the Humpty Dumpty of Christendom back together again. They may resign themselves to the change, with or without regret or sorrow, and simply allow the waves of transition to wash over them. Or they may seek to steward the change, asking for the positive meaning that is in it and endeavoring, on the basis of that perceived meaning, to direct the process toward its potential goal.

The latter response, so far as I am concerned, is the only one that is Christianly justifiable. Even apart from the question of its possibility, the idea of re-creating a Christian West seems to me repulsive theologically, and perhaps even wicked morally. But the rejection of that alternative does not just leave us adrift and redundant, doomed to eventual extinction. Rather than letting the process of disestablishment happen to us, we must discover, under the guidance of the divine Spirit, how to steer the ark of the Church so as to take best advantage of the winds and tides of the historical moment in which we find ourselves.

Such navigation, if for a moment I may continue to deploy the metaphor of seamanship, requires a far greater familiarity with the charts, and a far greater daring than most of us in these old churches have ever had. Until now we have relied primarily on sheer unthinking convention for our replenishment and renovation. To speak plainly, we need to learn a critical and constructive theology of the church that is based on the charter of Scripture and informed by the Holy Spirit, in contrast to one that is entrenched in the ecclesial conventions of Christendom.

Where is it written that the church must be a majority? Where are we told that the dignity, order, and authority of the *corpus Christi* can only be maintained if the church mirrors, in its internal structure and its mission, the accepted patterns of its host culture? Where, in our biblical charter, does it stand written that the Christian religion, being the only true one, must displace and repel every other claim to truth and goodness, and get the whole human populace onto its registers?

We have been giving to God what belongs to Caesar! We have been reading our scriptures with Constantinian eyes! We have made much of the so-called Great Commission, but little of the characteristic metaphors by which our Lord described his "little flock" (Luke 12:32). And we have made almost nothing at all of his question whether, upon his return, any faith would be found on earth (Luke

18:8). We have isolated and grossly exaggerated all the triumphal language of the Bible, and have paid little attention to the fact that the cross is at the center of our faith where it ought to condition the whole of our ecclesiology.

Salt, yeast, light, a little city set on a hill in a dark night, a small seed: these are the metaphors that belong to our charter. It was not Jesus who invented the imagery of the "mighty army." Reading of him in the gospels, I cannot imagine him plotting out the Holy Roman Empire, or Denmark as a Christian nation, or the United States of America becoming such either. Clearly, he was thinking of something far less grandiose, and, like a genuine pearl, far more precious.

And why would he not? He was a Jew. He understood the meaning of election, that in God's design it is often the few who are there for the many. He understood the logic of the covenant, that "through you all the families of the earth will be blessed" (Gen. 12:1-2). He knew that there are times when only minorities may be trusted as means to accomplish ends that majorities would never pursue, such as vigilance for the victims that they themselves, the majorities, inevitably create. He knew, having been reared in the tradition of the prophets, that prophetic consciousness is not born and nurtured in the houses of kings or of the priests who serve them, but only on the outskirts of power. This is the same type of consciousness that Martin Luther King, Jr. demonstrated so clearly in our own time and place. Jesus recognized, by the same token, that against all temptation to false glory and preeminence his little flocks would have to learn the humility of servanthood in order to represent his way in the world. No doubt he expected them to learn the way of the cross only with difficulty and backslidings. But do you suppose Jesus ever envisaged how enthusiastically the church of the ages would take up the very temptations that he himself resisted in the wilderness, temptations to power and glory of the most mundane sort?

The Jesus who gave the church its charter also assumed that such a witnessing community would have to separate itself again and again from the world, and that this could not occur without suffering. There is more in the New Testament about the suffering of the church than about any other single ecclesiastical theme. This has been, in many ways, the best kept secret of the Bible. As Dietrich Bonhoeffer taught us, this suffering is certainly not an end in itself. The cross is not to be sought out! The end is discipleship, not rejection and suffering.[4] We are aware that suffering and rejection are so typically the consequences of genuine discipleship that in their absence the church must wonder where its discipleship has gone wrong. The only indispensable mark of the church, said Luther, is the presence of the holy cross in its life.[5] By this he did not mean a mere liturgical symbol. And what, one asks, does Jesus the crucified one make of those churches that offer to end all suffering?

"Do not be conformed to this world" (Rom. 12:2), wrote the Apostle to the Gentiles, having himself learned the hard way of the suffering that belongs to nonconformity. But unlike those who glory in their nonconformity, as if it were the goal, Paul understood the meaning of the cross well enough to know that separation and even estrangement from the world are for the sake of the world. The world must not be prematurely written off. Of what use is the salt if it is not sprinkled on the food, or the yeast if it is kept apart from the dough, or the light if it is hidden under . . . our collection plates? The church that is simply of this world has nothing to bring to this world. It does not engage the world, it only reflects it. That, in a nutshell, has been and is the failing of all Christian establishments, and especially of the kind of cultural establishments that have been developed and promoted on this continent. But the alternative is not the holiness sect, the ghetto. The church that prides itself on its great distinctiveness has mistaken election for a tawdry version of elitism. Not *of* the world, then, but most decidedly *in* it, that is the dialectic that, informed by Scripture and the Spirit, we must recover (John 15:19).

My point is this: there is *potential* present in this enforced distancing from the world that is our present experience of disestablishment. Especially in the older, formerly more established of denominations, we may be enabled precisely to achieve the distance that we need to become the disciple community of the crucified one. Only in this way can we have any prospect at all of bringing to our world some perspective, some wisdom, some alternative, some redemptive word and deed that is not already there. Providentially, we are being pushed to the edges of the dominant cultures we have served so predictably.

4. Dietrich Bonhoeffer, *The Cost of Discipleship,* trans. R. H. Fuller (London: SCM Press, 1959), pp. 76-83.

5. Martin Luther, *Works of Martin Luther,* vol. 5 (Philadelphia: United Lutheran Publication House), pp. 270ff.; see also *Confessing the Faith: Christian Theology in a North American Context* (Minneapolis: Fortress Press, 1996), pp. 90-97.

We are now being cast into a position of redemptive self-doubt in which it may be possible for us to entertain once more the radicality of the gospel we have been talking about with such false ease.

This, I repeat, is a matter of potentiality. The great spiritual shift that is at work among us, contemplated in the light of a new exposure to the Scriptures and the best traditions of our past, untrammeled by Constantinian assumptions, could be the very jolt we need. It may allow these once-mainline churches to acquire a really vital function within a society that is itself undergoing unsettling changes. But such a potentiality can be made real only if we cease allowing these vast changes to wash over us like some great, unstoppable tide. We must grasp them for the opportunity they contain. Make no mistake, we *are* being disestablished. The message of the Holy Spirit to the church in our day is: "Don't wait to be wholly disestablished, disestablish *yourselves!*"

Theology: Disengaging in Order to Engage

Disestablish *yourselves!* But what does that mean, concretely speaking? It is a relatively straightforward thing to disestablish when establishment, in the primary sense, has meant a legal arrangement between the church and state. The famous Barmen Declaration required immense courage and a strong, biblically inspired theology; but it could come to the strategic point that it did come to with a kind of enviable immediacy. "Since we Christians are bound in obedience to the one Lord," said the drafters of that Declaration, in effect, "we cannot admit as ultimate the authority of any other leader, and (by implication) especially not this little self-proclaimed Führer whose agenda so obviously violates what we hear from our one Source and Sovereign."[6]

In the light of the suffering of the Confessing Church under Hitler one dare not suggest that Barmen was easy. But as the most dramatic instance of Christian disestablishment in modern European history, Barmen is premised on the existence of a *de jure* form of religious establishment. Its authors knew quite precisely where the *disen-*

6. See the Barmen Declaration, Article 1, in Arthur C. Cochrane, *The Church's Confession under Hitler* (Philadelphia: Westminster Press, 1962), p. 239.

gagement from culture had to concentrate its attention. Intentional disestablishment in North America is another story. How can churches disengage themselves from such nebulous things as worldviews, ways of life, moral codes, social values, dreams of happiness and prosperity?

There is only one way, and it is neither easy nor quick. It is called theology. The church, whose establishment consists in its legitimation and sanctification of the operative values, goals, and moral conventions of its host culture, may disengage itself from that culture symbolically through occasional acts of dissent and resistance. These must occur in relation to specific social practices, such as siding with labor against capital; or with ethnic and other minorities against oppressive majorities; or with the weak over against the powerful. I am assuming that such dissent and resistance must, in fact, accompany every serious attempt at Christian self-disestablishment in our context, and must do so more and more. But unless such acts of disengagement are accompanied by and grounded in renewed and sustained *thought* concerning our real identity and vocation as Christians, the acts will neither speak for themselves nor become the basis of an ethic compelling enough to inspire the whole people of God.

Here I am thinking of the fact to which many commentators on mainstream Protestantism allude, namely that in all of these denominations there are minorities that have grasped, in concrete ways, aspects of the resistance to which Christians are called. But in the absence of a deeper, biblically literate and theologically imaginative analysis, one into which earnest Christians of many different political and cultural backgrounds and persuasions may be initiated, the acts of the radical minorities within the churches only serve to alienate many who, with some sustained attempt at *thinking* the faith, might well become part of the resistance. This will involve earnest Christians of many different political and cultural backgrounds.

In other words, to quote a recent pronouncement of the Presbyterian Church USA, a pronouncement promulgated with an air, almost, of discovery, *"Theology matters!"*[7] We are living at a moment in history when the most practical thing that the churches can do is to become theologically serious. I trust it will be understood that by the-

7. Presbyterian Church USA, *The Minutes of the 206th General Assembly,* 1994, Part I, pp. 87-91.

ology I am not talking about mere theory, library research, or blood-less scholarship. Theology, if it deserves the name at all, is what oc-curs and may only occur at the point where the Spirit of Jesus Christ, testified to by Scripture and Tradition, encounters the spirit of the age — the *Zeitgeist*. It happens at the juncture, if you like, of text and context. One could be crucified for doing theology. Dietrich Bonhoeffer, Martin Luther King, and Archbishop Romero have, to mention only three.

Theology matters. It matters profoundly in the process of dises-tablishing ourselves as Christians in North America because our kind of establishment was precisely a theological establishment. It was the consequence of bad theology. We allowed the gospel of Jesus Christ and him crucified to become the unlikely bearer of a Promethean an-thropology, a progressive view of history, and a theology of glory. We allowed the idea of church to mean a gathering of like-minded, mid-dle-class people, meeting to celebrate their own way of life. And in their meeting together, they often do so as an act of symbolic and real exclusion of those with whom they do not wish to be associated.

We allowed the new law in Jesus Christ to be identified with suc-cessive moralities devised, and constantly revised, to accommodate the moral predispositions of the well-adjusted. To disestablish our-selves, then, given the nature of our establishment, we shall have to re-turn in all earnestness and in a spirit of critical self-awareness to our sources, and to learn together who we are and what we are called to become. This will require a long, intensive, and disciplined life of in-tellectual and spiritual contemplation. As such, it must never become an excuse for passivity or tardiness at the level of deeds, and it need not do so. But as we have been centuries in learning the rules of reli-gious establishment, we shall need at least decades to learn the basis of our new vocation as a witnessing community — as salt, yeast, and light.

Why must we undertake such an exercise in disengagement? Not, certainly, for the sake of being different. Not because some of us have grown ashamed of our middle-class roots and preferences. Not for the sake, either, of achieving some kind of Christian purity, un-stained by contact with this ambiguous and hell-bent world. Not even for the sake of exchanging a bad theology for a good one. No, there is only one reason why we must extricate ourselves spiritually and intel-lectually from the culture that we have come to serve so well and so predictably. It is that we might now serve that same culture faithfully — serve it, namely, as those who believe that we have something to bring to this society that it does not now possess, and who have acquired a certain confidence [*con* + *fide*] in their calling to be responsible for the fate of the earth. In a word, we must disengage in order to reengage. Or perhaps one should say more accurately, so far as corporate Christianity on this continent is concerned, we must distance ourselves from our dominant society sufficiently to achieve a new and meaningful proximity to it. This must be a proximity of true friends and not mere flatterers, comforters, or in-house priests.

I began with some words of a famous European Roman Catholic thinker. I shall end with a quotation from a great American Protestant, one who said nearly all of these things long ago, and who said them almost every day of his life, in explicit commentaries upon the life of this society seen from the perspective of biblical faith, Reinhold Niebuhr.[8]

> If the slogan "Let the church be the church" is to have a meaning other than its withdrawal from the world, must it not mean that by prayer and fasting it has at least extricated itself in some degree from its embarrassing alliances with this or that class, race and nation, so that it may speak the word of God more purely and more forthrightly to each person and nation, but also to each generation, according to the peculiar needs of the person and hour?

8. Robert McAfee Brown, ed., *The Essential Reinhold Niebuhr: Selected Essays and Addresses* (New Haven and London: Yale University Press, 1986), p. 99.

Cathedrals of Power: Engaging the Powers in Urban North America

CLINTON STOCKWELL

What follows is an interpretation of contemporary urban culture as illustrated by the city of Chicago. This article makes use of some key resources in Chicago, including: the First United Methodist Church; a visit with Cook County Clerk, David Orr, who works in Chicago's County Building; and a visit with Kristin Faust, Executive Vice President of Community Lending at the LaSalle Bank of Chicago. The purpose of this article is to examine how power is understood and used in metropolitan society.

Understanding the Powers

In 1924, the First Methodist Church in Chicago, also known as the Chicago Temple or People's United Methodist Church, erected a church building with a spire that reached 568 feet into the sky. It was the tallest building in Chicago at that time and is still the tallest church building in the world. Built of gray and white Bedford stone, it combines the grace of a French Gothic cathedral with the practicality of an American office skyscraper. Its height was not supplanted in Chicago until 1949, when the Prudential Building was completed.

The Chicago Temple was built by architects Holabird and Roche, the same people who in 1909 had built the neo-classical City

Hall/County Building located just across the street. For a moment in time, the Gothic church building overlooked all of Chicago, as well as the goings-on of City Hall. In fact, in 1949 a wood carving was placed on the top of the church steeple, prominently depicting a figure of Jesus looking over the city of Chicago. One is reminded of the concern shown by reformers such as William T. Stead, who in 1894 released his classic, *If Christ Came to Chicago.*[1] For reformers such as Stead, the church was responsible to address issues such as homelessness, unemployment, and corruption in high places.

Today, Chicago boasts of three of the tallest buildings in the world: the John Hancock Center, the Amoco Building, and the Sears Tower. These serve respectively as cathedrals to the corporate entities of insurance, oil, and a department store chain. The People's United Methodist Church is now dwarfed by numerous such skyscrapers, all of which serve as cathedrals to corporate empires. The Chicago of the 1990s is very different from the Chicago of 1924, when a church was still the tallest building in the city.

In contemporary global society, power is wielded mostly by big business, notably global corporations. The modern corporation has superseded not only cathedrals of ecclesiastical traditions, but even the authority and power of nations and states. The modern corporation, because of its global reach, is able to operate with minimal interference from the state. In short, the modern corporation has redefined the whole question of power in modern society.

In a recent book, *Power Shift,* author Alvin Toffler argues that the modern world has recently witnessed shifts of historical proportions. Whereas "power" was once viewed as political, military, religious, and economic, the current character in power dynamics has to do with information and information-control in cyberspace.[2]

Japan was perhaps the first country in the twentieth century, in the developed world, to realize that its best hope for the future was to invest in technology rather than in weapons. Just as the arms race contributed to the economic collapse of the Soviet Union, so also it has

1. William T. Stead, *If Christ Came to Chicago! A Plea for the Union of All Who Love on Behalf of All Who Suffer* (Chicago: Chicago Historical Bookworks, reprinted, 1990).
2. Alvin Toffler, *Power Shift* (New York: Bantam Books, 1990). For a discussion of power, see also Michel Foucault, *Power/Knowledge: Selected Interviews and Other Writings, 1972-1977,* ed. Colin Brighton (Brighton: Harvester Press, 1980).

led to the largest national debt in world history in the case of the United States, one that is now calculated in trillions of dollars.

In the wake of the changing role of military superpowers, corporations have waged a global battle that is just as militant, and designed to secure every possible economic advantage. In many downtowns, in what can only be described increasingly as postmodern corporate corridors, secular cathedrals of economic power dominate the landscape. Yet these powers, as illustrated in the case of Sears, Roebuck, and Company, can readily abandon even their architectural landmarks if greater profits can be realized in other ways. After Sears recently laid off 50,000 workers and moved its office from Chicago, the Sears Tower had one of the highest vacancy rates of any office building in downtown Chicago.

Corporations show great flexibility. After purchasing Marathon Oil in 1980, US Steel changed its name to USX. This change symbolized the fact that the company is not in the business of making steel, but rather is in the business of making money.[3] When this purpose becomes an ultimate value, what matters is not the products made, nor the welfare of society generally, nor the health of a nation, and certainly not the welfare of its workers, but rather the bottom line. According to James Meadows, vice president of AT&T, the corporation is trying to "promote the whole concept of the workforce being contingent." Meadows hopes for a "jobless, but not workless" world where "contingent workers" fill in as needed, but without the guaranteed benefits that labor worked hard to achieve through over a century of struggle.[4]

The result of "downsizing," or "rightsizing," according to the *Chicago Tribune,* is a disconnected economy, an economy whereby "Wall Street" profits at the expense of "Main Street." At the beginning of 1996, the corporate giant AT&T announced it would lay off 40,000 workers.[5] To put it bluntly: "A company announces mass firings, costing thousands of workers their jobs. The employees' pain is

3. Stanley Aronowitz and William DiFazio, *The Jobless Future: Sci-Tech and the World of Work* (Minneapolis: University of Minnesota Press, 1994), p. 16.

4. Carrie R. Leana, "Why Downsizing Won't Work. As American corporations cut payrolls to the bone, it's time to question the assumption that Wall Street knows best," *Chicago Tribune Magazine,* April 14, 1996, p. 15.

5. "An economy 'disconnected': As America Prospers, its work force continues to be hit with job cuts," *Chicago Tribune,* January 3, 1996.

overshadowed by Wall Street's endorsement of the decision and its impact on the bottom line."[6] Just as the announcement of massive layoffs occurred, AT&T's stocks rose $2.62 a share! The message: what matters is profits, not the workforce, for benefits given to laborers are too expensive. Although AT&T later reneged on the total number of layoffs, the downsizing of America continues to escalate and takes a costly toll. Is this a legitimate use of power, or does it represent an abuse of power? The result, as noted by Jeremy Rifkin, is an era characterized by the *End of Work;* or, as noted by Stanley Aronowitz and William DiFazio, it is *The Jobless Future.*[7]

During March 1996, the *New York Times* ran a series of articles on downsizing in America. According to the *Times,* some 24.8 million blue-collar jobs and 18.7 white-collar jobs were lost in the period between 1979 and 1995, a total of over 43 million jobs. About a third of these workers were able to find jobs of comparable pay, but the remaining two-thirds did not.[8] Many found themselves working more hours for less pay, or not working at all. Either "overwork" or "underemployment" seems to characterize many workers after being laid off from a previous job.[9]

The Clinton administration reported a net creation of 705,000 jobs for the month of February 1996. However, according to Irwin L. Kellner of the Chemical Bank, "The numbers aren't as good as they looked," for the majority of jobs "created" included "a high concentration of part-time and temporary employment" in the service sector. While approximately 25 percent of the workforce in the United States are now "temporary workers," the number of "contingent workers" could rise to 35 percent by the turn of the century.[10]

For Richard Barnet, the job crisis raises "the most fundamental question of human existence: What are we doing here? . . . Until we rethink work and decide what human beings are meant to do in the

---

6. Ibid.

7. See Aronowitz and DiFazio; also Jeremy Rifkin, *The End of Work: The Decline of the Global Labor Force and the Dawn of the Post-Market Era* (New York: G. P. Putnam, 1995).

8. See the series of articles, "The Downsizing of America," in the *New York Times,* March 2-9, 1996.

9. For documentation, see Juliet B. Schor, *The Overworked American: The Unexpected Decline of Leisure* (New York: HarperCollins-Basic Books, 1992).

10. Rifkin, *The End of Work,* p. 191.

age of robots and what basic economic claims on society human beings have by virtue of being here, there will never be enough jobs."[11]
Even *Business Week* had a cover story on the issue, where it was noted
that, "The restructuring of Corporate America has carried enormous
social costs."[12]

The real issue in the changes in the workforce reflects the transformation of the economy from an industrial-manufacturing base to a
global, information-driven one. However, for William Greider, a
transformation of power relationships has also occurred. It used to be
that power was in the hands of governments, and specifically in the
hands of the people. Now, governments often seem beholden to special interests, or to lobbyists such as the National Rifle Association,
the American Medical Association, or the tobacco industry. The new
question for Greider is, "Who will tell the people?" or more accurately, "Who will listen to and speak for the people?"[13]

If it takes millions of dollars for a Ross Perot or a Steve Forbes to
enter politics, what does that say for a democracy? For most Americans, the cathedrals — whether religious, political, or economic — do
not really represent them. These are institutions of wealth and power
that seem, on the contrary, to work against the interest of the people
and the public good. For Greider,

> Corporate interests, on the whole, still do not accept that they must
> comply with the new regulatory controls enacted during the last
> twenty-five years. . . . That's real political power — choosing
> whether to honor a law or resist it. Since the cost of resistance is of-
> ten quite modest compared to the cost of compliance, companies
> benefit in real dollars from any success at political stalling. . . .
> Thus, what looks like a legal contest on the surface is really a politi-
> cal struggle in its deeper dimensions.[14]

What is at stake here is democracy as a political institution and a
deliberative process. Corporate entities, and the cathedral-like aristoc-

11. Richard J. Barnet, "The End of Jobs: Employment is one thing the
global economy is not creating," *Harper's*, September 1993, p. 52.
12. Michael J. Mandel, "Economic Anxiety," *Business Week*, March 11,
1996, p. 50.
13. William Greider, *Who Will Tell the People? The Betrayal of American Democracy* (New York: Charles Scribner's, 1992), p. 110.
14. Greider, *Who Will Tell the People?*, p. 110.

racies they have created, desire to be immune from accountability to the public at large, or to the politics of nation-states. Like the Gothic cathedrals of a bygone age, modern corporations and their monumental structures seem to be impervious to change or to outside regulation. While they symbolize a certain stability and permanence in the way they present themselves (e.g., Prudential, a "piece of the rock"), they are anything but permanent as they vie for a competitive edge.

Corporations find it in their political and economic interest to insure, through legislation, free rein to operate in the market without restraint or accountability to any other earthly institution. They often try to do so without adequately considering possible social costs that might result from their decisions. The question on a pragmatic level is the extent to which democracy and people of goodwill are able to mobilize themselves to counter these trends with their accompanying abuses of power and privilege.

Understanding the Meaning of Power

Cathedrals, secular or religious, are institutional manifestations of power and authority. Many people are afraid, or timid, about power. But power is an omnipresent reality. It is the key issue for those who are concerned about social justice, or the practice of compassion toward those who are vulnerable. For Michael Lerner, editor of *Tikkun,* a progressive journal in the Reformed Jewish tradition, the problem is not so much an absence of power, but what he calls "surplus powerlessness."

> If people feel terrible about themselves and their lives, and they internalize those feelings in the form of self-blame, they develop what I call "surplus powerlessness." This is a sense of themselves being even more powerless than they actually are (beyond the reality of "real powerlessness") in the face of powerful economic forces dedicated to accumulating profits at all costs.[15]

For Lerner, there is nothing more incapacitating than internalized oppression. Lerner believes that activists, indeed even ordinary people,

15. Michael Lerner, *The Politics of Meaning: Restoring Hope and Possibility in an Age of Cynicism* (New York: Addison-Wesley, 1996), p. 251.

have more power than they are willing to admit. Lerner believes that such people need a connection to some form of transcendence, some form of absolute value which lies outside the self. Transcendence is the key to discovering one's power. "Surplus powerlessness" is the internalization of cruelty. It is the internalized conviction that "the way things are" now is the only way things can be. It is the lack of imagination, the lack of hope, the loss of an awareness of power that is the key human problem. "The deep structuring of surplus powerlessness makes the patterns and distorted consciousness embedded in the institutions and social practices of daily life difficult to dislodge."[16]

The first thing we need to do is to discover our own sense of power. Power is not necessarily a bad thing. Power is the ability to act. It is the ability to marshall the resources necessary for social restructuring. True, many people have made the world seem evil or sinister, what has often been described as Machiavellian. They have misquoted Lord Acton's famous phrase: "Power *tends* to corrupt, and absolute power corrupts absolutely." The tendency toward corruption is certainly present, but there is nothing more corrupting than "surplus powerlessness" and the pervasive cynicism of our culture. Despite the problems we are facing as a society, social change will occur only when we realize our surplus power.

We need to understand that power is actually a resource that can be used either for good or for evil. Communities often have more power than they realize, where it is normally organized either around money or people, or both. Power represents the ability to effect meaningful change. The late founder of community organizing, Saul David Alinsky, cited to this effect some of the saints of the Western tradition, persons we now refer to as DWEMS — Dead White European Males; for Blaise Pascal, "Justice without power is impotent, power without justice is tyranny"; for Jesuit founder St. Ignatius, "To do a thing well a man needs power and competence"; and finally, for founding father Alexander Hamilton, "What is a power, but the ability or faculty of doing a thing? What is the ability to do a thing, but the power of employing the means necessary to its execution?" Alinsky himself put it well when he concluded, "It is impossible to conceive of a world devoid of power; the only choice is between organized and unorganized power."[17]

16. Lerner, *The Politics of Meaning*, p. 112.
17. Saul Alinsky, *Rules for Radicals: A Pragmatic Primer for Realistic Radicals* (New York: Vintage, 1971), p. 52.

Of course, those with power, especially those who have the means to organize their power, have not always used it to promote what we might call the general welfare. As the familiar proverb states, "All it takes for evil to triumph is for people of good will to do nothing." This proverb might be better restated, "Evil triumphs when evil people abuse and misuse their power because people of good will don't utilize theirs."

In contemporary times, political and economic power have coalesced into the modern corporation. A "metastate" has emerged "in which the intersection of the largest transnational corporations and the international political directorates of many nations constitute a new governing class."[18] The result is a new arrangement of power in which leading business leaders, diplomats, academics, and other experts align with goverment leaders to insure that policies allow transnational corporations to operate freely without significant restraint, and without any substantive obligation to any people or governmental body. They are truly transnational corporations with little accountability to nations or states.

Hope, Power, and Social Change

The misuse of power and the reality of "surplus powerlessness" represent intensely modern phenomena. In a meeting of academics and community-based leaders sponsored by the Policy Research Action Group (PRAG),[19] a discussion arose as to the difficulty of attracting broad constituencies to address issues on a local level. Several problems were identified that become the target of reform work for a metropolitan area.

One problem is the matter of political retrenchment. Due to scarce resources, city governments are being forced to tighten their

18. Aronowitz and DiFazio, *The Jobless Future*, p. 22.
19. PRAG, "May Partnership Seminar," May 23, 1996. PRAG is a coalition of university scholars who care about communities and community-based organizations (CBOs). The universities include Loyola of Chicago, DePaul University, the University of Illinois at Chicago, and Chicago State University. The CBOs represent environmental, housing, job development, and advocacy organizations. PRAG provides a forum for discussion, links resources, and assists with research and the provision of technical assistance so that CBOs can better address issues of common concern.

belts and to protect, if not control, relatively fewer resources than in the past. The result for the Chicago City Council is that its budget contains few resources for addressing the major issues identified by community groups: youth, community development, and small business development. This has been further intensified by the restrictive government priorities at the state and national levels, and the disinvestment of private dollars in most urban centers.

Other problems noted by community-based leadership included underfunding, overwork, and overextension; "turf" battles among community groups; fragmentation among activist organizations; restrictive stipulations by funding mechanisms; and a suspicion of outsiders who wish to do good in local settings. These issues are difficult to address at the local level. But they are even further complicated when academics pursue such matters as primarily an objective analysis of urban issues. This keeps them from finding a way to be in solidarity with the people they purport to assist.[20]

The most significant problem to be addressed, however, is what one author calls the *Twilight of Common Dreams*.[21] According to Todd Gitlin, progressive groups are themselves isolated and competing with each other. The result, even among progressive groups, is the loss of a common agenda and a loss of a compelling, unifying vision that might unite groups to address common problems.

Many of the same sentiments were echoed in an interview with David Orr, County Clerk of Cook County in the State of Illinois.[22] Orr is a former Tenant Organizer, former Alderman in Chicago, and the former vice mayor for deceased Harold Washington, Mayor of Chicago, 1983-1987. He has long been a friend of progressive political forces in Chicago. When asked what his opinion was as to the "state of politics" in the city and elsewhere, his first response was "too much money."

Indeed, with many millionaires running for office, and the costs involved in buying media time, it is virtually impossible today for

20. On this matter, see the works of Richard Rorty, "Solidarity or Objectivity," in John Rajchman and Cornel West, eds., *Post-Analytic Philosophy* (New York: Columbia University Press, 1985), pp. 3-19; and Richard Rorty, *Contingency, Irony and Solidarity* (New York: Cambridge University Press, 1989).

21. Todd Gitlin, *The Twilight of Common Dreams: Why America Is Racked by Culture Wars* (New York: Henry Holt, 1995).

22. Interview with David Orr, Cook County Clerk, March 21, 1996.

someone without independent means to be elected. Further, according to Orr, the media does anything but discuss issues. Instead, attacks on personality or one's sex life often gets more media attention than substantive issues. The media, stated Orr, is "for hire." There is little free media air time for candidates. This represents a serious problem. When one adds to this such issues as economic anxiety, lobbyist control, and pervasive political partisanship, there is little wonder why widespread cynicism exists among the electorate. The problem, according to political journalist E. J. Dionne, Jr., is that neither political party is listening to what concerns the electorate.[23]

According to Orr, what needs to occur is more participation on the part of the electorate, despite the obstacles noted above. What is needed is more activity on the part of grass-roots organizations, including the church. Orr is the author of the Motor Voter Law, which would allow citizens to register to vote, if they aren't registered already, when they obtain their driver's licenses. This is opposed by some political forces, including Jim Edgar, Republican Governor of Illinois as of 1996, for fear that such might attract an uninformed electorate.

The actions of community-based organizations, however, on a grass-roots level may be the last best hope of democracy in America.[24] Orr also called for a Liveable Wage, not just a raise in the Minimum Wage. Such would allow poor working families to survive and cope in an age of downsizing and job dislocation.

For Jim Wallis, founder of Sojourners Community in Washington, D.C., what is needed is the rediscovery of "soul" in political discourse.[25] He believes that the rift between conservative Republicans and left-leaning Democrats of the Great Society years should be, and can be, bridged. Historical liberalism represented a top-down approach to social change. Recent conservative solutions attempt to let the market run its course, with the view that disparities between the wealthy and the poor will correct themselves. The legacy of liberalism is dependency. The legacy of conservatism is wholesale abandonment and neglect. What is needed is a third way, one that works at empow-

23. E. J. Dionne, Jr., *Why Americans Hate Politics* (New York: Simon and Schuster, 1991).

24. Greider, *Who Will Tell the People?*, p. 222.

25. Jim Wallis, *The Soul of Politics: A Practical and Prophetic Vision for Change* (New York: The New Press/Orbis Books, 1994).

erment. Empowerment involves the allocating of needed resources and opportunities to those at the grass roots so that people are better able to solve their own problems.

The soul of politics requires more than just technical tinkering or utilitarian methodology. The soul of American politics requires a spiritual base that rediscovers intangibles such as transcendent values and a sense of purpose, vision, and imagination. Such an approach would require the recapturing of the ability to dream new dreams that go beyond current political or social options, to a transcendent connection with values such as community, justice, compassion, and solidarity. Such a vision for a new community must transcend current party loyalties, allowing the people of this country a way to overcome cynicism and find new ways to hope.

Examples on the local level demonstrate that such a reenvisioning is possible. In community organization language, we must find ways to move from the world as it is to the world as it should be. For Wallis, hope is the doorway to change. "Hope is the great enemy of those who would control history. (It) is the door between impossibility and possibility. It is confidence in a vision, not in statistical probability. Hope is not nonsense, it is a community moving toward a dream. Hope is believing in spite of the evidence and watching the evidence change."[26] When optimism falls short, hope remains as a dynamic and unexpected force for change.

Politics is the ability to act, the responsibility to make decisions about how resources are allocated. According to William Greider, hope in relation to politics seems most manifest in the lives of community-based organizations, many of which are church-based institutions. Greider cites some examples, including The Nehemiah Project in Brooklyn, the Metropolitan Organization in Houston, BUILD in Baltimore, and COPS (Communities Organized for Public Service) in San Antonio, Texas.

For community-based organizations such as these, politics begins in personal relationships. In the populist tradition of community organizing, it is believed that community people are quite capable of assembling their own resources and deciding what is in their best self-interest without the interference of outside experts. This is the basis of true empowerment.

26. Wallis, *The Soul of Politics,* p. 240.

Empowerment means that leadership is identified and developed from within the communities, not imposed from without. Communities already have some of those resources, and already have leadership and institutions that can be organized for meaningful social change. The problem is that the people are not organized, resources are not effectively marshalled to address problems of concern. For those in power, there is an ignorance of the real needs and issues as articulated by community leadership. Communities must find a way to be heard again by the elected leadership. For Greider, "The overriding political objective . . . is to change the people themselves — to give them a new sense of their own potential."[27]

The public square must be reconstituted so that the electorate is able to articulate for itself what the issues are, and what it believes should be done to correct these issues. The current attempt to make government smaller is the *de facto* abdication of this responsibility. A new policy needs to be configured so that resources are made available to those institutions and organizations that are closest to the action. Such institutions and organizations are better suited to negotiate meaningful solutions and social change that address real issues as experienced in local communities.

It is helpful to work from a biblical understanding of the powers — that the powers, though now fallen, were created as good and are therefore capable of being redeemed.[28] From this perspective, it is possible for the church to work toward the transformation of the powers that they might contribute to redemptive purposes. An example of such transformed power can be seen in the South Shore Bank. Reoriented as a community development bank, it has virtually rebuilt the South Shore community in Chicago by way of housing rehabilitation and small business development.[29]

Thanks to the Community Reinvestment Act, which demands that lending institutions meet the credit needs of low- and moderate-income communities, other banks have also gotten into the act. Kristin Faust, of the LaSalle Bank of Chicago, has a 90-million-dollar portfolio of funds that have been lent to neighborhood groups and

27. Greider, *Who Will Tell the People?*, p. 225.
28. Walter Wink, *Engaging the Powers: Discernment and Resistance in a World of Domination* (Philadelphia: Fortress Press, 1992), pp. 84-85.
29. Richard P. Taub, *Community Capitalism: The South Shore Bank's Strategy for Neighborhood Revitalization* (Boston: Harvard Business School, 1994).

other developers committed to affordable housing construction. Faust, a graduate in Public Policy from Harvard University, states that communities have a role in educating banks and other lending institutions regarding the needs and opportunities for economic investment in low-income communities.[30] As it turns out, such investments are just as credit-worthy as those in middle-income communities, and the CRA is making money for the bank, even as disinvested communities, once redlined, are becoming capitalized and vital once more. Not-for-profit organizations can play a major role in community empowerment.[31]

In Pilsen, a Mexican-American immigrant community in Chicago, six Roman Catholic parishes have come together to sponsor The Resurrection Project (TRP). TRP has received numerous awards for housing development that has helped to stabilize this mostly Latino community on the city's Near West side. Some sixty-six single-family dwellings have been built, and another sixty are in the works. According to the founder, Raul Raymundo, "we are not just building houses, we are building community." TRP's work is replicated by other not-for-profits in Chicago, including Bethel New Life, Lawndale Christian Community Development Corporation, People's Housing, Circle Urban Ministries, Bickerdike Redevelopment Corporation, and Roseland Christian Community Development. These groups have discovered that with a little training and necessary resources, they can develop the capacity and competence to redevelop their own communities.

Local community-based organizations are in the best position to allow citizens to rediscover their power, define their dream, and work out strategies so that such dreams can become realizable, although corporate responsibility and government resources are still critical. This means not just a political restructuring so that issues can be addressed, but a reallocation of resources necessary for citizens to solve their own problems.

Just as in architecture, where ancient cathedrals have been over-

30. Interview with Kristin Faust, Executive Vice President of Community Lending at the LaSalle Bank of Chicago, in March 1996.

31. According to Jeremy Rifkin, the "social" or "third sector" is the remaining hope for community development, because the government is opting out and global corporations have divested of corporate responsibility. See Rifkin, chapters 16-17.

shadowed by secular cathedrals as structural manifestations of power, so power has shifted from religious and political institutions to multinational businesses. But perhaps the symbolic power and transcendent representation of ancient cathedrals can still have an important role to play for a counter reshaping of society. However, "power" alone is not enough if not accompanied by hope and some form of transcendent vision. While we may not have the resources to build the Gothic cathedrals of bygone centuries, we could do worse than trying to recapture their spirit, and representing the presence of the transcendent in ordinary life.

The medieval cathedral, with its massive stonemasonry, its gargoyles and steeples, its arched and vaulted ceilings, was essentially a product of community effort. Its frescoes and paintings retold ancient stories that gave the people identity and communal attachment. Further, in the best tradition of the cathedral, the rites and activities of the cathedral — including charity, the schools, and rituals of celebration — were done for the people. Something of that sacred and celebrative quality is needed today. Modern towers, including churches, public buildings, and secular embodiments of corporate power, often demand time and energy that could be better spent "in the neighborhood."

Yet, the ancient cathedrals carried a symbolic tradition that is still needed to reimagine or renegotiate sacred spaces, or for that matter secular spaces in public life. Cathedrals represented divine authority, absolute truth, and transcendent values and beliefs. They gave order, significance, and meaning to ordinary life. I am not advocating the building of new cathedrals, but I am advocating that communities everywhere seek to recapture the imaginative and aesthetic qualities that gave ancient cathedrals their grandeur and majesty.

In America, smaller-scale institutions are needed on a local level, institutions that allow ordinary citizens to participate in a meaningful way in safe spaces. Yet, for this participation to have more than temporary significance, a rediscovery of transcendent values is necessary. Unless we are able to do this, we will not be able to find sustainable dreams that allow people to redefine themselves as a community bound more by covenant than social contract.

Faith Twisted by Culture: Syncretism in North American Christianity

WALTER C. HOBBS

In Vietnam today, Cao Dai[1] is a modern religious movement that finds its ethics in Confucianism, its occult ritual in Taoism, its notions of *karma* and reincarnation in Buddhism, and its ecclesiastical structure in Roman Catholicism, including a pope.[2] Numerous saints are honored, including Buddha, Confucius, Jesus, Mohammed, Pericles, Julius Caesar, Joan of Arc, Victor Hugo, and Sun Yat Sen.

Macumba, an Afro-Brazilian religion,[3] melds animal sacrifice and the incantations of mediums with reverential display of the cross and the worship of Christian saints. One sect, Candomblé, is more African and flourishes in nonurban areas. Another sect, Umbanda, includes Hindu and Buddhist influences and has great appeal among the urban white middle class.

The Native American Church in North America, known best perhaps for its use of the hallucinogenic cactus, peyote, combines ele-

1. A more complete description of Cao Dai may be found in *Britannica On Line* at http://www.eb.com:180/.
2. Robert J. Schreiter, C.PP.S., "Defining Syncretism: An Interim Report," *International Bulletin of Missionary Research* (April 1993): 50-53.
3. A more complete description of Macumba and the Native American Church may be found in *Britannica On Line* at http://www.eb.com:180/.

ments of traditional Native American religion with Christianity. A common all-night ceremony begins late evening on Saturday, includes prayer and singing, contemplation and the sacramental use of peyote, then concludes with a communion breakfast the next morning. Some tribes base their moral teaching on that of the Bible; in others, Jesus is considered to be a cultural hero who turned to Native Americans after being killed by the whites.

On October 1, 1995, ABC Sunday News carried a brief story describing the growing popularity in the United States of the Afro-Caribbean Roman Catholic religion, La Santería. Although its adherents deny it is a blend of Western Catholicism with the traditional religious practice of the Yoruba (a West African people brought as slaves to the Caribbean), the name means "worship of the saints." The centerpiece of the news report showed a young man addicted to crack cocaine seeking release in a private ritual conducted by a priest of La Santería, during which three roosters were sacrificed and their blood used for purposes of purification. The setting was the basement of a pleasant suburban home in the Washington, D.C. area, where the religious artifacts surrounding the priest and petitioner included icons strikingly similar to those of Roman Catholicism.

Christian missiologists have long used the term "syncretism" to speak of such instances in which biblical concepts are mixed with traditional religious practices in places where the gospel has been newly proclaimed. Lately, another consideration has also pressed itself into the discussion in the concept of "inculturation," which speaks of the social processes by which a given people's particular expression of the gospel is rooted in their way of life. When any society adopts a new idea, a new technology, or a new technique for meeting a basic need, the new is not accepted completely without regard to what is tried and true. Usually, the new is incorporated within the old. Points of contact are identified between established verities and novel, often exciting notions so that the strange can be connected to the familiar. Once the gospel enters a culture, sooner rather than later its expression by people within that culture will reflect far more of the life experiences of the evangelized than of the evangelist. Coherence and continuity, not disruption, is the stuff of social identity.

Robert Schreiter argues that syncretism is the distortion of profound faith, and that inculturation is the process by which profound faith is given richness of local expression. These concepts are closely related, yet are quite distinct.[4] Three imperatives underlie the necessity of attending carefully to both dimensions. Theologically, we must be faithful to revelation, that is, we must avoid "syncretism" as it has been traditionally understood. Culturally, however, we must communicate the gospel not in terms that colonize others, but in terms that invite them into full participation within a community of faith. Missiologically, therefore, we must learn how to cross cultural boundaries in ways that develop genuine biblical identities which reflect their distinctive local circumstances.

Taken together, those are difficult assignments. A cursory review of the history of Western Christian missionizing discloses two problems. One is a colonizing tendency among those who have taken the gospel to other peoples. The other is an inclination among the evangelized to reshape the gospel along the familiar lines of their own traditional worldviews, values, and religious norms.

The task is perhaps even more difficult for the missionary who is a member of the culture to which the gospel is being proclaimed. North American Christians face a substantial challenge in this regard. The gospel we preach is too often shot through with Western sentiments, such as individualism, consumerism, security, personal happiness, and corporate success. North American culture has a tenacious grip on our expression of the Good News, and we face a formidable task in disengaging ourselves from its hold.

One method, albeit fairly painful, by which Christians in the United States and Canada might get a handle on the twin issues of syncretism and inculturation is to examine North American Christianity as if we had always been a *missionized*, rather than a missionizing, people. We might ask, for example, "If we were a people to whom the gospel had been preached by others from afar, would those others say that our (newfound) faith is rooted firmly in the Text? Or would it be obvious, at least to them, that our understanding of the gospel has been molded along the contours and emphases of our indigenous way of life?"

The thesis of this article is that North American Christianity is

---

4. Paul G. Hiebert, "The Gospel in Our Culture," Hunsberger and Van Gelder, eds., *The Church between Gospel and Culture* (Grand Rapids: Eerdmans, 1996), 139-57.

in great measure a faith *twisted by* culture. Too often, we have uncritically embraced many of the taken-for-granted presumptions and priorities that characterize the dominant worldview of Western civilization instead of testing our culture's values and perspectives against the biblical standards. And we have merged those cultural givens within our doctrine and practice, even though we are people who claim to be followers of the Way. North American Christianity bears a disturbing resemblance to Cao Dai, to Macumba, to the Native American Church, and to La Santería.

In pointed but clever fashion, the prophet Amos very slyly forced Israel to recognize how much like their pagan neighbors they had become. First he railed against the gross evil of the surrounding peoples:[5]

> 1:2This is what the LORD says: "For three sins of Damascus, even for four, I will not turn back my wrath. Because she threshed Gilead with sledges having iron teeth. . . . 6This is what the LORD says: "For three sins of Gaza, even for four, I will not turn back my wrath. Because she took captive whole communities and sold them to Edom. . . . 9This is what the LORD says: "For three sins of Tyre, even for four, I will not turn back my wrath. Because she sold whole communities of captives to Edom, disregarding a treaty of brotherhood. . . . 11This is what the LORD says: "For three sins of Edom, even for four, I will not turn back my wrath. Because he pursued his brother with a sword, stifling all compassion, because his anger raged continually and his fury flamed unchecked. . . . 13This is what the LORD says: "For three sins of Ammon, even for four, I will not turn back my wrath. Because he ripped open the pregnant women of Gilead in order to extend his borders. . . . 2:1This is what the LORD says: "For three sins of Moab, even for four, I will not turn back my wrath. Because he burned, as if to lime, the bones of Edom's king. . . .

Then, having "softened 'em up," the prophet spoke directly to the people of God:

> 2:4This is what the LORD says: "For three sins of Judah, even for four, I will not turn back my wrath. Because they have rejected the

5. *The Holy Bible: New International Version* (Grand Rapids: Zondervan, 1984).

law of the LORD and have not kept his decrees, because they have been led astray by false gods, the gods their ancestors followed. . . .

Consider several gods that our cultural forebears followed, and ponder the various ways in which the North American Church permitted the worship of such gods to become blended into our Christian faith. Three gods, in particular, seem to permeate the Euro-history that still dominates North American culture and North American Christianity. These are: (1) modern science, itself the progeny of the Enlightenment and rationalism; (2) economic liberalism and individualism; and (3) organization and professionalization. Each of these cultural themes has distorted a basic Christian doctrine. Science and rationalism have shaped our view of Scripture (revelation); the individualism of economic liberalism has shaped our view of salvation (soteriology); and organization together with professionalization has shaped our view of the church (ecclesiology).

Modern Science

The job of science is to produce reasoned, well-tested explanations of data concerning the world in which we find ourselves. The modern scientific enterprise is the product of both empiricism, which is the view that experience is the only valid source of knowledge; and of rationalism, which is the view that fundamental truth is reached by reason alone.

Western science shows itself in many colors, but virtually all its manifestations are traceable to the Enlightenment, that stirring intellectual movement of the seventeenth and eighteenth centuries. Religion took a beating in those days, for many of the prominent thinkers of the era were unabashedly hostile to traditional Christianity. Biblical affirmations such as the virginity of Jesus' mother, the Trinity, the resurrection, the Genesis flood *et al.*, all ran afoul of "reason" and were thus rejected by many thinkers as simply not credible. Not all persons pursuing the principles of science forsook religion completely,[6] but

6. C. A. Patrides, ed., *The Cambridge Platonists* (Cambridge, Mass.: Harvard University Press, 1970).

atheism, agnosticism, and deism enjoyed considerable ascendancy in that setting.[7]

On the face of things, one would not expect that science and religion could ever reach accommodation. However, major cultural themes that are disparate often grope their way to mutual toleration, and even to union. Religion and science achieved their conciliation, especially as rationalism imposed itself on the scientific venture via the almost purely rational academic discipline, mathematics.[8] Science's unrelenting and successful effort to explain the empirical world rationally forced religion to examine its taken-for-granted understandings of a created universe.

Although many Christians in North America, particularly those of conservative persuasion, harbor reservations concerning the legitimacy of modern science, few such Christians disdain the findings of such core academic disciplines as physics, chemistry, anatomy, and physiology. When aches and pains get us down, we pop an aspirin. If our maladies worsen, we consider very seriously the therapeutic possibilities offered by surgery or radiation. With scarcely a thought, we get into an automobile designed by mechanical and electronic engineers and hurtle at speeds in excess of sixty miles an hour across huge suspension bridges designed by civil engineers. Whether cognitively or subconsciously, we appreciate the value of theories carefully crafted by scholars in the physical and life sciences.

Similarly, most Christian ministries are now turning to bright young people trained in the new discipline of computer science to help them exploit the Internet.[9] Even the dismal science, economics, has found its way into the literature of estate planning by Christians,[10] just as marketing theory now informs church and parachurch fundraising.[11] Psychology and social work are studied and read by pastors

7. Gerald R. Cragg, ed., *The Church and the Age of Reason* (Grand Rapids: Eerdmans, 1962).

8. It was not a smooth ride. See Thomas S. Kuhn, *The Structure of Scientific Revolutions,* 2nd ed. (Chicago: University of Chicago Press, 1970).

9. E.g., Youth Specialties, InterVarsity Christian Fellowship, and Wycliffe Bible Translators.

10. See, e.g., Larry Burkett, *Investing for the Future* (Wheaton, Ill.: Victor Books, 1992).

11. See, e.g., Wesley K. Willmer, ed., *Money for Ministries* (Wheaton, Ill.: Victor Books, 1989).

and other professionals whose ministry is clinical counseling.[12] It is clear that modern science plays a major role within North American culture and within the everyday lives of typical North American Christians.

One is tempted here to warn of spiritual disaster by reciting the cliché, "The camel got his nose under the tent and it wasn't long before he was completely inside." Such a cliché, however, is off the mark. Modern science, whether taken in large doses or in small, is not *per se* injurious to Christian faith. But Christians inflict substantial harm on the integrity of the faith when they permit modern science to serve as an equivalent to Scripture where matters of doctrine or practice are to be decided. The line between inculturation and syncretism may be barely perceptible at such times, but it is always consequential.

A case in point can be seen in popular views regarding the character of the biblical record. North American Christians are often anxious to appeal to science — archaeology in particular, and ancient history *et al.* — to authenticate the trustworthiness of the Scriptures. Their intent is to use scientific evidence to substantiate biblical history and thus lead any person with an open mind to conclude that the Word is also reliable in matters of faith. To state the argument differently, the *reason* that Scripture can be trusted in its nonscientific pronouncements is that modern science corroborates it where its assertions can be put to the test. Such a claim is a far cry from the prophetic announcement, "Scripture is God's self-authenticated word to humankind; listen up!"

Taken alone, the two assertions ("science substantiates the reliability of Scripture" and "Scripture is self-authenticating") may appear to pose no serious problem, for they are neither incompatible nor mutually exclusive. But in today's North America, appeal to the persuasive authority of modern science as warrant for the believability of Scripture is to attribute only penultimate authority to the Word. Such an approach is syncretistic.

Unlike claims for the *trustworthiness* of the Bible which rest on science, arguments that Scripture was produced entirely without er-

---

12. Numerous seminaries today offer masters and doctoral level programs in counseling (e.g., Trinity Evangelical Divinity School and Fuller Theological Seminary), and numerous religious presses publish titles in the field (e.g., InterVarsity Press).

ror appeal to reason alone. Proponents of the inerrancy thesis rely heavily on the two principles, among others, of "the rule of the excluded middle" (a given proposition must be either true or false) and "the rule of noncontradiction" (a given proposition cannot simultaneously be both true and false). These principles are central to the system of reasoning articulated by the Greek philosopher Aristotle. His approach was incorporated full-scale into Western Christendom in the Middle Ages by Thomas Aquinas, and in later centuries by other Christian rationalists as well.[13]

The proposition that God's revelation (both written and oral) must be correct — a sloppy synonym for "true" — and never at odds within itself, occupies exalted status in the thinking of many contemporary North American Christians. Interestingly, such issues are a nonproblem to the logics of the East, which are known as "paradoxical logic" and "unitary logic." But among many otherwise thoughtful North American Christians, the veracity of God's Word is held hostage to the axioms of a particular system of reasoning. That is a dangerous syncretism. It tells the unbeliever that if he or she finds anything in the extant manuscripts which smacks of Aristotelian "error," then either the truthfulness of the texts we do have can sensibly be doubted, or one must believe not the Word as it is provided to us, but rather a lost copy that has been idealized to meet Western criteria of validity.

Perhaps the most common merger of Scripture with modern science by North American Christians is seen in our views about life and death. The controversial issue of abortion provides a useful illustration.

To know whether abortion is a prohibited taking of human life, one must identify the essential properties of a living being that biblically define it as "human." Arguably one such characteristic is possession of a life that survives mortality. But not many North American Christians pay a great deal of attention to whether there is textual evidence for the proposition that the Creator imparts such extra-mortal life to the preborn *Homo sapiens*. Instead, the genetic composition of the fetus, its viability outside the uterus, its remarkable morphology at

13. Both Aristotelian logic and science, however, have always had their critics, the most recent of whom are the deconstructionists and postmodernists. See Linda Hutcheon, *The Politics of Postmodernism* (London: Routledge, 1989).

the earliest stages of development, and other such biological realities are considered conclusive. The fetus is unquestionably human in the biological sense of that term, and biological humanness *ipso facto* connotes spiritual immortality (after all, the idea that a living entity might be human biologically but not spiritually is preposterous). It is evident, therefore, that the human fetus is a spiritual being. Case closed. There really isn't any need to consult Scripture in the matter.[14]

To turn to biologists, however, for a determination whether a given organism is the carrier of "spirit" is like asking an economist whether the tithe is still required of believers. Unhappily, that is no deterrent to many North American Christians, even though the academic disciplines are not capable of providing answers to such questions.

It is not my design here to argue either side in the abortion debate. The point rather is that North American Christians are all too likely to pay at least as much deference to biology as to Scripture in reaching whatever position they adopt. In a classic display of syncretism, modern science is raised to equivalent authority with God's Word in the address of a difficult moral issue.

Economic Liberalism and Individualism

To a contemporary westerner, the "L" word is probably tied more closely to the concept of the Welfare State than to the celebration of one's unfettered freedom to pursue his or her interests wherever they may lead. Nonetheless, the political-economic philosophy known to historians as Liberalism did in fact emphasize individual freedom, especially freedom from governmental restraint in possessing property and enjoying the use thereof ("laissez-faire"), and to think and act upon whatever one might find congenial to his or her interests ("civil rights"). John Locke, Adam Smith, Thomas Jefferson, Voltaire, Jeremy Bentham, and John Stuart Mill are all names associated with liberalism in that classic seventeenth- to nineteenth-century sense of the word.

14. One serious difficulty encountered by persons who do turn to the text for direction is the general silence of Scripture on the subject. The inquirer must reach conclusions on the basis of indirect clues from passages that address other issues, e.g., Exodus 21:22-25, which deals with penalties for injuries inflicted on a pregnant woman.

Such philosophic, economic, and political thinking was the seedbed of what Alexis de Tocqueville called individualism, that "moderate selfishness" whose boundaries enfold one's family and friends — and precious few others. Individualism prizes self-reliance, privacy, freedom of choice, and freedom's corollary, the minimal exercise of superior authority over individual conduct. Governmental authority is especially odious and should, in the liberal view, be directed chiefly to national defense and the maintenance of law and order.

Individualism runs rampant through North American Christianity. Not all the illustrations one might cite of the infection of faith and practice by individualism will be universally relevant because different faith communities emphasize different elements of doctrine and engage in various practices not pursued by every other religious fellowship. Nonetheless, anyone who has experienced even modest contact with North American Christians will recognize at least some of the following instances.

The greatest impact of individualism on Christian faith has probably been in soteriology, the doctrine of salvation. It is taken for granted by many people that to be saved means to go to heaven when one dies. For some persons, the decisive factor in one's attaining salvation is the deeds one does or fails to do. For others, attaining a higher level of sanctification is the key. For still others, accepting Jesus as one's personal Savior is the necessary and sufficient condition. And for still others, salvation comes by God's grace through the individual's faith.[15] The aforementioned differences, however, are concerned primarily with *how* one gets what he or she is after, not with what the "what" is. *What* many a person wants is to live the good life here and now, then avoid hell when at last this life must end.

In this perspective, it is the individual's gain or loss that is at stake. It is my eternal welfare that matters here, not the purposes and objectives of the God who created and who died for me, not the part I might play in the reconciliation to him of the world he loves, not the vitality that the spiritual gifts he invests in me bring to the Body of Christ, but me. *I* am the reason Christ died — it was for me.

North American Christians can be rather audacious about this,

15. See Donald W. Dayton and Robert K. Johnston, eds., *The Variety of American Evangelicalism* (Downers Grove, Ill.: InterVarsity Press, 1991).

to the point of Scripture-twisting. It is not unusual in some quarters, for example, to hear it said, "Read John 3:16 and where it states, 'For God so loved the world . . . ,' insert your name instead." Any sensible self-reliant person will recognize the value to oneself that inheres in this scheme of things and take advantage of the offer. It's free! Absolutely free.[16] Nor is there a need to be publicly embarrassed by all this since it is done "in the privacy of your heart." Mass evangelism, with its altar calls and invitations, is not as common in this age of television and the Internet as it once was. But such exercises can still be found in local churches where practitioners heed well the principle of "Heads bowed, eyes closed please, no one looking around, this is just between you and the Lord." How the individual responds and what that response may be are his or her business alone, no one else's.

As a point of departure for a lifelong walk in faith, such an individualistic soteriology sets the stage for a style of discipleship that is no less individualistic in nature. The case can be put by a few rhetorical questions that draw attention to several realities found not only in our host culture, but in the Christian subculture as well:

- How many jobs would be lost in the Christian book/tape/video industry if suddenly no one in that field were allowed to market Christian self-help material such as: strengthening your marriage; overcoming depression; losing excess weight; finding inner peace; getting along with your neighbors or coworkers or kids; deepening your devotional life; investing for retirement, and the like?
- What percentage of committed Christians in North America would maintain fellowship with a group that insists on seeing each other's federal tax return (or some equally revealing alternative) in order to evaluate each individual's discipleship in the use of financial resources? And why would many Christians argue that such an arrangement is unworkable and/or unwise?
- What priorities lead a Christian in North America to dress up for a meeting at which he or she hopes to consummate a lucra-

16. A current debate about what constitutes salvation can be found in the views of two authors who wrote with each other in mind. See John F. MacArthur, Jr., *The Gospel according to Jesus* (Grand Rapids: Academie Books, 1988); and Zane C. Hodges, *Absolutely Free!* (Grand Rapids: Academie Books, 1989).

tive business deal, and dress down for a meeting with sisters and brothers at which, he or she says, they will approach the God of the universe in reverent *worship?*

Such questions highlight various ways in which the basic tenets of individualism, that distinctively North American "moderate self-ishness" first described by Tocqueville, have infiltrated the world-views and religious practices of North American Christians. These tenets include: self-reliance, privacy, freedom of choice, and freedom's corollary, the minimal exercise of superior authority over individual conduct. But the Bible continues to confront us, "He died for all that those who live should no longer live for themselves but for him who died for them and was raised again" (2 Corinthians 5:15). It is difficult to escape the haunting indictment laid against contemporary Western Christianity by Dietrich Bonhoeffer that in our practical theology we have displaced costly discipleship with "cheap grace," and have given up far too much in the exchange.[17] Syncretism is at work once more in our midst.

Organization and Professionalism

Over the centuries most of church life within Christendom has been quite highly structured. Episcopacy was the organizational form adopted by virtually all the early and medieval bodies, surviving even the great schism between East and West in the eleventh century. In the wake of the Reformation movements of the fourteenth to sixteenth centuries, however, presbyterian configurations became popular with many Protestant communities. Congregationalists, on the other hand, rejected the view that local assemblies should be subject to any higher jurisdiction, such as a diocese, presbytery, or synod. They argued that each church is an autonomous, self-governing, and self-disciplining entity.[18]

In the late nineteenth and early twentieth centuries the German

17. Dietrich Bonhoeffer, *The Cost of Discipleship* (London: SCM Press, 1975).

18. Some denominations with a strong congregational polity did borrow from the episcopal tradition to create a mixture of governing structures, e.g., The Methodist Episcopal Church.

scholar Max Weber produced a remarkably clear catalog of the defining characteristics of "bureaucratic" organizations.[19] He drew his conclusions from what he observed in the behavior of government agencies in nineteenth-century Prussia. Later researchers found the model valuable in their attempts to describe and explain the ways in which many other large-scale organizations go about accomplishing their respective tasks. The principles underlying this model were applied not only to secular organizations but also to churches and their denominations.

Concomitant with the spread of formal structures created to organize and manage all sorts of enterprises — commercial, religious, governmental, charitable, health care, military, etcetera — was the increasing specialization of the work that organizational personnel performed. Technological advances encouraged and then demanded it, and educational opportunity in North America, especially following the Second World War, virtually guaranteed it. Not only were production and service tasks becoming more complex and sophisticated, so too were the duties and responsibilities of managers.

Churches and denominations have not remained aloof from these developments. Ministry today is specialized, where we find such roles as: Senior Pastor, Minister of Music, Minister of Worship, Organist and Choir Director, Minister of Youth and Christian Education, Director of Christian Education (there *is* a difference; ask any DEC), Associate Pastor for Counseling, Singles Ministries Pastor, Adult Ministries Pastor, Senior Adult Ministries Pastor, Minister of Missions, Minister of Evangelism and Discipleship, Church Administrator, Book Store Manager, Christian Day School Administrator, Day Care Administrator — etcetera *ad infinitum*. Typically, though not universally, at each level and for each general domain there is also an oversight board or committee whose membership is drawn from the general membership of the organization, such as the Council, the Board of Elders, the Music Committee, the Board of Christian Education, the Board of Trustees, the Board of Deacons, the Board of Missions, the Athletic Committee, the Outreach Committee, the Fi-

19. T. Parsons (ed.), A. Henderson and T. Parsons (tr.), *The Theory of Social and Economic Organization* (New York: Free Press, 1947). See also Peter Blau, *Bureaucracy in Modern Society* (New York: Random House, 1956); and C. Wright Mills, *The Sociological Imagination* (New York: Oxford University Press, 1959).

nance Committee, the Community Liaison Committee, the Ecumenical Relations Committee — etcetera *ad infinitum*. These functions and functionaries, in turn, are reflected in counterpart offices and officials at the diocesan, synodic, and denominational levels.

It has long been a matter of controversy how much organizational structure, if any, is biblically appropriate to the local church and/or its related bodies. But that issue need not detain us here. The more substantive question is: "What role does the concept 'organization' play in the minds of North American Christians when they think 'church'?" The answer appears to be, "A major role, one that can easily dominate the whole meaning of church." Organization constitutes virtually the exclusive understanding of the *ekklesia* among Christians as diverse as the parishioners of the Archdiocese of New York and the congregation of Fellowship Community Church in mid-Alberta.

George Hunsberger describes the contemporary vision of the church as "a vendor of religious goods and services."[20] His purpose is to lay bare the consumerism that characterizes North American Christianity. But his imagery also suggests the nature of the corporate model that Christians presume the vendor church to adopt.[21] Church members are tough customers. Many even believe they have a *right* to the religious goods and services that the church is expected to provide regardless whether they carry their share of the costs. No person should have to prove, for example, that he or she tithes, or even puts a few dollars in the offering plate on occasion, to expect a visit by the pastor when one is in the hospital. Being listed in the organization's roster is sufficient.

Professional staff are paid employees who had better measure up to the members' expectations or face serious repercussions, occupational and/or organizational. If the sermons don't meet my needs, or the music is not to my taste, or the youth program fails to hold my daughter's interest, or I don't think the Associate Pastor for Counseling did much for my brother-in-law, or . . . , or . . . , then either he or she must go, or I'm outta here. 1 Corinthians 13:4-7 is lovely, but it

20. George Hunsberger, "Sizing Up the Shape of the Church," in Hunsberger and Van Gelder, 333-46.
21. See Inagrace Dietterich, "A Particular People: Toward a Faithful and Effective Ecclesiology," in George R. Hunsberger and Craig Van Gelder, eds., *The Church between Gospel and Culture: The Emerging Mission in North America* (Grand Rapids: Eerdmans, 1996), pp. 347-69.

reads better in wedding ceremonies than as a prescription to govern our behavior with professional staff whose salaries we pay. 1 Corinthians 12:14-27 is great imagery with its detailed descriptions of the members of the Body of Christ joined to one another in the same way that eyes and feet and hands are connected. But when I decide to leave Harmony Baptist Church Inc. and join Melody Methodist Inc. because my gifts aren't appreciated at Harmony and I'm not happy there any more, don't tell me that what I'm doing is mutilating the Body — the equivalent of *amputation* you call it?!! Nonsense; you're taking that business about the church being the Body of Christ, the incarnation of God in its time and place, far too literally. If a person can't eat the food at Joe's restaurant, he goes to Mary's. That's all I'm doing. Besides, we're each one of us members of the Body of Christ, "one holy catholic church," that mystical universal invisible entity known only to God.

Churches which are viewed like that and are treated like that require equally tough yet godly leaders. Leadership, therefore, has become a buzzword in the lexicon of North American church life. For lay person and professional clergy alike, books and even whole magazines are devoted to the understanding of church leadership and the care and feeding of church leaders. What we need is better leadership by people who know how to develop more effective organizations.

Can a church get along easily enough without meeting regularly as a Body to pray — no other activity on the calendar than conversation with its Head? Apparently it can, if it's well organized into small groups that pray on their own, and if it's well managed by prayerful leaders. Can a Body worship *as a Body* even if it truncates itself into two or three "services" on Sunday morning and Saturday evening? Apparently it can, if capable worship leaders conduct the services: "See how God has blessed us with so many newcomers — and such a variety they are!" Can a church accept a talented new couple as members without insisting that they first be reconciled to the brother and sister in their former church who didn't include them in their wedding party? Apparently it can: "After all, there's certainly work for them to do here." Can a church get rid of a pastor because all he or she can do is preach and teach? Apparently it can: "Well, he's okay, as a preacher and teacher that is. But he can't manage the office staff, and we can't afford an administrator. It's time we tell him that he should start thinking of moving on to bigger and better things where he can concentrate on his speaking."

Bigger and better things. Office staff. Getting rid of poor managers. Finding tasks for talented newcomers estranged from brothers and sisters elsewhere. Holding separate services for the hands and eyes of one Body. No time to meet with the Head; we get together with him in small groups — sorta like, you know, committees. The telling language of the organized, professionalized "church."

Postscript

The purpose of this article has been to identify particular corruptions born of cultural themes that have marred the integrity of contemporary Christianity in North America. That is a doleful assignment, and one is tempted to consider the job unfinished until one also sounds a note of biblical hope, indeed joy.

There is good and ample reason for such hope and such joy. We have the confident expectation that the God we serve is the Gracious Juggernaut of history and that the church he lives to purify is his means to reconcile the world to himself — through us and even, at times, despite us.

Strangers but Not Strange: A New Mission Situation for the Church (1 Peter 1:1-2 and 17-25)

DAN DEVADATTA

I believe that there is a tension in our understanding of the gospel of Jesus Christ and how this good news shapes our understanding of the mission of the church in today's world. It is no secret that the world around us is changing. In turn, we are being changed. On the one hand, we want to believe that we are a religious people who can make a difference in the world. On the other hand, we often find ourselves helpless on what it means to make a difference because of our religious convictions. While we believe that the Christian message needs to have relevance in relation to our society, we are becoming increasingly aware that we have privatized the faith. While we cry out for a sense of community, we find it difficult to translate our individualized notions of the faith into a corporate identity as a community of faith.

The basic issue is that we are having trouble defining what it means to be the church. As we come to the close of this century, we are undergoing an identity crisis. The questions we must ask are: Who are we? And what does it mean to be a congregation and church in our time and place in history? This crisis of identity cuts across all parts of the denominational churches in the North American landscape.

What Is This Identity Crisis?

To state it briefly, I would say that this identity crisis is that in trying to grapple with our identity, we have tended to reduce the mission of the church to issues. We have become issue oriented. Let me give a couple of examples of what seems to be shaping our understanding of the mission of the church today.

Winning People to Christ

There are those who claim that the purpose of the church is to win individual people to Christ and to bring them into membership within the church. Here the church is often narrowly understood in terms of growth. The mission of the church is defined by numbers, and numerical growth becomes the central focus of the work of the whole church. Everything else the church is and does tends to become secondary at best, or unimportant at worst. From this stance, the church's mission is defined in terms of meeting the needs of people and answering the questions of the world. In doing so, the mission has been reduced to issues associated with the needs of lost people based upon "how they see it." This approach is usually implemented through the tools of demographic research, ministries that specialize in reaching target groups, and in the use of various marketing mediums to make the message of the church more palatable to people.

Addressing Social Issues

On the other side, there are those who focus their attention on such problems as oppression or injustice as the great social issues of our day. Here the church is often narrowly understood in terms of social justice. Whether the issue is homosexuality, the role of women, abortion, assisted suicide, or racial representation, the Christian message becomes reduced to matters of justice and advocacy in relation to a specific cause. In this approach as well, the issues become defined primarily in terms of how the world sees them. The church then seeks to understand its mission as one of trying to address these problems. Here too the world sets the agenda for the church.

111

In both of these perspectives, the mission of the church becomes "ours" as humans, and lines are drawn toward a particular course of action. I believe that this is one reason why we see such an intense competition between churches in North America. It is my conviction that such issue-oriented approaches to the mission of the church have weakened, rather than strengthened, the witness of the church today. Both perspectives rightly struggle with what it means to be "in the world but not of it," but by focusing on issues as the world defines them they fail to be faithful to the gospel of Jesus Christ. The mission of the church becomes *our* mission, not God's, and the church becomes a tool to accomplish *our* purposes, not his. To be faithful to the gospel, the mission of the church must be understood as the full participation in the mighty work of God in his world.

The church is a called-out community, called to participate in the mission of God in the world. The church's agenda is to be shaped by the purposes of God for this world. It owes its very existence to Jesus Christ and the life he brings to it as the cornerstone of the church. Its values are to be shaped by careful listening, and by obedience to the work of the Spirit of God. What makes the church distinct from all other social institutions is that it makes the bold, and yet humble, claim to live in such a way as to shed light in the midst of the world's darkness. It provides hope in the midst of despair. It shows how life was meant to be lived.

How Did We Get to This Point?

The development of an issue-oriented understanding of the mission of the church did not occur overnight. We arrived at this point over time. In the twentieth century, there has been a gradual erosion of the Christian message and the influence of the church within society. When Alexis de Tocqueville visited America during the first part of the nineteenth century, he saw religion as the foremost of all institutions shaping American social life. I wonder if he would say the same today.

One can experience the extent of the shift that has taken place by spending time with older relatives and asking them to reflect on the support that Christian values had some years ago. It is clear that a shared Christian ethos was taken for granted in earlier years, until not all that long ago. Much of Christianity was reinforced, not just in the church, but also in many of society's other institutions, such as education, the legal and political systems, and even the entertainment industry. In previous generations we would not have questioned the convictions and moral principles of Christianity, because to have done so would have undermined the most important forces shaping our lives and institutions. Now such public support of the Christian faith has eroded, and with this shift the church is struggling to relate to our society. This is creating an identity crisis.

How Have Some Chosen to Live?

Well, some have chosen to grieve for a day that has long gone by, and will again never return. The past is idealized and immortalized as if the traditions of yesteryear ought to be the defining character for the church today. When the forms of the past are unable to hold sway, these persons, rather than attempting to translate the meaning of these forms to a new context, continue to cling to them and to wish for a recovery of this bygone era.

Others have found the Christian message and the church irrelevant to their lives. In our changing context, some have given up on the church. They find the church to be an outdated institution that does not have the power or ability to make a difference in today's world. The message of the church is seen as quaint, and the demands of the gospel are seen as irrelevant, or as unnecessarily restrictive.

In order to bridge the gap between the past and the present, still others have adopted an activist view of the church. They have reduced the mission of the church to issues, but as illustrated earlier, these issues are usually defined by the world. Whether it is the evangelical or ecumenical side of the debate, the church is often reduced to programs that seek to address particular agendas. In all of this, we are struggling to regain our identity — what it means to be a living and vibrant Christian community. We all wonder what it means to be in the world but not of it — a question that goes to the heart of what it means to be a Christian community living in our world today.

The Community as a "Displaced People"

Two thousand years ago, the Christian community was struggling to understand her position, her role, her mission, and her identity. In this context, Peter, an apostle of Jesus Christ, wrote and circulated a letter we now know as 1 Peter. Let me highlight a section from this letter, 1 Peter 1:1-2, 17-25:

> I Peter, an apostle of Jesus Christ. To God's elect, strangers in the world, scattered throughout Pontus, Galatia, Cappadocia, Asia and Bithynia, who have been chosen according to the foreknowledge of God the Father, through the sanctifying work of the Spirit, for obedience to Jesus Christ and sprinkling by his blood; Grace and peace be yours in abundance. . . . Since you call on a Father who judges each man's work impartially, live your lives as strangers here in reverent fear. For you know that it was not with perishable things such as silver or gold that you were redeemed from the empty way of life handed to you from your forefathers, but with the precious blood of Christ, a lamb without blemish or defect. He was chosen before the creation of the world, but was revealed in these last times for your sake. Through him you believe in God, who raised him from the dead and glorified him, and so your faith and hope are in God. Now that you have purified yourselves by obeying the truth so that you have sincere love for your brothers and sisters, love one another deeply, from the heart. For you have been born again, not of perishable seed, but of imperishable, through the living and enduring word of God. For 'All men are like grass, and all their glory is like the flowers of the field; and grass withers and the flowers fall, but the word of the Lord stands forever.' And this is the word that was preached to you.

The Christian community in the first century was a displaced, scattered, suffering, and persecuted people. They were in pain and were struggling to make sense of the faith and hope they had placed in Jesus Christ. They had taken on his name (4:14), and because of that, they were being rejected, scorned, and looked upon with contempt by their neighbors. Peter encouraged them in the midst of their experiencing such rejection and suffering. His message was, "Don't lose heart." In fact, less than two years after penning these words, Peter himself experienced the final consequences of such suffering when he was killed and hung upside down on a cross outside the city of Rome.

We know the story of Peter well, how he protested when Jesus made it clear that his mission was to suffer and die a cruel death for the redemption of the world. Peter feared for his own life when Jesus was captured and even denied knowing the one who loved him so dearly. This same Peter became an apostle of the Lord Jesus. His selection as an apostle was confirmed by the risen Jesus, when he was identified as one who would proclaim God's love for all people. At the end of his life, Peter writes to suffering Christians so that they can find some sense of hope and meaning in the midst of their experience of rejection and suffering.

These Christians were scattered throughout the distant regions of Asia Minor. They were exiles who had been forced to relocate to areas which were not their homelands. They did not share the values of the people they now found themselves living among. They did not belong in these regions. They were aliens who were vulnerable, and they had to endure intense suffering because they were in a world that was not their own. Peter calls this community, "God's elect who are strangers in this world" (verse 1). How could this be? Their position in the world was now that of being strangers, chosen and yet aliens, elect and yet exiles.

This same tension is at work in shaping the identity of the North American church today, just as it has shaped the community of faith throughout the ages. Consider Abraham, the father of our faith, who went to the foreign land of the Hittites and said, "I am a stranger and sojourner among you" (Genesis 23:4). Or consider the Psalmist, who made confession of the fleeting nature of human life when he wrote, "I am your passing guest, a sojourner, like all my fathers" (Psalm 39:12). Or consider in our own time the familiar song we sing, "This world is not my home, I am just passing through." The picture of the normal Christian life and community is that we have been chosen to live our days as strangers whose citizenship is not on earth. Our citizenship, instead, is in a city that God himself is making.

How Should We Then Live?

What then does it mean for us to regain a sense of identity of being a faithful Christian community in our own time? How should we live as

God's chosen ones who are shaped, not by the fundamental beliefs of this world, but by the triune God — by the Father who called us even before our choosing of him, by Jesus Christ who frees us from the destructive power of sin, and by the Spirit who sets us apart to a totally different kind of life (1:2).

Called to Live Courageously

1 Peter 1:17 says, "Since you call on a Father who judges each person's work impartially, live your lives as strangers here in reverent fear." When you and I are adopted into the family of God, we are called to live a courageous life. It is to be courageous living because we can call the very Judge of the entire human race "our Father." There is something scandalous about calling God our Father. Who are we that we may meet God, let alone belong to the family of God? Yet God has chosen to invite us into his family. The one who judges all humanity is also our Father.

This is why we are called to live our lives as strangers — not to be strange, but to live as strangers in this world. The word "stranger" really means to live "alongside with." The Christian community has been called by God, out of the peoples of the world, to live "alongside with" the peoples of this world.

We are not called to be so much an alternative society, or a countercultural community, as a *parallel community* of God's family. The problem with defining the mission of the church as an alternative society, or as a countercultural community, is that its mission usually becomes something that is over against the world. One has to ask the question, "Alternative to what, or countercultural to what?" The answer to this question usually leads us into defining our priorities over against those of the world. In many cases it even leads us into using the tactics and methods of the world to try to achieve our agenda. How often, in the history of the church, have we seen so-called alternative societies or countercultural communities defining themselves *over against* something, rather than *living for* something.

The Christian community is called to live for God through living by a different set of values. We are to live parallel to our neighbors, but the rhythm of our existence is to come from above. This is why we are called to live in reverent fear of God. God shapes the values of the Christian community, and it is this shaping that creates the rationale for our existence as the people of God in the world. We are called to live for this purpose. We are called to demonstrate to the world and to our neighbors a kind of life that can only be explained by the supernatural workings of the living God in our midst. We should not be concerned about whether we are attractive to the world, or are relevant to its questions; rather, our concern is to live our lives with a reverence for God who has called us and elected us to live our lives for his purposes.

It takes courage to focus the mission of the church on living courageously in the midst of our neighbors. We are to demonstrate that we are living *for* something. This kind of living will not only call into question the fundamental beliefs of our world, but will also demonstrate to the world the way life was meant to be lived.

Called to Live Redemptively

The kind of demonstration we are to live in the midst of others is to be a redemptive life. There are two alternatives for a Christian community as it lives in exile in an alien land. The first is to attempt to go back to what is familiar and seek to reestablish the former order in an effort to cope with the incredible pressures of living in a new situation. The second is to choose to live redemptively in the foreign land.

Peter reminds this exiled community of God's people, "For you know that it was not with perishable things such as silver or gold that you were redeemed from the empty way of life handed down to you by your forefathers, but with the precious blood of Christ, a lamb without blemish or defect" (1 Peter 1:18-19). We are reminded of the great cost and value Jesus Christ paid when he gave up his life on the cross as a ransom for people like you and me. The world measures its life in terms of things that are perishable, such as silver and gold; but the Christian community is to measure her life and destiny by the precious blood of Jesus Christ.

I know that in today's society we find it difficult to talk about blood. We can be easily repelled because it is so closely related with images of crime on our streets, or with the war scenes that come to us on television. We have been taught to associate blood with death. While that is true, the very opposite is also true. Blood is life-giving

117

and life-sustaining. When Jesus Christ gave his life, he was actually giving his lifeblood to the community he had called to himself. This is why when one receives Christ, he or she is called a new creation (2 Corinthians 5:17). The old has passed away and the new has begun. The Bible calls this kind of life "eternal life."

This is the reason the Christian community, no matter where you find it, celebrates the faith and hope it has placed in Christ by observing the Lord's Supper. Though the forms and ways differ in how this is observed, when the Christian community celebrates the Lord's Supper it is demonstrating to the world the very act of Jesus providing his life-giving presence to the community of his people.

The mission of the church is to live redemptively. The church is not so much an agent of mission, as it is the place where people can see and experience the redemptive mission of God for this world. It is a place where God works secretly in the hearts and minds of people: a place where people are drawn to the person of Jesus Christ himself; a place where God's Spirit confirms the real meaning and goal of human existence; and a place that celebrates the presence of a new reality. This is a reality that cannot be bought with silver or gold, nor can it be understood through the empty alternatives offered by the world.

Let me illustrate. When one looks at the church in the countries of the former Soviet Union or China, one finds that the growth and vitality of the church had very little to do with what we commonly associate with missionary activities. The church was crushed to the point where public worship was prohibited. It was persecuted to the point that the Scriptures were banned. Christians were tortured, exiled, or killed if they were found to have beliefs that questioned the Communist system. Yet it is exactly in these situations that the church has survived, has been preserved, and is now thriving.

Have you ever wondered why, when there is a community of people who live by the gospel, various belief systems surface which seek to offer salvation on other terms? Whether it be the Marxist point of view that promises a new age through revolution, or Islam that offers a worldwide kingdom of God without a cross, or the blatant materialism of Western societies that offers consumption as a way of true happiness and fulfillment, at their core all these views reject any idea of redemptive suffering. Yet this is the essence of God's involvement in his world. His redemption involved the suffering and death of his own son. "For God so loved the world that he gave his only begotten son, so whoever believes on him shall not perish but have eternal life" (John 3:16). This was God's plan from the very beginning. Peter says, "Jesus Christ was chosen before the creation of the world, but was revealed in these last times for your sake" (1:20).

Jesus, who was chosen to reveal God's redemption, challenged the disciples to full participation in the same reality when he said, "As the Father has sent me, so I send you also" (John 20:21). Each generation of the Christian community is to live redemptively in its own time and place.

We share in the cross, we share in the utter weakness of Jesus Christ, we share the marks of rejection, humiliation, scorn, and, at times, even death; because the mission and purposes of God are accomplished through suffering. When men and women, boys and girls, take the name of Jesus Christ, they are baptized into this new reality. When they choose to pattern their lives according to the gospel, there will be opposition. This is why Paul said, "When we preach Christ crucified, we preach a message that is a stumbling block for some and a foolish way of living for others. But to those whom he has called, Christ is the power of God" (1 Corinthians 1:23-24).

Called to Live Wholly

The mission of the church means that we are to live with courage. It also means that we are to live as Christ lived — redemptively. In addition, we are called to live wholly (1 Peter 1:21-25). Too often our expectations of the church are such that our understanding of the church's mission begins with the individual. From this starting point, a move is often made directly to mission activities. Even though this might not be conscious or deliberate, an individual focus is implicit. Like a computer operating system, which exists unquestioned and assumed behind the screen, so too our individualistic focus lies hidden in the background; onto it we load the software of our Christian activities.

We need to start at a different point. We need to start with the Bible, and then proceed to understand how the Bible sheds light on a unique understanding of our humanity, our histories, and ultimately our destinies as people. Each generation of the Christian community is called to witness to the centrality of the life of Jesus Christ. That's why in verse 21 we read, "Through Jesus Christ you believe in God, who raised him from the dead and glorified him, and your faith and hope are in God."

The one who was called before the creation of the world and human history is also the one who became a human being and gave up his life. He is the one who was raised from the dead, who now sits glorified at the right hand of God, and who will some day come back to completely fulfill and consummate the purposes of God for this world.

The mission of the church is to live within these realities. It is to provide this new vision of hope as the backdrop of understanding our individual and personal lives. To do it any other way is to betray the good news of Jesus Christ. Peter makes this clear in verses 24-25, "All men are like grass, and all their glory is like the flowers in the field; the grass withers and flowers fall, but the word of the Lord stands forever."

When we envision the new heavens and new earth in the Book of Revelation, we see a slain lamb as the one who alone can unseal the scroll of history and declare its meaning and end. We see the vision of Jesus with a two-edged sword coming out of his mouth, showing us that it is the very Word of the Lord that has capacity to shed light between the truth and falsehood of our lives, our histories, and our destinies.

It is this new reality for which the world ultimately hungers. The world has its own questions, but the church does not necessarily have to answer those questions. That is not our primary business and mission. The church, however, has to answer this question, "What is the new reality that shapes the Christian community through the ages and in every place and time?" Kingdoms come and go, governments rise and fall, ideologies often crumble even within a lifetime, and customs change, but there is something in the church that endures. What is it? It is the presence of Jesus Christ himself. That's the good news. The very Lord of this creation, the Lord of our families, our nations, and our world, is the one who is present with us here today. He is the Lord of the Christian community which is called out in every place to demonstrate in a wholeness of living the promise and hope of eternal life.

This is why Peter challenges the Christian community to be a people of *truth and love*. This is the kind of life that goes beyond the superficial. This is the kind of life that comes from being born again, from being born anew into a new reality (1:22-23). This is the secret of the Christian community. By our words and deeds, by our total life as a community, we are to live "alongside with" our neighbors, reflecting what life was meant to be. We are God's elect who are strangers in the world. God has chosen us for this purpose.

Conclusion

In these times when the church grapples with its own identity in a changing world, it is important that we go back to the basics. Like a good coach who recognizes that when a team is falling apart, we must go back to the basic drills, not only to regain confidence but also to rebuild the team. The church today needs to go back to the basics. Let me remind the reader of three areas of renewal for the church if she is to be strengthened.

1. The church needs a renewed commitment to preach and teach the truth of the Word of God. A major reason for the lack of confidence in the church is that we have lost our confidence in the Word of God. The Word of the Lord stands forever (1:25), and it is for this very reason that it needs to preached and taught in our churches. The church will endure if the Word of the Lord of the church is taken seriously in these changing times.

The church is unique in that it is the only institution that gathers people from all walks of life around the Word. When the Word is compromised, so is the calling of the community. The Word not only serves as a source of nourishment; it also shapes the community in ways that God intends as it lives "alongside with" its neighbors.

This commitment to preach and teach the truth is the highest calling of the church. It is an awesome task that must be marked by humility. It must avoid triumphalism on the one hand and tendencies to divide the unity of the church on the other. When the Word is preached and taught, it brings true godly power and a unity to our witness.

In an age when the world seeks and hungers for meaning, the church must reaffirm this high calling without apology. To accomplish this, the church needs to return to a regular practice of the expository preaching and teaching of the Bible. In many circles today, the Bible has been reduced to a "how-to" manual. In the name of relevance, the Bible is used to answer people's questions as they see them. While connecting the Word to people is a crucial task, it is not the starting point. The order needs to be reversed. The starting point is God's Word, and people's questions need to be reoriented according to this Word. The best way to do this is through the careful and continual exposition of the Word of the Lord within the community of God's people. The Word alone has the power to shape people over time in fulfilling the call and purpose of God to be strangers in the world.

2. *The church needs a renewed commitment to communal discipleship.* The corporate character of Christian discipleship is missing in many churches. Even when discipleship is emphasized, it tends to focus on individual notions of such. However, discipleship that stems from biblical living is communal.

The communal disciplines of the church should be characterized foremost by praise and hope. The church should practice praise because, in spite of what the church is going through, it is an elect community (1:1) that is called to live its life for the glory and praise of God (1 Peter 2:9). The church should live in hope because the church is the supreme community where people not only find purpose for their existence, but also find meaning in the struggle of their common human frailties against the power of sin and its efforts to destroy their lives.

When the world sets the agenda for the church, discipleship tends to be viewed in pragmatic terms. Discipleship is measured by what works. If it works it must be good. However, Christian discipleship that is communal begs to answer a different question. It seeks to answer the question, "Is it right?" The quest for what is right and true is at the heart of Christian discipleship. The church is that body which gives its life for the truth. This leads to the third and final reminder.

3. *The church needs a renewed commitment to be the place that equips people for ministry.* The ministry of Christ in and through the church is a special calling. This ministry should be characterized by obedience to the truth and love for each other (1:22).

In these days, we have a tendency to devalue truth in the name of love, or to demand truth in an unloving way. Yet the call that is shaped by the gospel to minister to people includes both truth and love. If Christian discipleship, shaped by the twin poles of truth and love, is to become the rhythm of the community in each place and time, it will only occur when the church takes seriously the call to be a place that equips people for ministry (Ephesians 4:11-13). Ministry as defined in the Bible is simply the people of God doing good within society in the name of Christ. Its purpose is to regain in simple and profound ways the original goodness of God's creation. This can be done only when the community is communally equipped or prepared for works of service.

The church is called to the unique task of shaping people to be servants. It is not a political organization nor a social club, but a community that lives in service to others. If ministry or service does not characterize a church, it fails in its God-given mission. This equipping task of the church should be comprehensive in nature, with the sole purpose being for its members to become servants of the world community. We are called to live "alongside with" our neighbors as servants. We are called to serve people according to the purposes of God.

This kind of service looks at the issues of life facing all humanity through the eyes of the good news of Jesus Christ. How this takes place will be different in each church or congregation. This has to do with the work of Christ through his Spirit in each congregation that seeks to be obediently equipped for service in the world. The danger is to reduce the church to a rigid blueprint that "forces" people into a particular ministry or vision that is based on trying to answer the questions of the world. The service of the church in the world will be dynamic and multifaceted, depending on the church's ability to listen and obey the voice of God in its midst. This is a daunting task for the church.

The church today struggles with its identity in the world. But it is also "the church of Jesus Christ who has been chosen according the foreknowledge of God the Father, through the sanctifying work of the Spirit, for obedience to Jesus Christ . . ." (1:2). The world needs the church, and the church is called to live as "strangers in the world." How shall we live? Perhaps, as the wise author of Ecclesiastes concludes:

> "Now all has been heard;
> here is the conclusion of the matter:
> Fear God and keep his commandments,
> for this is the whole duty of man.

123

Dan Devadatta

For God will bring every deed into judgment,
including every hidden thing,
whether it is good or evil."

(Ecclesiastes 12:13-14)

Understanding the Gospel in the North American Mission Context

When the world all around is changing and the church is going through convulsions in trying to find its identity in the midst of a new social location, the only place to turn for both perspective and power is the gospel. The gospel is God's good news for every generation and for the church in every context, even a postmodern context. What does this good news sound like in our present location? The gospel is always a redemptive word, but it is one that brings with it the dual character of God's truth as both judgment and grace. In this section, we are introduced to ways of hearing God's gospel as good news in the midst of our postmodern context.

The provocative character of the cross as an instrument of torture and death is the theme that Jim Brownson unfolds in the opening article in this section. He offers some historical perspective as to the horrible pain and suffering associated with this instrument of death in the early centuries of the church. He also notes how this instrument was later cleaned up and turned into a symbol of faith. Jim suggests that it is in reclaiming the central character of the shame of the cross that we also can reclaim the essential meaning of our faith. The church that now lives on the margins in a postmodern context needs to understand that in God's economy there is joy in the midst of suffering; that the essence of grace is in the cross and crucifixion.

In order for the gospel to come alive within the church, it is essential that it be contextualized within the particular culture the church is located in. What is critical is to think about this task of contextualization while bearing in mind that the church today is being marginalized. In the second article in this section, Stephen Bevans provides some guidelines for thinking about the process of contextualization. After reviewing several approaches, he settles on a "cross-cultural model" as the most helpful for maintaining faithfulness to God while seeking to be relevant to a postmodern context. He proceeds to show how this approach can and should be used by congregations in North America as they struggle to redefine their mission.

The gospel requires that it be communicated in order for it to function as gospel. The function of preaching is central to the life of the gathered community, and the task of preaching is an essential skill for Christian leaders. In the third article in this section, Lee Wyatt offers some helpful procedures for preachers to draw on as they seek to develop this skill. His thesis is that for a text to come alive as a sermon, it must find its life within the dynamics of the context within which the church lives. He discusses ways in which our present postmodern context offers provocative opportunities for biblical texts to come alive. He also lays out the detail of his method, which he calls "agonistic preaching," and provides helpful suggestions for applying this approach to a variety of different genres and texts.

Globalization has introduced all of us to a multicultural world. This has raised important issues for the church that struggles to express its essential unity in the midst of increased diversity. In the final article in this section, Stan Inouye provides some helpful insights into intercultural relations by drawing primarily on his experiences as a Japanese-American. His thesis is that the gospel, because it comes to us within a particular cultural context, bears the marks of context, but still functions as gospel. What is critical is for the church to develop skills and capacity to hear the gospel through the culture of the other person. In doing so, the whole church can be strengthened in its ministry within a multicultural society.

Hearing the Gospel Again, for the First Time

JAMES V. BROWNSON

The topic I am addressing, "hearing the gospel again for the first time," is shamelessly borrowed from Marcus Borg's study on the historical Jesus, "meeting Jesus again for the first time."[1] Though I don't intend to wade into the whole historical Jesus debate, there is something about the recent interest in the historical Jesus that is instructive about trends in our culture. In the history of the church, there have been a variety of movements seeking to go back to the original sources — whether that source is the Bible itself, as in the Protestant Reformation; or the historical Jesus, as in the nineteenth- and twentieth-century pursuits.

Such movements characteristically arise when people believe that the gospel has become overlaid with cultural accretions that distort its original power and vitality. I suspect there are many, both inside and outside the historical Jesus debate, who believe that we are now in a situation like that. I believe we are at a point in time where we need to cut past institutional habits and forms, to recover the vital center of our faith. And we need to find fresh ways to live out that center in a new and changed situation.

---

1. Marcus J. Borg, *Meeting Jesus Again for the First Time: The Historical Jesus and the Heart of Contemporary Faith* (San Francisco: HarperSanFrancisco, 1994).

127

The Gospel in *Our* Culture

All this comes into focus in an essay by George Hunsberger entitled "Acquiring the Posture of a Missionary Church," where he discusses the little word "our" in the phrase "the gospel and our culture."[2] He argues that a missiological approach to our culture is concerned not only with how to deliver a gospel message to those "out there," but also with how the gospel and culture enter into conversation in *our* own lives. It is that inner conversation upon which I want to focus. What would it be for *us* to "hear the gospel again for the first time?"

My concern is not with the historical Jesus, nor with the authority of the Bible, important as those questions may be. Rather, I want to focus attention on the gospel, the center of our faith: the good news that in the life, death, and resurrection of Jesus, we see the culmination of God's saving purpose for the whole world. Within the context of the gospel, I want to talk particularly about the cross, that aspect of the gospel which we as North Americans find most difficult to hear and to embrace. In approaching this topic, I would invite you to consider two key scripture passages that are placed in a kind of antiphony to each other, which together illumine the gospel of the cross:[3]

> For the message about the cross is foolishness to those who are perishing, but to us who are being saved it is the power of God. For it is written, "I will destroy the wisdom of the wise, and the discernment of the discerning I will thwart."

> Blessed are the poor in spirit, for theirs is the kingdom of heaven.

> Where is the one who is wise? Where is the scribe? Where is the debater of this age? Has not God made foolish the wisdom of the world?

> Blessed are those who mourn, for they will be comforted.

> For since, in the wisdom of God, the world did not know God through wisdom, God decided, through the foolishness of our proclamation, to save those who believe.

2. George R. Hunsberger and Craig Van Gelder, *The Church between Gospel and Culture* (Grand Rapids: Eerdmans, 1996), pp. 289-97.

3. 1 Corinthians 1:18-30 and Matthew 5:3-12. Note that all Scripture quotations are taken from *The New Oxford Annotated Bible: New Revised Standard Version* (New York: Oxford University Press, 1991).

Blessed are the meek, for they will inherit the earth.

For Jews demand signs and Greeks desire wisdom, but we proclaim Christ crucified, a stumbling block to Jews and foolishness to Gentiles, but to those who are called, both Jews and Greeks, Christ is the power of God and the wisdom of God.

Blessed are those who hunger and thirst for righteousness, for they will be filled.

For God's foolishness is wiser than human wisdom, and God's weakness is stronger than human strength.

Blessed are the merciful, for they will receive mercy.

Consider your own call, brothers and sisters: not many of you were wise by human standards, not many were powerful, not many were of noble birth.

Blessed are the pure in heart, for they will see God.

But God chose what is foolish in the world to shame the wise;

Blessed are the peacemakers, for they will be called children of God.

God chose what is weak in the world to shame the strong;

Blessed are those who are persecuted for righteousness' sake, for theirs is the kingdom of heaven.

God chose what is low and despised in the world, things that are not, to reduce to nothing things that are, so that no one might boast in the presence of God.

Blessed are you when people revile you and persecute you and utter all kinds of evil against you falsely on my account. Rejoice and be glad, for your reward is great in heaven, for in the same way they persecuted the prophets who were before you.

He is the source of your life in Christ Jesus, who became for us wisdom from God, and righteousness and sanctification and redemption, in order that, as it is written, "Let the one who boasts, boast in the Lord."

The words in verse 18, "For the message about the cross is foolishness to those who are perishing, but to us who are being saved it is the power of God," are tricky words that have been used in a variety of ways. Over 1,800 years ago, all the way back to the second century, the church father Tertullian set Christian faith over against all the philosophical traditions of the Greek and Roman world. If it made sense to the rational mind formed by those traditions, it couldn't be central to Christian faith. In the Middle Ages, it became popular in some circles to speak of the "sacrifice of the intellect" as the highest act of devotion one could offer to God; Christian faith involved the willingness to believe in realities which utterly contradicted the rational mind. I remember my own college years as a student at the University of Michigan, trying to make sense of my studies as a Christian, and listening to someone trying to tell me that you couldn't bring together these secular ideas and Christian faith. You just had to believe, and forget about trying to make everything make sense.

I have to admit that I have never been terribly attracted to this way of understanding Christian faith. I've always thought that if the good Lord gave me a mind, he intended me to use it. If my mind got in the way of my relationship to God in Christ, then the appropriate thing was to discover how and where I was wrong, rather than just turning off my mind altogether. It's worth noting that Tertullian certainly didn't turn off *his* mind, regardless of his rhetoric about the worthlessness of philosophy. He was one of the sharpest intellects of his day.

I also don't think that a "sacrifice of the intellect" is really what Paul has in mind when he says that the cross is foolishness to the Greeks and a stumbling block to Jews. I don't think that Paul is concerned primarily with intellectual questions in this passage. Paul is talking about the *cross*, which in the ancient world is not so much an intellectual issue as something that hits you in the gut. For us today, the cross is the central symbol of Christian faith. But for many of us, it has become so commonplace that it no longer has generative power over our imaginations.

The cross today all too easily becomes — an empty symbol, something to put at the front of churches, something out of which to make necklaces, something to add to a charm bracelet, or something to reflect on in theological abstraction. This was not at all the case when Paul was writing this passage. The cross in Paul's day represented the most brutal kind of death by torture. It was not a source of comfort to people; the cross was not a religious symbol of any sort prior to Christianity. When Paul speaks of the foolishness of the cross, he is talking about the offensiveness of taking something so ugly and bringing it to the center of faith.

The Gospel and the Cross

To talk about a cross in the ancient world would be like talking today about instruments of torture. Listen to some of the ways people in the ancient world talked about crucifixion:[4]

> Punished with limbs outstretched, they see the stake as their fate; they are fastened and nailed to it in the most bitter torment, evil food for birds of prey and grim pickings for dogs.

Often by the time someone came to take the bodies from the cross, birds and wild animals had not left much to be taken. The Roman poet Juvenal writes, "The vulture hurries from dead cattle and dogs and crosses to bring some of the carrion to her offspring."[5] Another Roman writer, Seneca, speaks of the variety of creative options open to the sadistic executioner: "I see crosses there, not just of one kind but made in many different ways: some have their victims with head down to the ground; some impale their private parts; others stretch out their arms on the gibbet."[6]

Sometimes people would be nailed to a cross; at other times, they were simply impaled on a stake. Crucifixion was almost always preceded by some other form of torture that gave the executioner an opportunity to display his virtuosity. Jesus was flogged. Others would have their eyes gouged out, or their tongues cut out, or have limbs broken.

I don't write these things to titillate or offend, and I don't mention them to try to magnify our appreciation for the death of Jesus, important as that may be. Instead, I'm trying to evoke something of what it must have been like in the ancient world to hear talk about

---

4. This translation is drawn from Martin Hengel's helpful book, *Crucifixion in the Ancient World and the Folly of the Message of the Cross* (Philadelphia: Fortress Press, 1977), p. 9. The reader of Hengel's monograph will easily discern how deeply indebted I am to his fine research throughout this paper.

5. Juvenal, *Satires* 14.77f, as translated in Hengel, p. 54.

6. Seneca the Younger, *Dialogue* 6, 20.3, as translated in Hengel, p. 25.

crucifixion. I'm trying to gain some grasp of what people in Paul's day would have thought and felt when you used the word "cross." It wasn't pretty. It wasn't nice. Once that reality is clearly in our minds, we are better prepared to understand the social implications of worshiping someone who was crucified.

Crucifixion was not the general form of capital punishment in the Roman empire of Jesus' day; it was rarely done to Roman citizens. It was reserved instead for particular classes of people: people who committed especially violent or repugnant crimes; people who engaged in sedition against the Roman government; and slaves who rebelled against their masters. In other words, crucifixion was essentially a device used by the Romans to terrorize potentially dangerous populations into submission. It was used against those groups who posed the greatest threat against the security of society, and was designed — intentionally — to be so horrifying and gruesome that these groups would not dare to act against the establishment. That's why the executioner was to display all his virtuosity in making the death as miserable and offensive as possible.

Consequently, many people in the ancient world had a kind of instinctive revulsion to anyone who had been crucified. To be crucified meant to be in the class of subversives, the worst of criminals, and rebellious slaves — in other words, to be at the bottom of the societal heap, to be a danger to society. You get a feel for what it was like to talk about someone who was crucified from this quote from Cicero:[7]

> How grievous a thing it is to be disgraced by a public court; how grievous to suffer a fine, how grievous to suffer banishment; and yet in the midst of any such disaster we retain some degree of liberty. Even if we are threatened with death, we may die free men. But the executioner, the veiling of the head and the very word "cross" should be far removed not only from the person of a Roman citizen but from his thoughts, his eyes, and his ears. For it is not only the actual occurrence of these things or the endurance of them, but liability to them, the expectation, indeed the very mention of them, that is unworthy of a Roman citizen and a free man.

So the crucifixion represents an emotionally shocking, shattering, and disconcerting event for early believers. It also represented a

7. Cicero, *Pro Rabirio*, ch. 16, as translated by Hengel, p. 42.

real problem in missionary preaching, because you might not get a hearing after saying that Jesus had been crucified. You might be suspected of being a subversive yourself.

What is especially striking, however, is that the early church made no attempt to diminish the offensiveness of its message by downplaying the crucifixion. One could imagine a quiet sweeping under the rug of the details of the circumstances of Jesus' death. In fact, precisely this happens in a story of a Roman general, Regulus, who was captured and crucified by the enemies of Rome, and became a kind of national martyr. Only the earliest accounts of his life mention the fact that he had been crucified. In later, more developed accounts of his death, there is no mention of the fact that he was crucified.[8]

Christianity, by contrast, *focused* upon and preoccupied itself with this offense. Early Christian preachers, rather than accommodating themselves to normal human tastes and sensibilities, threw this offense into the face of the world. Madison Avenue would never have counseled such a move: too many negatives to make the cross so central. But there it is, at the center of Paul's discourse.

The question, of course, is *why?* Why couldn't the early church have just said that Christ died for our sins, without talking about *how* he died? We come at this point, of course, to the very center of Christian faith, and we could probably give dozens of answers to the question of why the cross of Jesus is so central. But let me offer at least a few possible answers.

First, and perhaps most importantly, the message of the cross means that Christianity is, in very fundamental ways, a reality that radically calls into question the *status quo.* Any group that worships a crucified person will have difficulty functioning within the Chamber of Commerce. Any community of people that celebrates the fact that God redeems the world through a crucified Messiah will also be a community that celebrates how God continues to work in unexpected, unconventional, and unpredictable ways. The message of the cross invites us to look to a God who works from the bottom up, and from the margins inward, rather than from the top down. Christianity has seldom functioned with spiritual vitality when it has been in the mainstream of a culture. There's something about this location that often seems to blunt the energizing and disruptive power of the cross.

8. See the discussion in Hengel, *Crucifixion,* pp. 64ff.

This does not mean, however, that the gospel must always spawn a sectarian and separatist life in order to have integrity. It's rather the case that the message of the cross jars Christians loose from normal assumptions and expectations. It gives them an odd, quirky way of looking at the world, in whatever social location they may find themselves. The cross not only creates a kind of dislocation with respect to the dominant society; it also creates an internal dislocation and turbulence. It cuts across our normal hopes, dreams, and expectations for our own lives. It suggests that God's work in our lives emerges in the most surprising and unexpected ways: in the brokenness; the darkness; and the loneliness of our lives.

We must remember, though, that there is more to the gospel than just oddness. This is not some romantic vision of walking to the beat of a different drummer. The cross is not merely *counter* cultural, not merely a critical and negative principle; it also has its own constructive message. In the midst of all its disturbing offensiveness and strangeness, the cross speaks powerfully of *radical love and radical trust.* It shows just how far God is willing to go to show his love to us, in the life of Jesus who gives up his life for his friends. And it shows just how far humanity can go in trusting obedience to God in the life of Jesus, who trustingly obeys God's will, even when it costs him his life. The cross shatters our conventional understandings of what it means to love, and of what propriety and decorum are all about. It breaks the boundaries that enclose how far we think we can trust God. It calls us to a profoundly different kind of life: loving, trusting, and risking more deeply than we otherwise would have thought possible.

If we want to "hear the gospel again for the first time," we need to hear it from the perspective of the cross. If we want to peel back the cultural accretions and clear off the barnacles of institutionalization and tradition, we do not need only a new kind of philosophical or cultural or historical analysis, as vital as those things may be (and I do believe they are essential). What we need, at an even deeper level, is an encounter with the message of the cross that changes the frame of reference we use to make our way in the world.

Counter-cultural Gospel

I want to try to spell out a bit more how this counter-cultural thrust to the gospel changes, in very basic ways, how we think about God. The gospel of the crucified and risen Jesus is not merely a doctrinal proposition to be given assent. Paul speaks of the ministry of the gospel as an *aroma* that pervades everything (2 Corinthians 2:15). What happens when all our thinking about God becomes pervaded with the aroma of the foolishness of the gospel? I want to look at each person of the Trinity, in an effort to reread our theology from the perspective of the gospel of the cross.

The Gospel Changes the Way We Think about God

The gospel presents to us a God who takes the initiative with human beings, and does not merely sit back, waiting to be discovered. That's central to the Bible's portrayal of God: God is always active and dynamic, never simply sanctioning the status quo, but always calling us to something deeper. The God of the gospel is a God of surprises who catches people off guard. What happens when God acts? Young folk have visions and old folk dream dreams. Water turns into wine. Mustard seeds grow into huge plants. Treasures get discovered in unexpected places. Holy people and prostitutes sit down for meals together. That's what the kingdom of God is all about.

North American culture is not terribly comfortable with this perspective. Our culture believes that religion needs to stay in its place, and God needs to stay in God's place. We're perfectly content with diffuse, vague notions of God: the force; the void; the guarantor of national pride; or the ticket to heaven. Our culture doesn't like to be surprised by God; God needs to stay in heaven, not come to earth on a cross.

Think about the effect of that! A God who never surprises can never inspire someone to radical love, or to radical trust. How can you trust a God who never actually touches human life in any real way? What kind of love would be willing to upset the apple carts of this world, if God is always upholding order, and never doing the unexpected?

One of the ways in which this issue of radical love and radical

135

trust comes to a head in our culture is in the way we handle risk. In our culture, an enormous amount of energy and time is devoted to managing and anticipating risks, and in developing contingencies. Think about it. Most of the major political crises, at least in American society, revolve around the handling of risk: health insurance; pensions; disaster relief; governmental intervention; farm price supports — all these things revolve around the reduction of risk and the elimination of contingency. In a world that is changing at an unbelievable pace, we crave security as much as we crave anything. No wonder it is difficult for us to hear the gospel of a God of surprises!

The tragedy of our lives, however, is that rather than trying to handle the contingencies of our lives with a deeper love for others and a deeper trust in God, we do exactly the opposite. We insulate ourselves from others. We try to deal with all those contingencies ourselves. What we can't handle ourselves, we entrust to faceless corporations and bureaucracies. The goal in life is to get to the point where you no longer need anyone, other than your insurance agent.

I had an experience in my own life a few years ago that captured for me this insulated character of life in North America. I lived for seven years in a typical American suburban neighborhood. Folks in my neighborhood generally kept to themselves, didn't see much of each other, or engage each other in conversation. The neighborhood was like thousands of others: at the end of a cul-de-sac; single-story ranch-style houses; two-car garages; big back yards; immaculate lawns. I have always been a somewhat reluctant gardener, and after two years of living in this neighborhood, my lawn had fallen below the lush and verdant standards set by my neighbors. I decided that if I wanted to retain some respect from my neighbors, I would need to fertilize my lawn. The problem, however, was that I had no fertilizer spreader.

So I went out on a Saturday morning (the only time when all the automatic garage doors are up for chores) and walked around my neighborhood, peering into garages to find a neighbor who might have a fertilizer spreader I could borrow. As I walked around the block, I realized that *every single house* had a fertilizer spreader in its garage! And suddenly the thought occurred to me: here is a neighborhood where people don't know each other very well. Most of them are two-career families, driving themselves to the limit of their time and endurance, desperately trying to earn enough money *so that they won't need anyone else.* They had reached the American dream, and it had left them almost completely cut off from each other! The goal of the American dream is "material and financial security," guaranteed by your pension fund and the federal government. A recent TV ad by a major insurance company expresses the ethos. Three captions appear on a screen, against the backdrop of family life: "Live Well." "Make a Plan." "Be Your Own Rock."

I surely don't intend categorically to reject such supports for human life. But I do want to note what happens when our whole center of trust and allegiance shifts in that direction. How vastly different is a community of people devoted to radical love and trust, who are willing even to lay their lives down for each other! That's the power of the gospel.

I also tasted something of that reality when I was a student in graduate school. I lived in the married student apartments, where everyone was getting by on borrowed funds, as they tried to scrape together a living. Strangely, although it was the time when our family was the most financially stressed, it was also the time when we experienced the deepest sense of community and connectedness with others. The fact that all of us in that complex *needed* each other led us to love and trust each other much more deeply than we otherwise would have done. I learned more about radical love and trust there than I learned in the comforts of suburbia.

The Gospel Changes the Way We Think about Jesus

The gospel does not express merely the abstract idea that God is a God of surprises who calls us to radical love and trust. The gospel presents to us the life, death, and resurrection of one particular person, Jesus Christ. The gospel invites, even demands, radical allegiance to this person, to this way in which God has been made known. In that particular life, we find enormous wisdom about how to live a counter-cultural life in our own world. How much we need to meet this Jesus again, for the first time!

Think about some of the characteristics of his life, and how they resonate with the needs and crises of our culture. His example of *nonviolence* offers powerful alternatives to our violent society. The recent movie "Dead Man Walking" raises in profound ways the question of alternatives to violence — the terrible violence of criminals, and the sanitized institutional violence of capital punishment. The central character, a nun, repeatedly evokes the example of Jesus as she tries to live in the midst of this terrible pain and violence, loving both the victims and the perpetrators of violence. There's wisdom there for us.

I think of the constant tendency of Jesus to penetrate to the genuinely *core values* at stake in controversies, rather than focusing on external structures. That perspective can be powerfully liberating for us at this point in our history. The first century, in many ways like our own, was a time of intense and competing pluralism and change. In the midst of so many competing proposals for how life should be lived, Jesus was able to penetrate to the fundamental questions. Such questions always remain, whatever we may do with the details. That freedom from rigidity frees us to live more redemptively in the period of transition and change we are now experiencing in our culture and in our churches.

We need to rediscover Jesus' delight in *parable and paradox*. Jesus, at many points, seems congenitally incapable of giving a straight answer to any question. In our postmodern world, we understand that. We understand that questions often already carry within them their own ideological biases. We understand that many of the most important truths can be gotten at only indirectly. Jesus is a teacher we can listen to.

Think of the constant tendency of Jesus to *see the hidden ones: the children, the sick, the lame, and the blind.* What a powerful message that is, in the context of a glamour culture obsessed with the thin veneer of beauty that masks all pain, all sickness, all aging, all deformity, all loss. Think of his *love for enemies,* which offers a way out from the cycles of retaliation, hate, and bitterness that hold us in their grip. His emphasis on *detachment from wealth* frees us from the grip of acquisition and greed, and enables us to find a new source of fulfillment and meaning.

To hear the gospel again for the first time is to think afresh about what discipleship might mean in our world, in light of the radical love and trust revealed in the cross of Christ. But perhaps all this feels a little overwhelming to you. I must confess, it does to me. Every time I hear the beatitudes, something in me gets uncomfortable. I wonder what I will have to give up, what I will lose, what unhappiness I must endure if I am to follow Jesus Christ. I think that at precisely that point, when the defenses start to rise, we need to hear again about the promise and help of the Holy Spirit.

The Gospel Changes the Way
We Think about the Spirit

We need to hear about the Spirit, because one of the most important things the Bible has to say about the Spirit is that the Spirit forms us into the image of Jesus Christ. Paul presents the work of the Spirit in relation to the body of Christ, where differentiation is what enables the body to function. There is not just one way to live out a life under the sign of the cross. The Spirit inspires many ways. A look at the early church gives some ideas. In living out its life under the cross, the early church found a variety of ways to say "no" to human assumptions and values. Some early Christians lived lives of radical voluntary poverty. A good example is found in Jesus' commission to his own disciples before their preaching tour in Matthew 10:5-10 and Luke 10:1-12. Here they are to take no money, not even a spare set of clothes. They are to be living examples of a radical trust in God, a kind of trust that shatters our ordinary assumptions about what we need to get by. They are to be a living sign that shakes the world loose from its anxious reliance on possessions. In this sense, they are a precursor to the cross itself.

But notice something. Who takes care of these itinerant poor preachers? It was believers who had homes, families, and food to spare! Without them, the preaching missions would have been impossible. Hence, this call to radical poverty is not a call to the whole church; it is a call to *some* in the church as an expression of the cross. Likewise Paul calls some to celibacy in 1 Corinthians 7:32-35. These are a sign to the world that sex is not the be-all and end-all of life. But again, this call is not for everyone. The Christians in Acts 4 pooled their possessions as a radical challenge to the world's tendency to horde and isolate. But again, there is no evidence that this pattern was normative in early Christianity.

Diversity is scattered throughout the pages of the New Testament. Some gave up their lives in martyrdom. Others opened wide the doors of their houses in hospitality to whole congregations. They poured themselves out in concern for the poor; they experimented with whole new patterns of relating to each other — patterns that cut against the static hierarchies of the day. In countless ways, both great and small, they challenged with their lives the prevailing assumptions of the day, and like a prism they refracted the light of God's grace into many colors.

139

I believe that the church today needs both the radicality *and* the diversity of early Christianity. We need people who are called to a radical simplicity of lifestyle, to remind the rest of us that we don't need what we think we need. We need people committed to celibacy, to tell us that sex is neither a necessity nor a god. We need people who continually open their homes to others, to cure the rest of us of the idolatry of our privacy. We need devoted parents who sacrifice career advancement for the sake of time with their children, so that the rest of us can keep our priorities straight. We need people who are lavish in prayer and spiritual disciplines, in order to remind those of us with harder spirits of where our real help comes from. We need communities of Christians willing to commit themselves to support each other in risky, venturesome ways, to goad the rest of us out of our autonomy. We need Christians willing to resist the many ways in which the dominant in our world crush the weak.

In short, we need Christians who find a thousand joyful ways to take the screwed-up values of this world and turn them upside down — Christians who aren't afraid to walk down a path the world calls madness, but which is really the road to life. In this, each of us has a unique calling. It is vitally important that we not carry someone else's cross, but rather, with our eyes fixed firmly on Jesus, to discern the call by which he is calling us. Then, and only then, will we discover the resolution to one of the greatest paradoxes in all of Scripture. We are all to take up our crosses daily, and yet, what Jesus says is absolutely true — "my yoke is easy, and my burden is light" (Matthew 11:30).

My desire for Christians is simply this: that we never become so sophisticated, so learned, so literate, or so professional, that we cease speaking of this horror, this obscenity, this Cross of Jesus, which alone has the power to shatter our world. Only in this way can the hope of resurrection and new life spring forth within us, and through us to this world which our God so deeply loves.

Living between Gospel and Context: Models for a Missional Church in North America

STEPHEN BEVANS, SVD

In the book *Models of Contextual Theology,* I outlined five "models" of contextual theology being practiced by contemporary theologians from both the first and the third worlds.[1] The underlying conviction of the book was a *methodological* one. In doing theology today, and for theology to be genuine theology, theologians need to take into account not only the *scriptural* witness, and the witness of the *Christian Tradition* — Christianity's creeds, confessions, and official church teachings; they need also to take into account the *context* in which they live.

In this essay, I want to reflect a bit more in detail about this process of doing theology, and to develop a kind of analogy for a reflection on the theme to which the title of my essay points. In other words, I would like to reflect in these pages on how an understanding of the nature and methods of contextual theology might help us understand more deeply the ways in which people of faith might live *as church,* as a missionary people, in the midst of our contemporary culture. I will outline four models of interaction between church and context that

1. Stephen Bevans, SVD, *Models of Contextual Theology* (Maryknoll, N.Y.: Orbis Books, 1992).

might be used by a missional church in North America in our turn-of-the-millennium era as it tries to be faithful to both gospel and context. After sketching out the general features of each model, I will propose that one model — which I will call the "counter-cultural model" — might be the one that will ensure the double fidelity to which the church is called in living out its missional nature.

Contextual Theology

The Centrality of Human Experience

In what we might call "classical theology," theology is conceived as the attempt to understand more deeply and reasonably what we as Christians believe. According to this notion of the theological process, there were just two sources of theological reflection: Scripture and (in various senses, depending on one's ecclesial and theological commitments) Tradition. Theology was the investigation through faith into God's revelation, and Scripture and Tradition were where God's revelation was found. One did theology, therefore, first by trying to understand what Scripture really said and really meant, and by trying to determine what the Tradition *was* — what, in other words, the church proposed for our belief. This was called the *positive moment* of theology. Then, in a second moment of *speculative theology,* theologians attempted to understand what the data of faith found in Scripture and Tradition *meant* in terms of (mainly) philosophical reasoning.[2]

When we speak of *contextual theology,* however, Scripture and Tradition are not the only sources for theological reflection. *Context* is a theological source as well. What this means is that contextual theology considers not only Scripture and Tradition to be the sources where God's revelation is to be found. Revelation is also encountered in the midst of human life, in human history, in *human experience.* Theology's source, therefore, is not just in records of God's revelation

2. See René Latourelle, *Theology: Science of Salvation* (Staten Island, N.Y.: Alba House, 1969). Also note that this description of "classical theology" is admittedly Roman Catholic in substance. However, I would imagine that Protestant and Evangelical "classical" theologies would have similar descriptions of their method.

given in the past. Theology's source is the whole human and cosmic reality of people's present existence. There are not just two sources of theology, as a more "classicist" theology proposed, but three: Scripture, Tradition, and Context.

Such an understanding of how context serves as a theological source is, from one point of view, hardly new and quite traditional. After all, what are the four gospels but four different theological portraits of Jesus, developed from four very different early Christian contexts? How can one understand Aquinas if one does not understand his medieval background where church was vying with state and Aristotle had been freshly rediscovered? Would Luther have been Luther without the context of a corrupt Catholicism? Would Barth have been converted from liberalism if there had been no First World War and no Hitler?

From another point of view, however, contextual theology is something radically new. Not until our own time (as we have reaped the positive benefits of the Enlightenment's discovery of subjectivity and the nineteenth century's discovery of historical consciousness)[3] have theologians been so aware of the importance of context in constructing human thought, and — at least in the minds of some — of the sacredness of context in terms of God's revelation. Indeed, when we say that there are three sources for theology, we are not just adding context as a third element; we are changing the whole equation.

When we recognize the importance of context for theology, we are also acknowledging the absolute importance of context in the development of both Scripture and Tradition. The writings of Scripture and the content, practices, and feel of Tradition did not simply fall from the sky. They, themselves, are products of human beings and their contexts. They have been developed by human beings, written and conceived in human terms, and conditioned by human personality and human circumstances. As we study Scripture and Tradition, we not only have to be aware of their inevitable contextual nature; we have to read and interpret them within our own context as well.

3. See Karl Rahner, "The Hermeneutics of Eschatological Assertions," in *Theological Investigations IV* (Baltimore: Helicon Press; London: Darton, Longman & Todd, 1966), p. 324; and Jeffery Hopper, *Understanding Modern Theology II: Reinterpreting Christian Faith for Changing Worlds* (Philadelphia: Fortress Press, 1987), pp. 4-31.

We can say, then, that doing theology contextually means doing theology in a way that takes into account two things. First, it takes into account the faith-experience of the past that is recorded in Scripture and kept alive, preserved, defended — and perhaps even neglected or suppressed[4] in Tradition. A major part of the theological process, insists Douglas John Hall, "is simply *finding out* about the Christian theological past."[5] Second, contextual theology takes into account the experience of the present, the *context*. While theology needs to be faithful to the full experience and contexts of the past, it is authentic *theology* only "when what has been received is appropriated, made our own. For that to happen, the received tradition must of course pass through the sieve of our own individual and contemporary-collective experience: we cannot give it, profess it as ours, unless such a process occurs."[6]

The Manifold Nature of Context

This "individual and contemporary-collective experience," or context, is rather complex, and represents a combination of several realities. First, context involves the experiences of a person's or group's personal life: the experiences of success, failure, births, deaths, relationships, etc., that allow persons to, or prevent persons from, experiencing God in their lives. There are also the experiences of life — personal or communal — in our contemporary world: political discussions in an election year; tragedies such as the crash of TWA 800; or moments of wonderment like the heady times in Europe at the end of 1989.

Second, personal or communal experience is possible only within the context of culture, that "system of inherited conceptions expressed in symbolic forms by means of which people communicate, perpetuate, and develop their knowledge about and attitudes toward life."[7] Such

4. Douglas John Hall, *Professing the Faith: Christian Theology in a North American Context* (Minneapolis: Fortress Press, 1993), pp. 34-36; and Rosemary Radford Ruether, *Sexism and God-Talk: Toward a Feminist Theology* (Boston: Beacon Press, 1993), pp. 12-46.

5. Hall, *Professing the Faith*, p. 33.

6. Hall, *Professing the Faith*, p. 33.

7. Clifford Geertz, *The Interpretation of Cultures* (New York: Basic Books, 1973), p. 89, as quoted in Gerald A. Arbuckle, *Earthing the Gospel: An Inculturation Handbook for the Pastoral Worker* (Maryknoll, N.Y.: Orbis Books, 1990), p. 28.

culture, it seems to me, can be either "secular" or "religious." A "secular" culture might be a culture like ours in North America and would comprise the values and customs of a particular group of people. A "religious" culture might be a culture like that of India, where values and customs are permeated with the symbols and myths of a religious system such as Hinduism. Not only the values and customs of a people need to be engaged, therefore, in contextual theology; often the religion of peoples needs to be understood and engaged.

Third, we can speak of context in terms of a person's or a community's social location. It makes a difference, both feminist and liberation theologians have insisted, whether one is male or female, rich or poor, from North America or Latin America, at the center or at the margins of power. Social location can be a limiting factor in some ways, but it can also be a position from which one can detect flaws or riches in the tradition. It can be a position from which one can ask questions never before asked or entertained in theological reflection. As theologians do theology, their social location needs to be acknowledged, and even embraced. We can certainly move beyond our social locations, and our "etic" insights can be important in particular situations.[8] However, we disregard who we are only at the risk of doing poor theology.

Finally, the notion of present experience or context involves the reality of social change. No context is static, and even the most traditional culture is one that is growing, improving, or declining. In today's globalized world of compressed time and space,[9] two factors in particular are having an impact on social change within cultures. First, there is the cultural impact of modernity, with the revolutions brought about by electronic media and the contemporary expansion of global connectedness. Benjamin R. Barber names this "McWorld," and describes it as a "product of popular culture driven by expansionist commerce. Its template is American, its form style. Its goods are as much images as matériel, an aesthetic as well as a product line."[10] Second, the idealist side of modernity has had a worldwide impact as well. Many societies who have been ruled by oppressive

8. Bevans, *Models of Contextual Theology,* pp.13-16.
9. Malcolm Waters, *Globalization* (London and New York: Routledge, 1995).
10. Benjamin R. Barber, *Jihad Vs. McWorld* (New York: Times Books, 1995), p. 17.

forces now recognize the rights and dignity of oppressed peoples who are struggling for their liberation. This is the case politically in societies in Latin America or Asia, or in situations of marginality such as among women, people of color, or homosexuals.

Theology today needs to take into account all of these aspects of context. It needs to realize that many of these aspects were already at work in the development of both the witness of Scripture and the witness of Tradition. It needs to realize even more that context in all its dimensions is the inevitable starting point of theological reflection today. How that context is interpreted, however, and how it interacts with Christian faith as it is expressed in the classical sources, gives rise to another methodological question that might be explored with the use of models.

Models of Contextual Theology

Doing theology is not only a matter of identifying one's sources; it is about how these sources are employed, about which source receives a certain priority, and about which source serves as its starting point. Having identified three sources for the construction of a contextual theology, the question of *procedure* arises. The answer comes in the form of various models that emerge as theologians make procedural choices dependent on prior theological or doctrinal commitments.

In my 1992 book I identified five such models, and subsequently I have identified one other,[11] but for the purposes of this essay I will focus on only four of these six. If theologians stress the authority and normativity of Scripture and Tradition, while still *valuing* the context, they tend to develop a "translation model" of contextual theology. If, however, theologians stress the basic authority and even normativity of the context, while not denying a certain authority and normativity to the received scriptural and doctrinal tradition, they theologize out of what might be called an "anthropological model." Other theologians lay stress on the importance of participation in and learning from the movements of social change in a particular context, and

11. Stephen Bevans, "Taking Culture Seriously in Religious Education," *The Catholic World,* September-October 1994, pp. 236-40.

work at rereading the scriptural and traditional witness out of that experience. Such a procedure might be called a "praxis model" of doing theology. Finally, if theologians approach the context with a hermeneutics of suspicion, while at the same time recognizing its importance in theological expression, they work out of a "counter-cultural model," in which the scriptural and traditional witness functions in a critical manner in relation to context.

Let me make two additional remarks about these models. First, all of these models are valid ways to come to an understanding of Christian faith. There are no "wrong" models sketched out above. The question is not one of a wrong model in theory or in the abstract, but one of the choice of the most *appropriate* model in terms of the context. In a certain sense, the method of contextual theology demands that, in a kind of pre-theological move, theologians always begin with an analysis of the context.

Second, models are *models.* They represent relatively simple, artificially constructed cases that are "found to be useful and illuminating for dealing with realities that are more complex and differentiated."[12] The value of models certainly can be *constructive,* and indeed this is the way I treat them here. The original intent of my reflection on models of contextual theology, however, was *descriptive.* I discerned that various contextual theologians spoke of contextual theology in different ways, and that the reason for such difference was on account of the various ways Scripture, Tradition, and Context were regarded in terms of their authority and theological normativity. In actual theological activity, the models sketched above and outlined at the end of this essay are not used exclusively, but inclusively. That is, when one does theology that takes context seriously, two or perhaps even more of the models can be used simultaneously, and in all sorts of combinations. One can, for instance, employ the counter-cultural model together with the praxis model, as does Douglas John Hall in his essay in this volume.[13] Or, as I will propose, the counter-cultural model might also be paired, in a kind of mutually critical correlation, with the anthropological model.

12. See Avery Dulles, *Models of Revelation* (Maryknoll, N.Y.: Orbis Books, 1992), p. 30; also Bevans, *Models of Contextual Theology,* pp. 24-26.

13. Douglas John Hall, "Metamorphosis: From Christendom to Diaspora," pp. 72-76.

Stephen Bevans, SVD

Contextual Models for a Missional Church

From Models of Theology to Models for Mission

It seems to me that if we substitute the notion of pastoral strategy, or the church's mission, for theology, there would appear to be four distinct ways (or models) of living out the missionary nature of the church. In the past, we might have conceived of the church's mission as simply "preaching the gospel" or "living out the Christian life" as a witness to the world. The context in which we lived had little impact on us, whether it was France, or East Los Angeles, or Thailand. There was basically one gospel, one body of Christian Tradition, one way of living a Christian ethical life. This was reflected in our church architecture, our hymns, and our relatively uniform structure of worship, which was more noticeably Lutheran, or Catholic, or Presbyterian than it was African, or Asian, or particularly North American.

If we think contextually, however, we recognize the need to be church and live out the Christian mission by allowing our architecture, our forms or worship, and our style of preaching to be influenced by and engaged with the events of our lives and our world. Such things need to reflect the shape and values of our culture; our social location as white, or African-American, or middle-class; and the effect of social change as it is transforming our culture and our consciousness.

If we have begun to think in this way, the next question will be — as it was for theology — how do we engage this multidimensional context? Do we *translate* the gospel in terms that the context can understand, or at least not misunderstand — the translation model?[14] Do we study the context with faith that it is the place of God's continuing revelation and so find ways to deepen our understanding of the scriptural and traditional witness — the anthropological model? Do we reflect on our efforts to bring about gospel values such as justice and peace in the context within which we live, and let what we learn ground our further efforts in mission — the praxis model? Or do we

---

14. The importance of preaching the gospel in a way that people might be offended by it for the right reasons is a point made recently by Darrell Whiteman in his keynote address at the 1996 annual meeting of the American Society of Missiology, June 20, 1996.

confront our context with the culturally conditioned, but nevertheless divinely sanctioned, gospel and traditional Christian message in order to unmask what is counter to the gospel in the context, and call for its transformation — the counter-cultural model?

Before I propose what I consider the most appropriate model within our North American context, let me briefly define each model, keeping in mind that for a particular context any one of these models — or some combination of them — might be the most appropriate.

Models for Mission

A *translation model* for mission would have as its starting point that the essence of the gospel — what is recorded in Scripture and affirmed in the Tradition — is both supracultural and complete. It is a message, a content, that through its words is intended for and can be understood by all peoples in all contexts, provided only that it be expressed in the proper way in the particular context. It is a message to which nothing need be nor can be added. Given such a supracultural and complete nature, the only way it can engage the context is to take on the context's specific expressions.

To use an agricultural image that will recur in each model's description, it is as if the church brings the seeds to be planted in a particular plot of ground. As the seeds sprout, they will take firm root in that particular place, but if they are carrot seeds they will be carrots; the ground, the *context,* doesn't make any difference as to the ultimate identity of the seeds, although it has a lot to do with the quality of the plant. In citing the example of the "Peace Child" in his essay in this volume, Richard Mouw gives a striking example of how the church might preach the gospel in the particular context of Papua New Guinea.[15] As Bruce Fleming expressed it some years ago, this way of preaching the gospel functions by "putting the gospel into" the contextually conditioned and incomplete forms of a particular situation.[16]

15. Richard Mouw, "The Missionary Location of the North American Churches," pp. 9-10.
16. Bruce Fleming, *Contextualization of Theology: An Evangelical Assessment* (Pasadena, Calif.: William Carey Library, 1980, 1996).

An *anthropological model* for mission, in contrast, would start from a conviction that the context in which the church evangelizes is where God's revealing Word is most likely to be found. Here the witness of Scripture and Tradition needs to be read in its light, and is always open to fresh understandings and angles of interpretation. As we plan ways to evangelize a particular cultural context, the often-quoted words of M. A. C. Warren need to be prominent in our mind: the first task of evangelization, "is to take off our shoes, for the place we are approaching is holy," not forgetting that "God was here before our arrival."[17]

Context, therefore, whether human experience, culture, or social change occurring within a culture, is basically good and trustworthy. This model would hold that only by "listening" to it carefully[18] can we know not only how the gospel needs to be preached, but also what the content of the gospel is. The church does not so much furnish the seeds, as it were, as it waters the soil in which the seeds have already been planted. What grows up may be a surprise, but since the soil is good soil and the seeds have been put there by God, the harvest will be an authentic one. If one were to look for an example of such a missionary consciousness in North America, the phenomenon of the Willow Creek church might qualify.[19]

A *praxis model* of the church in mission is distinguished as one that believes that the gospel is to be found neither in static, content-oriented notions of Scripture or Tradition, nor in interpretations of the Context as a receptacle of thought-forms, values, or experiences. Rather, one finds the Christian God in the midst of history, beckoning those who believe to join in the struggle to create it. Scripture, particularly, is the record of God's active and saving presence in Israel's history, and it serves not so much as something to be believed as something to be imitated. While the praxis model would generally re-

17. Warren is speaking in his Introduction of the foreign missionary, but, as is the point of this volume, the work of the church in any context needs to pay attention to the context in which it ministers. On this point, see the essays of George Hunsberger in Hunsberger and Van Gelder, eds., *The Church between Gospel and Culture* (Grand Rapids: Eerdmans, 1996).

18. Robert J. Schreiter, *Constructing Local Theologies* (Maryknoll, N.Y.: Orbis Books, 1985).

19. Charles Trueheart, "Welcome to the Next Church," *The Atlantic Monthly* 272: 37-58.

gard the context as good and trustworthy, it realizes, as well, that quite often the content can be distorted and dehumanizing.

The context in many cases needs to be approached with some suspicion, and needs to be transformed. This is the case particularly in Latin America where the praxis model was originally developed, and it would certainly be the case in situations in North America. This would be true, for example, in our inner cities or in immigrant communities, where human rights are being violated, or where people suffer under racial prejudice. Like seeds that need constantly to be watered and soil that needs to be constantly weeded, preaching the gospel according to this model calls for continual concrete action (lobbying, picketing, boycotting, etc.). It requires continued reflection on such action in the light of Scripture and Tradition, and renewed action in light of that reflection. One does not so much preach the gospel with words according to this model, as it engages in "doing the truth in love" (Ephesians 4:15).

A church that chooses to carry out its mission by means of a *counter-cultural model* would be one that recognizes the importance of the context in which it lives. It would also point to the gospel — found in Scripture, in the church's doctrinal Tradition, and in the warp and woof of human experience as well — as having a critical function over against the context. As Paul Hiebert expresses it, "the gospel must be contextualized, but it must remain prophetic. It must stand in judgment of what is evil in all cultures as well as in all persons."[20] The mission of the church according to this model would be to unmask the context of its anti-gospel elements, and confront it with the truth of the gospel. Such unmasking would include not just the context outside the church, but also the context inside the church. Before the seeds can be planted, and as the seeds are growing, the soil — both inside and outside the church — needs to be weeded.

There is a kind of continuum along which various forms of this counter-cultural model might be placed.[21] At one extreme would be the thinking of Stanley Hauerwas and William Willimon, whose focus is strongly ecclesiological and who view the context outside the

20. Paul G. Hiebert, "Critical Contextualization," in *Anthropological Reflections on Missiological Issues* (Grand Rapids: Baker, 1994), p. 86.

21. My understanding of this continuum has developed over the years, particularly as the result of conversations with Dr. Michael Goheen. I am deeply grateful to him for challenging my rather unnuanced position, particularly in regard to Lesslie Newbigin.

church with the strongest suspicion. "As Jesus demonstrated," they write, "the world, for all its beauty, is hostile to the truth."[22] And so the church must live as a "colony of resident aliens within a hostile environment."[23] The mission of the church is simply to be the church, to cultivate itself as a counter-cultural sign in the world, not to transform it. "The very idea that Christians can be at home, indeed can create a home in this world, is a mistake."[24]

While Lesslie Newbigin would basically agree with Hauerwas and Willimon's analysis of contemporary Western society, he would say that it is not simply a secular society, but it is truly *pagan*.[25] He would hold that the church "cannot without guilt absolve itself from the responsibility, where it sees the possibility, of seeking to shape the public life of nations and the global ordering of industry and commerce in the light of the Christian faith."[26] To cite one more position on this continuum, Catholic theologian John Coleman would argue that while preaching the gospel "always involves counter-cultural moves," the culture or context — and Coleman is speaking of the North American context in particular — always contains within it "goods and values of the [U.S. American] tradition."[27] Being counter-cultural for Coleman means retrieving a sense of gospel values that are often hidden within a context, but which have been lost as that context is corrupted by anti-gospel influences.

A Contextual Model for North America

All of these models are valid as such, and all could be valid in the context of contemporary North America. However, I would suggest that

22. Stanley Hauerwas and William H. Willimon, *Resident Aliens* (Nashville: Abingdon Press, 1989), p. 47.

23. Hauerwas and Willimon, *Resident Aliens,* p. 139.

24. Stanley Hauerwas and William H. Willimon, "Why *Resident Aliens* Struck a Chord," *Missiology:An International Review* 19 (4 October 1991): 421.

25. Lesslie Newbigin, *Foolishness to the Greeks: The Gospel and Western Culture* (Grand Rapids: Eerdmans, 1986), p. 20.

26. Newbigin, *Foolishness to the Greeks,* p. 129.

27. John A. Coleman, "Inculturation and Evangelization in the North American Context," in *Proceedings of the Forty-Fifth Annual Convention of the Catholic Theological Society of America,* George Kilcourse, ed. (Louisville, Ky.: Bellarmine College, 1990), p. 26.

serious consideration should be given to what I have called the "counter-cultural model" for carrying out the church's mission in this context. Pope John Paul II has described certain aspects of our contemporary context as a "culture of death," in which "the values of *being* are replaced by those of *having*," and the notion of "'quality of life' is interpreted primarily or exclusively as economic efficiency, inordinate consumerism, physical beauty and pleasure, to the neglect of the more profound dimensions — interpersonal, spiritual and religious — of existence."[28] Probably nowhere is this culture of death stronger than in Europe and North America, and its existence both outside *and* inside the church should call the church to commit itself to becoming a "people of life and for life"[29] who work to create a "civilization of love and life."[30] Doing this means that the church needs to take a deliberately counter-cultural stance as it works out ways to live out its mission.

The position of Hauerwas and Willimon has much power and is quite attractive in many ways. But it seems to me that more positive attitudes toward the "transformability" of the world (as in Newbigin), and to the goodness and sacredness of the context (as in Coleman), need to be considered as the church seeks ways to witness to the gospel in today's North American situation. A counter-cultural preaching of the gospel, in this understanding, would involve all the "disengagement" from culture that Douglas John Hall calls for.[31] It would also involve a call to reappropriate the deepest values that made up the vision of the founders of the United States, as well as those that inform the Canadian *ethos*.

Coleman gives as an example of good contextual church minis-

---

28. John Paul II, *The Gospel of Life (Evangelium Vitae)* (New York: Times Books, 1995), 41 (#23). Pope John Paul II's encyclical letter referred to here, *The Gospel of Life*, focuses particularly on the moral issues of abortion, euthanasia, and capital punishment. While not all Christians might agree with the pope's position on these issues, his description of the context, or atmosphere, in which they are debated is, in my opinion, extremely accurate. The first number in the citation of the encyclical refers to the page in the edition cited; the number in parentheses refers to the paragraph of the encyclical, which will be the same in all editions.

29. *The Gospel of Life*, 142 (#79).

30. *The Gospel of Life*, 49 (#27).

31. Douglas John Hall, "Ecclesia Crucis: The Theologic of Christian Awkwardness," in Hunsberger and Van Gelder, eds., *The Church between Gospel and Culture*, pp. 198-213.

try in the two pastoral letters of the U.S. bishops that were issued in the 1980s on peace and the economy. These were truly counter-cultural documents "in the sense of opposing powerful new forces eroding older values and institutions in American life."[32] Nevertheless, their being counter-cultural does not make them documents that are condemnatory of the U.S. cultural context as such. "Inasmuch as the bishops appealed, beyond confessional warrant, to reasoned discourse and to a broader public, they could actually reawaken in other Americans (recall the many letters by Protestant churches which came in the wake of the bishops' pastorals) what many claim to be the truer and deeper American values." In other words, says Coleman, "we can appeal to countervailing forces already available in the culture or for defense of deep-rooted cultural ideas and institutions now under threat."[33]

This particular model of mission might be characterized as a combination of both the anthropological model *and* the counter-cultural model in its more austere forms (Hauerwas, Willimon, and Newbigin). It recognizes the neopagan, even diabolical nature of the contemporary North American context, which is caught in the grip of a hedonistic and narcissistic individualism. But it nevertheless recognizes that North Americans still yearn for the values of community and responsible freedom that are embodied in documents like the U.S. Constitution and in the writings of thinkers like Thomas Jefferson. The task of the church, like the task of the prophets of Israel, is to call North American people *back* to their roots, not to destroy them.

It is important to be *counter-cultural,* but to do that we do not have to be *anti-cultural.* Rather, it will be for the sake of the context that we speak and work against it. The church today needs to be a prophetic church, but it is important to recall that the prophets stood against Israel not because, in the final analysis, Israel was evil, but because Israel was God's holy people. Prophecy arises not out of hate of a context, but from a love of its deepest possibilities. It is this *gospel* vision that will guide the church in fulfilling its missionary nature today.

32. Coleman, "Inculturation and Evangelization," p. 29.
33. Coleman, "Inculturation and Evangelization," p. 29.

Preaching to Postmodern People

LEE A. WYATT

"Will it preach?" That's the question which is always close to the surface for preachers! This volume of essays presents the argument that we need to revision the church as a missionary body within the mission location of North America. One primary reason is that our mission location is now characterized by the postmodern condition. This article will attempt to address the issue of preaching in this new context. It is my conviction that we need to respond with theological integrity to the issues raised by postmodernity, and that we need to allow this to inform our preaching. As we do so, we will better equip ourselves to revision the church as a missionary people in this context.[1]

We will begin with a brief overview of postmodernism. This will be followed by a discussion of how to move from text to sermon in postmodern times. The third section will present a model of what I call "agonistic" preaching, and the final section considers the theological location of such preaching. I intend my remarks as being suggestive and exploratory, as ideas that are still in process of development.

---

1. This material is part of a larger project I am working on titled "Preaching Is Stranger than It Used to Be: The Gospel and Postmodern People," which is a play on the title of J. Richard Middleton and Brian J. Walsh, *Truth Is Stranger than It Used to Be: Biblical Faith in a Postmodern Age* (Downers Grove, Ill.: InterVarsity Press, 1995).

Postmodernity

Descriptions of postmodernity abound.[2] To get a firsthand feel, however, one should consult philosophers like Derrida, Lyotard, Rorty, Foucault; read novels like Douglas Adams's *Mostly Harmless*;[3] and watch MTV and rock videos from groups like the Indigo Girls and R.E.M.

For our purposes, I suggest the following as agenda items that postmodernism confronts us with as preachers of the gospel: rejection of Story, identity formation, and community. It is essential, I believe, that we wrestle with these issues in light of the gospel. We must do so if our preaching is to substantively address our present North American culture.

Jean-François Lyotard, a leading postmodern theorist, declares, "Simplifying to the extreme, I define postmodernism as incredulity toward metanarratives."[4] In postmodernism, there is no universally applicable account of humanity, its goals, or its purposes. There is no Story, only stories in all their bewildering variety and contradictoriness. All of us see things our own way. And we experience extraordinary difficulty communicating across our singular perspectives.[5] In particular, the western Story, which has often been violently imposed on other cultures since the dawn of the modern age, must be rejected. Obviously, for people who preach a message that we understand as a Story or a metanarrative, this must be a central concern.

If we reject the Enlightenment Story of reason, progress, and success on which our culture is built, along with the Christian Story that undergirded it much of the time, where do we go from there? What resources can we draw on to reconstruct a sense of self that

---

2. Two different, but helpful, delineations are found in Stanley J. Grenz, *Primer on Postmodernism* (Grand Rapids: Eerdmans, 1996), pp. 5-9; and Craig Van Gelder, "Postmodernism as an Emerging Worldview," *Calvin Theological Journal* 26 (1991): 415-16.

3. Douglas Adams, *Mostly Harmless* (New York: Ballantine Books, 1992).

4. Jean-François Lyotard, *The Postmodern Condition: A Report on Knowledge,* trans. Geoff Bennington and Brian Massumi (Minneapolis: University of Minnesota Press, 1994), p. iv.

5. See the discussion between Arthur Dent and the Hawalian sage in Douglas Adams, *Mostly Harmless,* pp. 110-11.

can withstand the rigors of postmodern life? Finally, in an age where we are continuously reconstructing ourselves willy-nilly, what can community mean? Can we have a church constituted by ersatz selves?

These three concerns — the rejection of Story, identity formation, and community — form the horizon and the challenge for our reflections. How we respond to that challenge as preachers of the gospel of Jesus Christ will be the measure of our faithfulness!

From Text to Sermon in Postmodern Times

How preachers move from text to sermon is heavily dependent on how they understand the church, in addition to the church's relation to its culture. During the hegemony of Christendom, the church assumed its role was to shape the private moral life of its people in ways consonant with the presuppositions, values, and goals of America.[6] This move was relatively unproblematic because there was a shared vision of life in America supported by the churches. Preachers experienced little dissonance in applying Scripture to this culture — what could be described as a "churched-culture."

This consensus, however, began to unravel in the sixties, grew increasingly ghettoized in the seventies and eighties, and in the nineties is largely a nostalgic cultural artifact. Even the recent retrenchment from among those on the right has failed to fan its remaining embers to full blaze again.

Many of us experience a double alienation as we move through this collapse of Christendom into postmodernity. First, the culture we now live in is no longer "ours" in the sense it was to our parents. It's not ours demographically or ideologically. America as a quarry of cultural diversity, rather than being a melting pot of assimilation to WASP values, is a reality we did not grow up in, and is one to which we do not readily take.

Second, there is an alienation from Scripture itself. As long as the biblical text was nursemaid to the American ethos, this alien-

6. See especially John Howard Yoder, "The Constantinian Sources of Western Social Ethics," ch. 7 in *The Priestly Kingdom: Social Ethics as Gospel* (Notre Dame: University of Notre Dame Press, 1984), pp. 135-47.

ation was largely hidden. But as that ethos fell apart, we suddenly discovered that we weren't any more at home in the Bible than we were in our changing culture. Our dominant "plausibility structure"[7] collapsed, leaving us with a Book that we no longer knew what to do with. The church, now bereft of its former social function, finds itself caught in the swirling vortex of postmodern currents without a sense of identity or mission. Therein lies our dilemma.

In this cultural wilderness, we face a decisive moment full of promise and peril. We stand at a threshold of choice, not unlike Joshua's challenge to his people — *"choose this day whom you will serve"* (Joshua 24:15). If we respond with Joshua's people, declaring our desire to follow the Lord, a promise attends our way into the unknown and uncertain wilderness of postmodern North America. It is this: beyond our wildest hopes, stretching farther than our most imaginative proposals, outdistancing our fear and confusion, the Spirit of God will do a new thing in our midst. In this new context, we will rediscover a new gift of identity as God's people that will render us the missional people God intends us to be. My mixed imagery of "rediscovering" a "new" gift is an intentional allusion to the two poles of memory and hope within which we live as disciples — and as preachers!

George Hunsberger, in summarizing the missiology of Lesslie Newbigin, develops a helpful notion of a "three-cornered pattern of relationships" between gospel, church, and culture which is reproduced in Figure 1.[8] It pictures our location in the mission context and the key dynamics we experience there.

7. Peter L. Berger and Thomas Luckmann, *The Social Construction of Reality: A Treatise in the Sociology of Knowledge* (New York: Anchor Books, 1966), pp. 92-128.

8. George R. Hunsberger, "The Newbigin Gauntlet: Developing a Domestic Missiology for North America," in Hunsberger and Van Gelder, eds., *The Church between Gospel and Culture* (Grand Rapids: Eerdmans, 1996), p. 9.

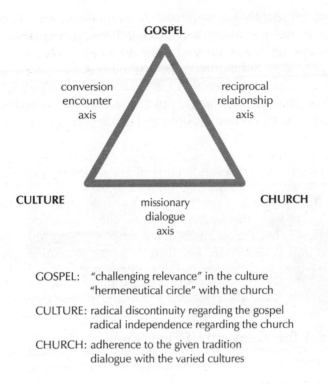

GOSPEL: "challenging relevance" in the culture
"hermeneutical circle" with the church

CULTURE: radical discontinuity regarding the gospel
radical independence regarding the church

CHURCH: adherence to the given tradition
dialogue with the varied cultures

FIGURE 1. A Triangular Model of Gospel-Culture Relationships

The point to grasp is that the church does not simply stand with the gospel in its missionary approach to culture. Rather, the gospel incites conversation with both the culture and church simultaneously. It confronts the culture about its godlessness, while it confronts the church about its worldliness. As preachers, we stand with the church, which means that the gospel's confrontation with the church's worldliness also implicates us. We relate to culture as former lovers, who having returned to our spouse, nevertheless carry inside us an intimate awareness of the hurts, hopes, lures, and lies of our former relationship with this culture. We know that we have not yet completely broken free of its hold on us. Our spouse's unfathomable love enables us to honestly face and explore these parts of ourselves. Out of the intense dialogue between culture and gospel within ourselves, there grows a compassion that animates the missionary conversation as a

159

dialogue, not merely a monologue. This double conversation of the gospel with both the culture and the church forms the heart of our being "in" but not "of" the world (John 15:19).

It also constitutes the *agon* (from the Greek word meaning "struggle," "fight," "compete") out of which *agonistic* preaching is born. This kind of preaching, I submit, is the most credible way to move from text to sermon in our time. Let me offer a brief description of it.

> Preaching is the struggle to proclaim the gospel in such a way that it "frames" the entirety of our ministry in light of the context we live in. To preach out of touch with one's context and/or how the gospel interacts with that context is to be either nostalgic or utopian. Preachers live the questions of our time, as it were, questioning the text from where we are, and then reshaping or counter-questioning those questions in response to God's Word. Out of such an "encounter with the culture," a sermon is born.

A Model for Agonistic Preaching

What will *agonistic* preaching look like in postmodern times? What marks will it bear? The following model suggests a narrative-based approach with four primary marks: iconic, midrashic, parabolic, and poetic. As a whole this model constitutes a response to the concerns raised for preachers by postmodernity that we identified earlier — the rejection of Story, identity formation, and community.

The fundamental shape of biblical faith is narrative. The nonnarrative portions — such as laws, poetry, epistles, hymns, and prophecy — all grow out of, or respond to, the gracious story of what God has done, is doing, and will do in human history.[9] If we allow the shape of this Story to inform our preaching, then we will be primarily storytellers. No longer will we simply dip into the Scriptures to find a text, or use the lectionary readings in isolation from their larger contexts. Specific texts will be embedded in a larger Story. We will tease out the ways in which the nonnarrative portions of the Story gain

---

9. See Eugene H. Peterson's exposition of the relation of Torah, Prophets, and Writings in the Old Testament, in *Working the Angles: The Shape of Pastoral Integrity* (Grand Rapids: Eerdmans, 1987), pp. 30-43.

their coherence and intelligibility from the baseline established by the narrative. And the Story will be told again, and again and again, in as many different ways as we can imagine.

It is important to be clear about this. We need to allow the shape of the Story itself to determine both the form and function of our preaching. This chart reflects the model I have in mind:

FORM	Re-telling	Forth-telling	Fore-telling
FUNCTION	Reframing	Refining	Retooling

Our preaching is fundamentally a re-telling of the grand Story of Israel and Jesus. Within the parameters of this Story, we learn to discern the key moments in the plot — creation, call, election, land, exodus, exile, diaspora, prophecy, fulfillment, Jesus' death and resurrection, Spirit, peoplehood, and mission. Our preaching moves from re-telling into forth-telling as we dare to identify where those key moments are being played out in the life of our people. The plot line of the Story also guides us in imaginatively extending it into our future. It suggests, evokes, envisions, and even at times predicts what issues we will face. It defines the dynamics that will impact us, the nature of the struggle in that new time and place, and the costs of faithlessness both to us and to the creation our God dearly loves.

Function follows form here. Re-telling the Story enables our people to catch a fuller sense of God's will and his characteristic ways with us. This amounts to a reframing of all of life within the horizon of the will and work of the triune God. A perspective develops that enables a greater integration of life and experience, a decompartmentalizing of who we are and of what we do, as we embrace as our own the identity God offers us in this Story. In computer lingo, such reframing is equivalent to "defragging" your hard drive. Just as files from the same program are pulled together from various parts of the hard drive to improve efficiency, so the Story helps us reframe things, pulling together more and more pieces of our lives into a coherent whole. Thus, our sense of identity as God's people is solidified. Re-telling/reframing primarily answers the question: Who are we?

The function of forth-telling is refining, that is, bringing the insights and implications of reframing to bear on our current situation.

When we identify the moments in the biblical drama that illumine our present struggles, we are able to take our place within that drama. Our assumptions and expectations about God, ourselves, our hopes, and our needs are thus seasoned by the dynamics of those moments. This gives us the vantage point we need for creative missional response. An obvious example is Liberation Theology's use of "exodus" as a defining moment for the people of Central and South America's participation in the biblical drama. "Exile" and "Diaspora" are "refinements" currently under exploration for the North American church.[10] Forth-telling/refining primarily answers the question: "Where are we?"

Retooling is the function that correlates with fore-telling. Once we have begun to internalize the Story (re-telling), and have identified the moments of that drama in which we live (forth-telling), then we are ready, theologically and contextually, to envision the future. We are ready to move forward and start preparing for what is coming. Fore-telling/retooling thus responds to the question: "What are we to do?"

If we are to survive the twenty-first century as Christians, it will be necessary for us to become mystics. In reading the signs of postmodernity, and the culture shaped by it, we will not only be scattered and fragmented, but surface-bound as well. What was said of the oratory of William Jennings Bryan will very likely be true of our experience in postmodern North America — "We will live a mile wide and an inch deep!" Fore-telling helps us to retool for that future. Preaching that fore-tells will point to, recommend, and even embody the necessary retooling.

Meeting the challenge of postmodernity's perspectivalism requires a firmer, surer grasp of our own Story. This Story, as we preach it each week, will be challenged in the heads and hearts of everyone present (including us!) by a multitude of other stories that impact our lives. We must persevere in telling and re-telling the Story, be discerning in forth-telling its contextual significance for our churches, and be specific and concrete in fore-telling where we are going, and

10. See Daniel Smith, *The Religion of the Landless: The Social Context of the Babylonian Exile* (Bloomington, Ind.: Meyer Stone Books, 1989); and Stanley Hauerwas and William Willimon, *Resident Aliens: Life in the Christian Colony* (Nashville: Abingdon Press, 1989).

what we must do to prepare for that future. *Agonistic* preaching affords us a wide-angle perspective within which we can tighten and untighten our focus as needed without losing the big picture. Without that big picture, our sermons float free of both theological and cultural reality. They end up being either the easy moralisms of nostalgic Christianity or the progressive platitudes of a utopian Christianity.[11] Such attenuated stories cannot carry conviction in a postmodern setting.

Now I will fill out the model by adding the questions to which each aspect responds, as well as their attendant marks.

FORM	Re-telling	Forth-telling	Fore-telling
FUNCTION	Reframing	Refining	Retooling
QUESTION	Who are we?	Where are we?	What are we to do?
MARK(S)	iconic	midrashic/ parabolic	poetic

The four chief marks of agonistic preaching — iconic, midrashic, parabolic, and poetic — are, of course, versatile and fulfill a variety of functions in preaching. There is considerable overlap between them. For our purposes, I want to consider them in terms of their primary function in *agonistic* preaching.

Iconic

As we have seen, identity formation is an uncertain process in the postmodern ethos. This represents a key tension that agonistic preaching wrestles with week-in and week-out. How we respond to the question "Who are we?" continually confronts us with increasing pressure.

I have borrowed the term *iconic* from Orthodoxy and use it in one of its secondary senses within that tradition to refer to the biblical

11. Ephraim Radner effectively critiques the utopian use of the motif of "liberation" in "From 'Liberation' to 'Exile': A New Image for Church Mission," *Christian Century* 106 (October 18, 1989): 931-34.

"Word."[12] This use of *iconic* invites us to move in our preaching toward the postmodern emphasis on images, and to craft our sermons to leave our people with a verbal icon of Jesus Christ that will go with them into their homes, schools, and workplaces. The Apostle Paul's commitment to "know nothing among you except Jesus Christ, and him crucified" (1 Corinthians 2:2) is definitional for our identity as Christians.

This kind of icon is more than a rhetorical flourish, or a particularly vivid image, or a metaphor. Rather, it reaches out to us through its aesthetics and takes root within us. It evokes a moment of insight, often one that is removed in time and place from its sermonic origin. It takes on a life of its own, spawning new insights beyond the scope of its use in the sermon. In a recent sermon, I reread the crucifixion story as the coronation of Jesus. With the cross as his throne, I interpreted his declaration of forgiveness of sin as his new foreign policy — Jesus' way to make enemies into friends, and his affirmation of trust in God's goodness to the repentant thief as his new domestic policy — the way to do things in Jesus' kingdom. Several members of the congregation repeatedly told me how that image continues to be definitive for their understanding of discipleship. This is what I mean by "iconic."

Whether it be the primary intent of any given sermon or not, we need to find ways to provide an iconic focus on Jesus Christ as the One in whom the story of Israel, the story of the church, and our story come into focus. These verbal icons, which stay with us and continue to do their work in us, provide postmodern people with a durable resource through which they can come to the gift of identity in Christ. If it be true that integrity depends on identity, then these icons may even take us a step further down the road of faithfulness as well!

Midrashic

This suggestion of the ancient Jewish interpretative technique of midrash as an appropriate mark for Christian preaching might at first

---

12. Daniel B. Clendenin, "From the Verbal to the Visual: Orthodox Icons and the Sanctification of Sight," *Christian Scholars Review* 25 (1995): 32.

strike you as odd. Yet, as we consider it briefly here, I hope to make a case that it is an important resource for us, particularly in times like ours.

Midrash is a varied phenomenon with a complex history.[13] I want to highlight only the fundamental thrust of "Haggadic" Midrash (the kind applied to narrative and non-legal materials). This style of interpretation is much of what I have in mind under the rubric "forth-telling," which in certain respects is the linchpin of the understanding of preaching I am developing. It intends the same purpose as the Haggadic midrash. "If thou wishest to know Him at whose command the world came into existence, learn *Haggadah,* for thereby thou shalt know the Holy One, blessed be He, and cling to his ways."[14]

Midrashic interpretation was intended to help sustain the understanding of life found in the Torah in the ever-changing cultural contexts within which Israel found herself. It is important to note that Haggadic midrash did not try to apply Torah to a new situation in a propositional way (this was the province of Halakic midrash). Rather, it sought to interpret the current experience of life within its narrative categories. Necessarily open-ended, Haggadic midrash tried to subsume the present under the vision for life laid out by Moses, with the ultimate aim of unveiling the presence of the Holy One as decisive for Israel in its present existence.

Preaching as midrash is, at one and the same time, a sustaining and a subversive activity. It nurtures us into a deeper residence within the biblical world, while nudging us awake along the way to notice how many of our perceptions, assumptions, and expectations of both church and world are grounded in commitments to principles and powers other than the sovereign love of Yahweh. Born out of that awareness is a renewed equipping for cultural engagement. This kind of preaching keeps alive the three-cornered dialogue we looked at earlier.

Midrashic preaching answers the "Where are we?" question in terms of where we are in God's Story. This kind of answer not only locates us in terms of the movement of that Story. It also places us

13. See C. A. Evans, "Midrash," in *Dictionary of Jesus and the Gospels,* eds. Joel B. Green, Scot McKnight, I. Howard Marshall (Downers Grove, Ill.: InterVarsity Press, 1992), pp. 544-48.
14. Sifre to Deut. XI, 22.

within the stream of a community, one that has a long history, deep roots, and a promised-filled future. In the deepest sense, midrashic preaching locates us by reinforcing our sense of participating in the heritage and mission of the people of God.

Though interpretative rules were established for Haggadic midrash, at its best, it was more an art than a technique. To develop a feel for midrashic preaching requires our submission to a process like the one described earlier as re-telling, forth-telling, and fore-telling. The fragility of the postmodern self and world require the "narratives of a vulnerable God."[15] Such narratives need interpreters skilled in the art of "the renarration of a text for the good ends of a community."[16]

Parabolic[17]

"Whoever can give his people better stories than the ones they live is like the priest in whose hands common bread and wine become capable of feeding the very soul."[18] Often, however, we are not open to such stories. That's where parabolic preaching comes in. It usually happens in two movements. First, a known world, a settled situation, a self-sufficient life, a closed system are deconstructed. Even postmodernity's deconstructive Story that "there is no Story, only stories," gets deconstructed by parabolic preaching as it "makes room for God"[19] amidst those stories. Then, a new and better Story becomes imaginable for us, a new world dawns, and we become captivated by its horizons and possibilities. Parabolic preaching has done its work.

Whereas midrashic preaching primarily locates us within God's Story, parabolic preaching primarily dislocates us from our certain-

15. The title of William Placher, *Narratives of a Vulnerable God: Christ, Theology and Scriptures* (Louisville, Ky.: Westminster/John Knox Press, 1994).

16. Stanley Hauerwas, *Unleashing Scripture: Freeing the Bible from Captivity in America* (Nashville: Abingdon Press, 1993), p. 40.

17. Much of this section is indebted to William H. Willimon, *The Intrusive Word: Preaching to the Unbaptized* (Grand Rapids: Eerdmans, 1994), pp. 59-77.

18. Hugh Kenner, cited in *A Primer on Parables for Prophets,* compiled by Hal M. Warheim for a class in Prophetic Ministry at Louisville Presbyterian Theological Seminary, Louisville, Ky.

19. Willimon, *The Intrusive Word,* p. 65.

ties and idolatries. It brings us face to face with the living God whose presence destabilizes all that we thought was secure and well-founded (see Isaiah 6). Change, unnerve, contradict, subvert, reverse expectations[20] — these are characteristics of parables. They lure us to ask anew, sometimes in spite of ourselves, questions we thought we had answered long ago. The moment those questions are asked, our defenses are lowered, our certitudes are reopened for examination, and our world has been breached! Space opens up within and among us for the Spirit of God to blow, but we "do not know where it comes from or where it goes" (John 3:8).

This mark of agonistic preaching brings into sharp relief the oddness, or peculiarity, of our world and culture vis-à-vis God's Story. Indeed, that very oddness is catalytic for the revaluation of all values parabolic preaching aims at. Refining the church's sense of its present location as God's missional people requires continual parabolic nurture so that the supposed normalities, sanities, practicalities, and regularities — the "principalities and powers" (Ephesians 6:10) which delude us into believing that chaos is really order — cannot lay claim to our hearts and imaginations.

Parabolic does not necessarily refer to a genre. Rather, it points toward any story, narrative, situation, or saying that can function parabolically in opening us up to questions God has about the answers we have constructed for our lives. Jesus may finally be the answer, but we have to learn to ask the right questions. This is just what parabolic preaching does for us.

Like midrashic preaching, parabolic preaching answers the "Where are we?" question. Its characteristic answer is "You're not where you think you are!" This mark, more than any of the others, gives preaching in postmodern times its edge. Parabolic preaching reaches out and grabs us, crying "Gotcha!" Whether we respond positively or not, we are never quite the same again. We have been disenchanted, and our postmodern world with all its stories can never feel quite the same to us again. We have, in truth, been deconstructed!

20. Willimon, *The Intrusive Word*, p. 65.

Poetic

The poetic mark of preaching is the source of our passion. Exhortations only rarely light our fire; appeals and analyses even more rarely. What gets our juices going are visceral articulations of our hurts and powerful visions of our hope. It's the poetic in our preaching that massages these nerves of faith.

I am using *poetic* not to refer to a genre, but to the capacity to dream and evoke visions on behalf of God's people. The poetic in our preaching gives compelling voice to what it's like to be a marginalized and demoralized people. It makes the pain and helplessness accessible by speaking it, not allowing it to remain mute. Our poetry helps us to grieve.[21] When we articulate our grief, we feel our complicity in the dynamics of our culture. We sense our disobedience, the coercive nature of the forces arrayed against us, and we cry to God for deliverance, for forgiveness, and for help. Somewhere in the recesses of our hearts something stirs. Out of our reframed identity we remember what happened when the Israelites in their distress in Egypt cried out to God for deliverance. And we take heart. We lift our eyes and look to the future — *our* future, our culture's future, even the world's future, with renewed expectation. We begin to understand that "The poet hears voices at a deeper level . . . (his) vocation is to bring these voices to expression so that we may listen to the voice of God speaking into the situation of our marginality."[22]

Sometimes the energy of poetry is needed to image our hope in a way that refires the imagination and ignites our passion for God. An obvious example is Martin Luther King, Jr.'s "I Have a Dream" speech. He brought hope to life for many African-Americans in concrete, memorable images that needed no further explanation and that hooked into the larger symbolic world of America's democratic aspirations.

Poetic preaching not only points the way to hope, it sparks critical reflection on what we are to do as God's people in this time and place. Alan Roxburgh says it well, "the poet writes so that the congre-

---

21. See Walter Brueggemann, *Finally Comes the Poet* (Philadelphia: Fortress Press, 1989).

22. Alan J. Roxburgh, "Pastoral Role in the Missionary Congregation," in Hunsberger and Van Gelder, eds., *The Church between Gospel and Culture,* p. 330.

gation hears their story as God's pilgrim people."[23] Poetic preaching helps us retool for the future. It envisions by moving us into deeper engagement with the pain and possibilities of being God's people in this kind of world.

This, then, is my model of *agonistic* preaching. It offers us ways to tell our Story that bring us face to face with the three concerns of postmodernity — the rejection of Story, identity formation, and community. It offers us, as well, an opportunity to re-vision ourselves as a missionary people in the mission field of neopagan North America.

The Place of Preaching

One further matter needs attention. It concerns the place of preaching. It is misleading, I think, to consider the pulpit as the place where preaching happens. I suggest a reconceptualization. Visualize, if you will, the space between the Baptismal Font and the Lord's Table. Now visualize yourself as preacher standing in that space preparing to deliver the sermon. Now, I think, you are properly located to preach.

The importance of this reconceptualization is this: it puts the preacher in a place where he or she must be disciplined by the distinct shape and contour of God's Story. In a missional eschatology, the nexus of Font and Table is where the presence of God in sovereign love decisively shapes our lives and destiny. Characteristic of this God, his love comes to us in the form of a bath and a meal. These undeserved, welcoming actions bind us into community with God and all others so bathed and fed. This community does not exist for itself; rather in the presence of God, it finds itself gifted and ordained to a mission. This mission is to share the presence of God with the rest of creation. It is a prototype, as it were, of the creation's destiny; and all along its way it offers provisional samplings of that destiny by its very inclusiveness and the quality of its community.

At the nexus of Font and Table, this community discovers a form of life distinct from the culture it inhabits. Instead of performance and merit, gifts determine the distribution of leadership and roles. Forgiveness and healing constitute its internal politics. Justice

23. Roxburgh, "Pastoral Role in the Missionary Congregation," pp. 330-31.

and evangelism embrace the range of responses this community generates to incarnate its mission to its culture.

We need to help ourselves and our people understand that Christian existence is lived between Font and Table. This does not, of course, imply a lessening of engagement with the world. On the contrary, it intensifies it! Between Font and Table, we discover the gifts of identity, vision, and courage that equip and enable us for proper engagement in the world as God's people. In our postmodern era, nothing is more urgent than discovering those gifts and graces appropriate to mission.

Preaching is a central way that this discovery can be made. However, this can be done only if it reconceives itself as a practice disciplined by the mutually reinforcing realities of Font and Table. For that reason, it is essential for preaching in a postmodern world to find its place between the two.

Will it preach? You bet it will! If we preach and model the kind of engagements with the text and the world that are suggested here, we will find ourselves irresistibly pulled toward a reconceptualizing of the overall shape of our congregations. As we address the issues posed by postmodernity — the rejection of Story, identity formation, and community — with a proclamation emerging from the missional eschatology outlined above, we open up the nature and calling of being God's people. We may rediscover the resources in the biblical text and the church's heritage for a renewal of the church itself as the embodiment of the *missio Dei!*

Hearing the Gospel with Asian-American Ears

STANLEY K. INOUYE

God's Spirit is working in unprecedented and amazing ways among certain segments of the Asian-American community. Yet, in spite of this, well over 90 percent are still without Christ. Among Japanese-Americans, like myself, 97 percent are not yet Christian. There is an urgent need to develop more effective ways of relating the gospel to this rapidly growing, and increasingly influential, minority population in the United States.

To do so, we need to focus on the people who are hearing the gospel, rather than on those who are sharing it. We need to be hearer-oriented. We need to know the hearer's hopes and dreams, needs and dysfunctions, values and relational patterns, spiritual perspectives and ways of decision making. This is necessary if we are going to know how to shape both the gospel message and our approach to be deeply relevant, profoundly convicting in making a joyous presentation of the message of good news to those who do not yet know the living God.

The Asian-American population is incredibly diverse, and is ever changing. This article will provide a concrete example of how a more effective means of evangelism can be developed for all Asian-Americans. It will do so, however, by focusing on how to develop a more effective evangelistic approach for one segment of the Asian-American population, namely Japanese-Americans.

171

Stanley K. Inouye

Bicultural Nature of Japanese-Americans

One important characteristic we must understand about Japanese-Americans is that they are bicultural. They are on a journey from being culturally Japanese to becoming culturally American. To understand them, we must know where they are on that cultural journey. We need to understand how both their Japanese-ness and their American-ness influences them.

Relative Acculturation Rates

Most people of Japanese ancestry living in America are early in their journey from their Japanese-ness to their American-ness. Typically, this journey takes many generations to complete. Paul Hiebert provides some estimated rates of relative acculturation.[1] For northern Europeans like the Germans, Swedes, British, and French, middle America's closest cultural cousins, Hiebert speculates it takes three to five generations for immigrant families to acculturate completely to American culture. For southern Europeans like the Greeks, Italians, Basques, and Spanish, America's second cousins, he projects it takes five to seven generations. For those from Asian cultures like Japan, China, and Korea, which are cultural polar opposites to Western cultures, it takes in excess of seven to nine generations for complete cultural meltdown to occur.

At the same time, all these groups typically lose their cultural language between the third and fifth generation. Apparently, long after many outward cultural distinctives disappear, such as food, dress, patterns of behavior, and even language, a considerable part of what makes them members of their original cultural group continues to exist. This is because what makes a person cultural is not just a matter of language, or food, or dress. At deeper levels, culture functions in terms of "notions of right and wrong, good and bad, beautiful and ugly, true and false, positive and negative, and so on."[2] These notions

1. These estimates were shared with me by Dr. Paul G. Hiebert when he served as my faculty advisor at the School of World Mission, Fuller Theological Seminary.

2. Larry A. Porter and Richard E. Porter, *Intercultural Communication: A Reader* (Belmont, Calif.: Wadsworth, 1972), p. 7.

of how to think, behave, and relate are more caught than taught during early childhood development. They are largely in place before the acquisition of language skills. It is these notions that tend to persist generations after persons have immigrated to this country.

Hiebert acknowledges that many factors, such as intercultural marriage, can significantly accelerate acculturation and shorten his estimates. His purpose in making these projections is to stress the slow nature of acculturation at deeper levels. These deeper levels function as what might be called "culturally derived notions" or "basic cultural assumptions." In many ways they function as absolute values.

All of this is to say that most Japanese in America are influenced far more by their Japanese background than they themselves might think. Even though each successive generation of Japanese-Americans is further along on the journey from total Japanese-ness to total American-ness, whether Issei, Nisei, Sansei, or Yonsei (first, second, third, or fourth generation), still they are all predominantly Japanese at the "notions" level of culture.

Comparative Studies on Childrearing

Caudill and Weinstein provide us with a study that offers profound insight into how culturally derived notions become part of our "intuitive" selves and get passed on from generation to generation. In their study, they compared the differences between Japanese and American childrearing practices.[3] It was found that American mothers tended to designate certain times for certain activities. When it was playtime, the infant was to learn it was time to play. Likewise, when it was time to eat, or sleep, or was time for Mommy to have her time, baby was to learn what was appropriate for baby to do at that particular time. If, however, baby was in dire need, baby had to experiment with different cries until it found out what would convince Mommy or Daddy that death was imminent unless they came quickly. As a consequence, baby learned early the art of verbal negotiation.

---

3. William Caudill and Helen Weinstein, "Maternal Care and Infant Behavior in Japan and America," *Psychiatry* 32:12-43, reprinted in Takie Sugiyama Lebra and William P. Lebra, *Japanese Culture and Behavior: Selected Readings* (Honolulu: University Press of Hawaii, 1974), pp. 225-76.

Japanese mothers, on the other hand, are almost in constant physical contact with their babies. It is not unusual for the mother not only to lie down with the baby until it is asleep, but actually sleep with the infant all night. The father will often sleep with the second youngest. The parenting objective seems to be to keep the baby from crying as much as possible. It is not as necessary for the baby to verbally express its needs and desires, in order for these needs and desires to be met. This is accomplished by the parents' trying to anticipate the baby's needs and desires, and to meet them before the baby feels it necessary to express them.

This study helps us understand why American babies and Japanese babies tend to turn out to be such culturally different adults. This study also gives us valuable insight into why the Japanese, even third- and fourth-generation Japanese-Americans, turn out to be what we might call "omoiyari" people.

Japanese-Americans as Omoiyari People

"Omoiyari" is a key concept Christians must grasp if we are ever going to be effective relating the gospel to people of Japanese cultural backgrounds. The Japanese word *omoiyari*, roughly translated, means *empathy*. In *Japanese Patterns of Behavior*, Takie Sugiyama Lebra writes:[4]

> For the Japanese, empathy (omoiyari) ranks high among the virtues considered indispensable for one to be really human, morally mature, and deserving of respect. I am even tempted to call Japanese culture an omoiyari culture. . . . Omoiyari refers to the ability and willingness to feel what others are feeling, to vicariously experience the pleasure or pain that they are undergoing, and to help them satisfy their wishes.

I believe this reflects the natural outcome we would expect from the Japanese childrearing practices revealed in Caudill and Weinstein's study. According to Lebra, there are four behavioral patterns characteristic of *omoiyari* people.[5]

4. Takie Sugiyama Lebra, *Japanese Patterns of Behavior* (Honolulu: University of Hawaii, 1976), p. 38.
5. Lebra, *Japanese Patterns of Behavior*, pp. 38-49.

Maintaining Consensus

First, they seek to maintain consensus or agreement by deferring to the fulfillment of each other's needs and desires. Let me share an example from my personal experience. When a group of Japanese-Americans tries to decide where to go for a bite to eat, we will take an informal poll. We will each tend to make our suggestions in order of personal preference, but end by saying something like, "But it really doesn't matter to me. Wherever is fine." When we have probed each other for some sense of consensus, someone poses the apparent leaning of the group. With the favorable nodding of heads, it is decided. Chances are, the final selection is not everyone's first choice. This process protects each person from feeling guilty for not deferring enough to someone else. This process is in contrast to what white-majority Americans tend to use in reaching a similar decision. They tend to poll one another, but once this is done, they vote, with the majority winning. The winners are not made to feel guilty for being insensitive to the desires of others, as is the case with Japanese-Americans.

Providing Pleasure/Preventing Displeasure

Second, they seek to optimize each other's comfort by providing pleasure or preventing displeasure in anticipating the other's needs, and in taking initiative to meet those needs without the other person having to overtly express them. For instance, when Japanese are dining in a group, others are responsible to notice when someone no longer has something to eat and offer it to them. In response, that person must refuse the offer several times before accepting. If the quantity of what is being offered is limited, the person should also offer it to others before accepting it, especially to the person offering it. There is a good chance the person making the offer wants most what is being offered. The more adamant the offer the more insistent the response of refusal should be to eat it. Consistently, a bit of every dish should remain at the meal's end; this keeps the host, if there is one, from feeling there wasn't enough to satisfy everybody. Whoever finishes a dish is considered self-centered or unsophisticated, the opposite of an *omoiyari* (empathetic) person.

In contrast, white-majority Americans function on the premise that mealtime guests are invited to "help themselves," "dig right in," and "not stand on ceremony." Within a short time, the food is usually gone. When this happens, the host is happy, and the guests are pleased that they have shown their appreciation to the host in having eaten all that is available.

A variation of this theme involves preserving another's pleasure or preventing displeasure by not revealing one's own discomfort or suffering. For Japanese, it is the other person's responsibility to realize when someone is uncomfortable or suffering. When asked if they are in such a state, the sufferer is to nobly reply that they are "fine." It is only after repeated probing that they may admit to any discomfort or suffering. Their pain is to be communicated in such a way that it is read from behind their forbearance. If their discomfort is too obvious, they will be viewed as self-centered, or immature, or inconsiderate of others. If they are too subtle, their need for help or consideration will go unheeded, and they will be left to suffer alone. This nonverbal means of asking without asking is referred to as *amaeru*.

White-majority Americans, on the other hand, are typically treated quite differently when they get sick. Their brand of empathy functions in guarding one another's individual freedom by leaving each other alone unless one explicitly asks for help. Self-determination is a high value. However, once help is requested, aid and comfort are usually given immediately and generously.

The term mentioned earlier, *amaeru,* which means asking without asking, is very important here. When my American wife asks me whether I am fine, and I answer "I am," she may not realize that I'm not. In my mind, the inflection of my voice and my nonverbal behavior tell her in no uncertain terms that I am *not* fine. Japanese culture values the implicit and nonverbal, while American culture values the explicit and verbal. American culture is a "tell it like it is" culture. My wife can often be heard telling me, "Well, why didn't you just say so," or "All you had to do is ask." For the Japanese inside of this American me, that's much easier said than done.

Nonverbal Control

Third, they can control each other very effectively in nonverbal ways. One of the ways Japanese-Americans can punish one another is by refusing to respond to another's expression of *amae*. When another person nonverbally expresses their need for assistance, and you want to punish or constrain them, you simply refuse *omoiyari* and do nothing. I remember the distraught puzzlement of some Christians involved in campus ministry when they were confronted with the suicide of a Japanese-American student. He had been both a Christian and a leader in their predominantly Caucasian ministry group on campus. Before he ended his own life, this student seemed so together. Many commented on how sensitive he was to the needs of others. He always cared for others so much, they assumed he didn't have need of much care. A lot of miscommunication was going on in this cross-cultural situation. How does a person from an empathetic culture ask for empathy? — by giving empathy. This is what Lebra refers to as *sentimental vulnerability*.[6] Japanese are extremely vulnerable in this way, while Americans generally are not. A Japanese-American may attempt to control or punish a Caucasian-American by withholding empathy or *omoiyari*, and the Caucasian will entirely miss it.

Nonverbal Communication

Fourth, they believe that nonverbal communication is the most powerful form of communication. The following quotes are from Lebra, who expresses this dynamic of Japanese culture:[7]

> . . . (the Japanese attach priority) to implicit, nonverbal, intuitive communication over explicit, verbal, rational exchange of information. . . . Omoiyari makes explicit, verbal communication redundant and superfluous. . . . The Japanese find aesthetic refinement and sophistication in a person who sends nonverbal, indirect, implicit, subtle messages. . . . The message of a conversation is not what is said, but what is not said; silence is communication. . . . Among the reasons for the priority of nonverbal communication is that an intu-

6. Lebra, *Japanese Patterns of Behavior,* pp. 43-44.
7. Lebra, *Japanese Patterns of Behavior,* pp. 46-48.

itive, roundabout form of communication is based upon empathy as necessary to maintain the Japanese way of life; a verbal, explicit form may disrupt it.

How are these people going to be reached with the gospel when so many of the traditional approaches to doing evangelism are contrary to what is culturally natural to them? The evangelistic method and message must be in forms appropriate to the audience if it is to be effective in relating the Good News to them. Western approaches to evangelism have tended to be verbal, explicit, abstract, apologetic, individualistic, and confrontational. These are all characteristics that fit dominant American culture quite well, but they go against the grain of Japanese people. We must begin with who we are called to reach, and then shape our ministry accordingly.

Major Traits of Omoiyari People

So then, what are the major characteristics of Japanese-Americans that should determine the shape of effective evangelism among them? *Omoiyari* people are relational, group-oriented, consensual, nonconfrontational, nonverbal, and concrete/situational. They are relational because they are concerned about what other people think about them, and they desire to meet the needs of others through reciprocity. They are group-oriented in that the welfare of the group is more important to them than their own welfare, especially when it comes to family. They are consensual in that the goal of their decision making is for all to agree and to maintain relational harmony. They are nonconfrontational in that they tend to avoid bringing up anything between themselves that will jeopardize valued relationships. They are nonverbal in that they believe talk is cheap, and measure what is said by the integrity of the person saying it. They are concrete and situational in their orientation in that what will maintain relationships is what dictates how they respond to a given concrete situation. They tend to be pragmatic and practical rather than abstract and philosophical.

178

Implications for Evangelism

Having identified the primary characteristics of *omoiyari* people, we can now explore the implications of these major traits in relation to the component parts of evangelism. In the following, we will examine the method, message, messenger, media, and milieu of evangelism. The purpose of our discussion is to try to help maximize evangelism effectiveness to Japanese-Americans.

Method

What approaches to evangelism are most appropriate and effective among relational, group-oriented, consensual, nonconfrontational, nonverbal, and concrete/situational people? Evangelistic approaches which are most effective among these people are more relational than rational. They tend to focus more on being and belonging than on believing. Although the content of the evangelistic message is important, the character of the Christian sharing it is pivotal. In this cultural context, the credibility of the content is evaluated almost completely on the character of the communicator. The non-Christian's receptivity to the gospel is dependent on the integrity of the witnessing Christian, making the depth and quality of the relationship between them crucial. They need to be close enough to enable the non-Christian to judge the quality of the Christian's life. Their relationship must be sufficiently deep or be built to that level for conversion to become a serious option for the non-Christian.

Corporate witness is also a key element of effective evangelism to omoiyari people. Because they are group-oriented, non-Christians even slightly open to becoming Christians will almost immediately begin to assess the consequences of a decision for Christ on their relationships to family, friends, and the groups to which they belong. Such close relationships with other non-Christians offer the greatest obstacles, as well as the greatest opportunities, to evangelism. Effective evangelism to such extremely group-oriented people must either overpower the groups to which they belong, or embrace them.

In order for them to become Christians, omoiyari people need to be able to weigh the differences between their current non-Christian family and group relationships and those of Christian families and groups. For this to occur, they must be allowed a glimpse into Christian family, church, and group life. Just as we explored earlier how important it is for Christians to develop personal relationships with omoiyari people so they can become Christians, so it is also important for Christian families and groups to embrace non-Christian families and groups to help them grasp how much closer they can become through Christ's Spirit. The gospel will then be viewed as a way of making their family life stronger, rather than as something that will split them apart.

It is important for Christians and non-Christians, both as individuals and as groups, to relate in side-by-side situations where they are working, playing, and struggling with life together. This needs to be pursued in contrast to face-to-face confrontations where persons are challenged to compare abstract beliefs and seek to change each other's minds. Omoiyari people are empathetic people. As Christians live their lives as salt and light along with such people and share naturally and consistently what life with Christ is like along the way, non-Christians will read the message of their lives and respond to Christ.

In the United States, most of us have been taught to do evangelism by communicating the truth of the gospel (the abstract plan of salvation) through challenging the individual to make a conversion decision, and then, once the decision is made, to incorporate that individual into the church. For those who are culturally group-oriented, the process has to be reversed. We need to incorporate these people into relationships within the church first, with Christians and Christ himself, and then focus our attention on conversion. What I am encouraging is the need to see conversion for omoiyari people as a relational process. We need to enable non-Christians to get to know Christ better and better, little by little, becoming more and more committed to him as they come to appreciate, admire, and trust him in small relational increments. We need to be careful not to demand that the non-Christian be on a fast track to a commitment that encompasses primarily a pat set of beliefs and an abstract apologetic for faith.

This relational process to evangelism is, after all, consistent with the way Jesus himself related to those around him. He invited people to discover who he was. Jesus asked Peter, "Who do you say I am?" To which Peter replied, "You are the Christ, the Son of the Living God!"

(Matthew 16:15-16). How did Peter arrive at this discovery? By spending time with Jesus.

Message

What should be the content, emphasis, and particular interest, issue, need, or desire addressed when sharing the gospel with our particular audience in order to be most effective? It is in living with non-Christians side-by-side as individuals, groups, and families that we communicate much of the content that may motivate them to consider becoming Christians. Much of our evangelistic message is non-verbal and nonconfrontational. We communicate it by our attitudes and actions in everyday relational situations.

This kind of quiet witness is only effective if our non-Christian friends are aware that we are Christians. This is accomplished by naturally sharing with them our experiences with our Lord, as Christ helps us deal with both the mundane and the monumental challenges of our lives. We give reason for the hope that is within us in small bits. If God answers a prayer, we tell them. If a particular verse from the Bible rattles our cage, either affirming or convicting us, we share it. If we pray for them, we mention it. But we don't make a big deal of any of it. We share the stories of our spiritual journey, just like we share the story of our recent vacation. Then, incidentally or when such persons are in personal crisis, we invite them to ask us how they too can know Jesus Christ.

When they do ask, we introduce them to a living person, not to a plan of salvation or a set of airtight philosophical arguments. We introduce them to a person who came to reconcile us to his heavenly Father, to one another, and to the whole of his creation. Just as we share his life as revealed in the Bible, so also we share his life as it is revealed in our lives, especially our families. Repeatedly, Japanese-Christians have been told by non-Christians, "If my family won't be in heaven, I don't want to go there." It is my belief that Jesus must be presented and seen as able to save and bond families before widespread openness to the gospel will occur among omoiyari people.

It is critical that we do not push too soon for an individual conversion decision, but rather that we guide persons toward a closer relationship with God through Christ while helping them influence oth-

181

ers they love to do the same. As a result, they do commit their lives to Christ, but do so in a form that will not alienate them from others who are close to them.

Messenger

Who or what group is most appropriate and effective when sharing the gospel with people of Japanese ancestry? Omoiyari people are so relationally oriented that it is difficult for them to separate the message from the messenger. To them, the messenger is the message. They believe those whom they trust. "So-and-so says it, it must be true, so I believe it." They are extremely hesitant to question or disbelieve the views of those they admire for fear of damaging their relationships with them. The group they belong to is thought undermined by any seeming disloyalty through questioning the beliefs of others in the group. It is very difficult for them to perceive truth as something abstract and absolute, separate from relationships. To them, what is true unites. What is true serves relationships.

It has been stressed throughout this discussion that a Christian's power to influence an *omoiyari* person toward faith in God is directly proportional to the degree to which the Christian's life reflects the truth of the gospel. Essentially, we are Christ to these people, who see message and messenger as synonymous. Since our ability to reflect Christ will always be limited no matter how close our relationship with him, our primary responsibility is to introduce the *omoiyari* non-Christian to Jesus Christ himself, who is "the way, the truth, and the life" (John 14:6). He alone is the perfect match between message and messenger.

The incarnate Christ is God's ideal way of communicating all he desires to omoiyari people. By becoming familiar with Jesus' life, death, and resurrection as recorded in the Bible, they can come to empathize with the anguish Jesus suffers as he yearns to embrace them with his love. As Japanese theologian Kazoh Kitamori envisions it, our Lord's love is so great that the cross of Christ is but a window, a passing glance, into the pain our God has suffered and endured from the fall of humankind until now in order to bring us back to himself.[8] With such a bent

---

8. Kazoh Kitamori, *Theology of the Pain of God* (Richmond, Va.: John Knox Press, 1965).

for *omoiyari* (empathy), the non-Christian Japanese will join the centurion "who stood there in front of Jesus, heard his cry and saw how he died" and be moved to exclaim, "Surely this man was (and is) the Son of God!" (Mark 15:38).

It is interesting to note that after the incarnate Christ died, rose, and ascended, he and the Father sent the Spirit to indwell the lives of believers that they could become parts of one body — the body of Christ. In this way, they could as a group give witness to God's love and forgiveness. This action of the Spirit built upon the initial sending by the Father of his only begotten Son. In these works, God provides a family paradigm for family-centered people. God demonstrates that he is an omoiyari God who knows how to communicate most convincingly to family-centered people — to omoiyari people. He wants believers to do likewise, to communicate his love as groups and families to non-Christian groups and families.

Western evangelism has largely been an individual matter with individuals witnessing to other individuals. Even at large evangelistic gatherings, the evangelist is primarily one individual appealing to isolated individuals in the audience to make isolated individual decisions for Jesus Christ. Among omoiyari people, we must learn how to function as a Christian group that appeals to non-Christian groups and families to become Christians as families and groups. We need to see the Christian group and family as messenger and evangelist.

Media

In what forms should the message be encapsulated to most appropriately and effectively share the gospel with relational, group-oriented, consensual, nonconfrontational, nonverbal, and concrete/situational people? If omoiyari people tend to see the message and messenger as synonymous, then the messenger is also the most effective medium for the message. This is what I believe Christ was saying when he said, "I am the way, the truth, and the life" (John 14:6). Essentially, he was saying that he is message, messenger, and medium all wrapped into one. "What you see is what you get." So, also, the Christian family and group are the most effective evangelistic media for omoiyari people.

Non-Christians need people and groups to model concretely for them the difference Christ can make in areas of life they value most, namely family and group life. Therefore, the Christian family and group must be visible to non-Christian omoiyari people in ways that do not threaten their solidarity. Christians need to be genuine. They need to be who they are together in Christ while being with non-Christians in loving and serving them.

While life-on-life witness, whether person-to-person, group-to-group, and family-to-family, is most effective for communicating the gospel to omoiyari people, sometimes it is not possible. At times it needs to be supplemented with other forms of witness. Other media, such as audio or video tapes and reading material, can be effectively used if the content is appropriate. But these evangelistic tools will be effective only if they enable non-Christians to empathize with the lives of those Christians focused on in the media content. This content needs to give an inside look into the lives of Christian individuals, families, and groups, and to document their life stories.

Over a decade ago, the organization I work with, known as Iwa, conducted a research project among Japanese-American churches in Los Angeles and Orange Counties. They found that those active in Japanese congregations overwhelmingly preferred biographies over any other form of reading material.[9] Why is this so? I believe it is because they prefer to identify and empathize with real-life people. Drama can also be powerfully used for the same reason. Such material enables non-Christians to have close encounters with the lives of Christians without any risk to their present relationships. They can be confronted with their own need for Christ, and be invited to ask him into their lives as Savior and Lord, without any immediate threat of estrangement from others who are significant to them.

An apparent contradiction to much of what has been said up to this point is the fact that God will sometimes use a Christian stranger to finally bring an omoiyari person to Christ. Similarly, at times, such impersonal means as Christian radio and television programs and public evangelistic events may be used to enable an omoiyari person to make a Christian commitment. The probable reason for these occurrences is there is no significant relationship that is directly threat-

9. See Stanley Inouye, Arlene Inouye, and Sharon Uyeda Fong, *Final Report of the 1982 Survey of Japanese Churches in Los Angeles and Orange Counties* (Pasadena, Calif., 1982).

ened by making such a faith commitment. Prolonged exposure to Christians and Christian relationships, together with the work of the Holy Spirit, probably preceded such an act of commitment. The anonymity of the crowd, or the inconsequential nature of one's relationship to the Christian stranger, is what made it easier for such a person to take the step to accepting Christ as Savior and Lord.

Milieu

What situations and relationships are most appropriate for effective evangelism to take place among omoiyari people? By this time much has already been said regarding the situations and relationships most appropriate for effective evangelism among omoiyari people. We have observed that effective witness will tend to occur in settings where Christian individuals, families, and groups can be observed and where relationships with such persons can be experienced by non-Christians. Initial exposure should occur in life-on-life personal, group, and family situations that are common to the everyday experience of both Christians and non-Christians, whether these be at work, school, or play. As non-Christians and Christians develop relationships in these settings, Christians can reach out and invite non-Christians to participate with them in informal activities, such as going on a picnic, seeing a movie, or coming over for a barbecue. Thought should be given as to whether several non-Christians from the same group or network should be invited so that persons don't feel alone or outnumbered. Omoiyari people often decide whether they will go to a particular event based on whether they know anyone who will be there. The assurance that others they know are likely to attend has a lot to do with whether or not they will attend an event that is new or unfamiliar to them.

Gradually, doors will open to invite non-Christian omoiyari persons to participate beyond such informal, non-threatening activities to events that are more specifically Christian in nature. These might include fellowship groups, Bible study meetings, or church retreats. The problem has often been that the last place to which we should invite omoiyari people is the first place we tend to invite them. And, we tend to invite them alone. No wonder that many, who would otherwise be open to the gospel, seem closed because we naively intimidate them into declining our rightly motivated invitations to the wrong activities and events.

185

Ironically, when all is said and done, the omoiyari non-Christian may well make the decision to follow Christ when alone, with a Christian stranger, or at a mass event like an evangelistic crusade. Anonymity is the common reason for each case. Consistently, they probably won't go forward for an altar call at a crusade for the same reason, to guarantee their anonymity. They don't want others to know prematurely of their decision. They want to see what happens first, making sure their commitment is genuine and validated by their experience. Once sure their Christian experience is real, they will try to carefully control how their decision is communicated to others.

They do this, not because they are ashamed of their decision or Christ, but because they don't want to estrange, disappoint, or dishonor anyone, whether non-Christian, Christian, or even Christ himself. They make sure, as much as possible, that the outcome will be positive, honoring to all and shaming none. That's their desire and objective, even though it may not always be possible. They are not risk-takers, especially when it comes to relationships. Once bonded to the Lord, this bent in human relationships is directed toward Christ, where their relationship with him is viewed as permanent and their principal motivation is not to embarrass, but to bring honor to his name.

Conclusion

In this article, we have focused on how to develop more effective ways of reaching Japanese-Americans for Jesus Christ and seeing a spiritual breakthrough to the 97 percent who do not yet know him. In examining this, insight has been gained into how we might improve our effectiveness in evangelism to other Asian-Americans. What I am referring to focuses more on the process we should use than the outcome of the process. While there are many similarities between Asian-American subgroups, there are also many differences. Chinese-Americans, Korean-Americans, and other Asian groups should each be examined in terms of ministry implications that are worked out for each unique group. My prayer is that what I have shared about Japanese-Americans is of practical help so that the gospel will be communicated in a way that it will be heard by Asian-American ears and responded to by Asian-American hearts.

Relating the Gospel to Ministry in the North American Mission Context

A changed context, a changing church, rehearing the gospel on its own terms — all of these themes lay the foundation for rethinking the ministry of the church to its community. The most basic challenge facing congregations is how to make sense of the gospel in seeking to communicate it to others in its broader community. What will congregations do to present a confident witness in terms of specifics within their ministry? This is the focus of the fourth section of this volume. The reader is offered some practical ways of thinking about congregational ministry in a changing context.

This discussion is introduced by Bill Burrows in the opening article in this section. He uses his own journey as a way of telling the story of the collapse of Christendom in our North American setting. He suggests the language of "refounding" as a way of helping congregations reengage this changed context. Drawing on lessons from his experience as a missionary in the world church, he focuses on the importance of rediscovering Christian community as central to the task of refounding the church. Tied to the establishment of community, Bill notes, is the importance of cultivating capacity to know God personally and intimately, something that is not easily pursued in our consumer culture. Finally, he outlines some of the dimensions of what confident witness will look like in the refounded church.

Religious pluralism is a reality that confronts almost all congregations today, whether they are consciously aware of it or not. Learning how to bear confident witness in the midst of religious pluralism is an important ministry skill for congregations to acquire. Mary Lou Codman-Wilson draws on the seminal work of E. Stanley Jones to present, in the second article in this section, a helpful model for bearing confident witness in the midst of religious pluralism. The examples given from Jones's life come alive in her review, and provide easy access for congregations to consider in developing their own ministries in this area.

One ministry opportunity that presents itself to many congregations is to engage in working with and/or in impoverished communities that lack resources. The church has a unique opportunity to bring resource and need together in a way that invites redemption for all who are involved. In the third article in this section, George Beukema provides a helpful journey into one such community, the Church of the Good News in the Lathrop Homes community of Chicago. George has persons from the community share their stories in this article as a way for the reader to enter into this congregation's experience of learning to bear confident witness in a community of need. One of the most unique aspects of this congregation's ministry is its extensive influence within the whole fabric of the broader community.

Another way for congregations to rethink their ministry approach is to partner with congregations from other cultures, whether at home or from abroad. In the final article in this section, Isaac Fokuo and Patricia Lloyd-Sidle offer some practical suggestions for doing this. They share some of their experiences in working in partnership ministries within the Presbyterian Church (USA). Their accounts broaden our understanding of the barriers that tend to keep peoples apart, and convey the power experienced in this work of bringing diverse peoples together.

Witness to the Gospel and Refounding the Church

WILLIAM R. BURROWS

In this article, I will attempt to reflect on the nature and form of witness by churches that believe the gospel has a role in God's plan in today's multicultural, fragmented North American context. I will seek especially to identify the forms and attitudes of heart and mind that will ground the sense of vocation among such churches, and thus shape their particular approach to witness.

The nature of this task, identifying forms and attitudes of witness, is not the purview of one person's analysis. It demands corporate discussion and discernment in concrete local churches. What I hope to do is establish the frame of mind and heart that a church needs in order to carry on that discernment process at the local level.

Introduction

Each of us takes a winding spiritual road to anywhere, including participation in the Gospel and Our Culture Network. God, of course, is able to write a coherent narrative with the crooked lines of our lives. Tracing some of the crooked lines from my own life seems important before I begin.

I come from a small town in Iowa. Everyone, of course, was Christian. It was generally assumed that belief was a good thing and, although the various churches officially had distinct emphases, in the end theological nuance was little attended to. Why? Because, I think, the church in Belle Plaine, Iowa, was firmly embedded in a self-confident white, Anglo-Saxon culture, wherein both Protestants and Catholics had a clear and accepted place. The Belgians to the South, the Bohemians to the West, and the Germans to the North and East picked no major quarrels with the Anglo-Saxon hegemony, even though they were culturally distinct. There were no Jews or Hispanics in Belle Plaine, although there was one person of African descent.

The United States had just won World War II. There was a consensus among the people I lived with that our Christian faith had given us the strength to accomplish this. If there were a few admirable non-Christians in the world, like Gandhi, they were the exception rather than the rule. Communism, in addition, now gave us a comfortable enemy, having displaced the evil of Nazism.

When I went away at the age of fifteen in 1958 to join the Society of the Divine Word, that basic faith was intact. However, by the time I went to Rome for theological studies eleven years later, something had happened. Much of it stemmed from the civil rights movement, which had revealed that the cultural confidence we whites had was illusory. The women's movement, the rising profile of the Hispanic, and the widespread immigration of non-Western peoples deepened our realization that the United States was pluralistic in ways few whites had imagined in 1946. It is important to say from the start that these events *made manifest* a situation that had always existed, but which had previously been invisible except to those who suffered exclusion.

These movements, however, did not *cause* the cultural meltdown decried by so many today. Instead, they made Anglo-Saxon hegemony visible and thus vulnerable to denunciation. In the crumbling of an old order, whose hollowness few saw early on, the supports for traditional morality and control systems disappeared.

Like a lot of men who went off to seminary, I was transplanted from my roots and became very sophisticated. By the time I was ordained, indeed, I had read Barth, Lonergan, Whitehead, Tillich, Cobb, and Rahner. I knew it was the role of a priest, as teacher, to filter the insights of the masters down to the masses. Vatican II was for me a clarion call to theological updating, not spiritual renewal, despite my own verbal espousal of both ideals.

Five years in Papua New Guinea, about a third of it working in rural mountain areas and two-thirds of it teaching in a seminary, almost turned me around, but not quite. I was a stubborn man, and had ever so much education to overcome.

Despite its reputation for theological rationalism, seven years of working on a doctorate at the University of Chicago Divinity School — living much of the time in a poor black, inner-city parish — began to take me in the right direction, but not quite home again. Still, in the parish church of Our Lady of the Gardens, I began to see in the lives of poor African-Americans a depth and vitality of faith that had little to do with book learning. What really kept me from learning all they had to teach was my inability to deal with my shock at the chaos of their world. It frightened me, and so I lost a chance for fellowship, much to my own detriment.

Ultimately, it was the confusion I underwent in leaving my order, marrying, and working for several years at the American Medical Association that helped me internalize what really mattered. During this time, I came to understand what it meant to refound the church. As I live today, a somewhat schizophrenic Catholic pietist, I have a rather simple creed. It holds that what Christianity must be about in our age is what the Holy Spirit is always about: transforming lives; helping people cast out hearts of stone and replacing them with hearts of flesh filled with the hope that empowers men and women to overcome the world. It is belief in the truth of Romans 5:5, that there is a hope that "does not disappoint us because God's love has been poured into our hearts through the Holy Spirit that has been given us."

Church is not the plaything of leaders. It is rather a school for laity, the *laos tou theou,* the People of God. In the three years I was clearing my head of religion while working at the AMA, I began to experience what it was like simply to be one of those people. Being defrocked and learning the discipline of marriage concentrates the mind wonderfully. To be schooled in the ways of God in the world is to see the everyday as portal to the divine. The Spirit is central to that process.

In Matthew 16, Jesus preached to the disciples but they did not understand. This is clear even in verse 16, where Peter gives Jesus a textbook-perfect, christological title. The rest of the Gospel of Matthew shows how little Peter understood what he had said. Church occurs not when Jesus teaches disciples, but when the Spirit reveals to the inner person what Jesus means.

I realize that a church must be about many things. But I was deeply struck one day by the words of my friend and colleague, Professor Samuel Escobar. Sam said that churches should certainly be concerned about health care, liberating the oppressed, inculcating civic virtue, and feeding the hungry; but he observed that in our highly compartmentalized, bureaucratized, and professionalized society other groups can usually do these things better than churches. What no one else can do, Sam said, is preach the gospel and offer people a place to worship God. And I would add, in the context of our frazzled culture only the church can offer a zone of quiet and respectful space where the Spirit can lead us to a fuller understanding. In the spirit of Ephesians 1:16-19, it is "a spirit of wisdom and revelation resulting in knowledge of [God] . . . with hearts enlightened to know the hope that belongs to his call."

As conservative as that may sound, my own experience leads me to think that in large swaths of the American church, preaching, teaching, and worshiping, if truly practiced, would be radical actions. Doing them creatively and faithfully is the cornerstone of refounding the church.

The Terminology of "Refounding"

I borrow the term "refounding" from my friend and colleague Gerald Arbuckle, with whom I worked in Papua New Guinea in the early 1970s. In his book *Refounding the Church*,[1] Arbuckle uses the term to concretize the Reformation adage "Ecclesia semper reformanda" for Catholics who are caught between the poles of fidelity to their tradition on the one hand, and a felt call at times to follow the Spirit in ways different from those of the official church.

The term, Arbuckle feels, captures the central Protestant insight into the need for continual renewal and conversion, precisely to make the church faithful to Christ in changing circumstances. In that vision, the church lives *in relation to a living Christ,* and therefore needs

---

1. Gerald A. Arbuckle, *Refounding the Church: Dissent for Leadership* (Maryknoll, N.Y.: Orbis Books, 1993).

to change in order to accompany him in new circumstances. His sanctifying, healing, and forgiving activity meets people where they are in new circumstances. His church, as the members of his body to whom he entrusts his reconciling office (2 Corinthians 5:18-20) in the world at large, seeks to bring all things and peoples together in unity in the Spirit of God. Because Christ is in fresh relationship with new peoples in new circumstances, those who follow Jesus need to answer anew the question in each generation, "Who is he?"

Precisely in order to be faithful to its identity, a church must always be in reformation to the extent that it confronts situations different from those in which it was originally founded. Refounding does not mean finding a founder different from Christ and the Spirit. Rather, it means meeting Jesus in the living Spirit and having the courage to tear down old structures when necessary. What is even harder in a social organization is to tear down cultural habits and manners of doing things that no longer fit new circumstances.

At the risk of offering an opinion that may seem gratuitously offensive, I've gradually formed a perception that there is a certain kind of Protestant rigidity that is the functional equivalent of the Roman Catholic insistence on Tradition with a capital *T.* It is clear that after four hundred years Protestants have had time to build up interpretive and conceptual structures around Scripture that are every bit as rigid as Roman Catholic Tradition. Instead of having to cope with one Pope like Catholics, every individual is his or her own pope. This gets complicated in times like ours when the regnant cultural dogma appears to be skepticism, and when individuals fear surrendering to God as the core of faith.

For liberals, conservatives, and middle-roaders — whether they are Catholics, Protestants, and Orthodox — Arbuckle's notion of refounding involves interpreting Scripture in new ways. It is like mustering the courage to meet Jesus as the pair of shaken disciples did on the road to Emmaus. It is not interpreting Scripture away so it no longer bites, but rather surrendering autonomy and dying to self. Turning oneself over to God, which is the core of the act of communion in Eucharist, is a surrender of autonomy. It is an invitation to Christ to become our very life. The two disciples on the way to Emmaus recognized Jesus in the breaking of bread; they recalled that their hearts had burned within them as Jesus revealed the meaning of the Scriptures while they walked together on the road (Luke 24:31ff.). Thus Luke taught the first generation of Christians that they were to let Christ become their very food and drink.

To grasp the problem of refounding the church in North American culture, it may help to recall the teaching in Johannine theology (John 19:30-35).[2] Here the church is formed when Christ surrenders his life to the Father, and blood and water flow from Jesus' pierced side — blood the sign of his life given for the world, and water the sign of the Spirit being poured out.

Similarly, in Luke's two-volume theological interpretation of the life and meaning of Christ, the crucial event *for us* occurs on Pentecost in volume 2. There the Spirit comes upon the quaking disciples and welds them into a body that is empowered to follow the invitation of the Jesus of volume 1. Until that empowerment, however, they can neither understand Jesus nor follow him. Grace may, as Catholics are fond of saying, build on nature; but with natural eyes and a natural mind, one does not enter into Christian life in its fullness.

Why retell this familiar story and invoke this familiar dogma? Because it is a quintessentially American frame of mind to pass over the role of the Holy Spirit in the foundation of the church. We are people whose forefathers took matters into their own hands and founded a new nation. In today's spirit of inclusion, many are aware that both the deeds of our foremothers and the role of Spanish America also need to be recited. Some see deeper still and admit that a huge part of the labor that made the nation grow was African. America as a whole must acknowledge both this African contribution and White America's sin against Africans and Native peoples. They know that if we fail to come to grips with this original sin, and fail to include the richness that Africans, Asians, and Hispanics bring to us, we will be caught in a denial of our true nature as a people. But no matter how inclusive we become, Americans know this nation was founded by human beings and is a voluntary organization.

The trouble starts when we bring that attitude into our understanding of the church. Nevertheless, it is probably America's most characteristic contribution to Christianity — if it truly be a contribution — to imagine and then to act on the proposition that the church itself is a voluntary organization. Does our culture not tell us one joins

2. John evokes Ezekiel 47, where the spring stream flows out from the temple; and a similar theme in Zechariah 12 and 13.

the church with which one is most comfortable? Does it not tell us that one should leave it when it no longer meets one's needs, or one is unable to get the preacher fired? Thus, the American canon, "It matters not where you worship or what you believe. Worship in the church of your choice; in effect, be your own pope."

Although the voluntary principle has freed up amazing creativity within American Christianity, it has also given us a set of cultural eyes that is very likely not to see what makes church be church. After all, if my culture tells me that I can go out and start my own church when I disagree with the minister or a faction in my congregation, then where is the sense of a church being more than merely an organization enlisting members? Where is the sense of church being called by God's Spirit?

Directly counter to this American cultural attitude toward church and religion is the call of Christ. The most important element in the refoundation of the church is the recovery of a biblical insight that the church occurs as Christ invites persons to follow him and become his people. In so doing, they become an *ekklesia,* a term used in Christian Scriptures for the church as a people called to a specific mission. This mission is to become Christ's very body in the world to bring about a relationship of shalom with God and throughout all of creation, including all humankind.

I know it is both fashionable and important to pay attention to culture, particularity, inculturation, context, and contextualization. The Gospel and Our Culture Network, indeed, is dedicated to that proposition. The challenge to refounding, though, cuts far deeper. It remains one of following Christ, becoming part and parcel of an assembly called by God in Christ to bear witness to God's reign as the true destiny and ultimate ground of the whole of the world. The goal of the Christian message is not merely an I-Thou relation between the individual soul and God, but is rather a community wherein justice and love prevail over selfishness and all forms of egoism. As a pastor I once sat in a focus group where another pastor said, in a spirit of profound disillusionment, "though all that's *theologically* true, the problem of finding parking places for my parishioners' Lexuses tends to crowd out the theological."

What I want to underline is this: The Kingdom we seek is not something we create, but is rather a reality we discern when the Spirit of God gives us eyes to see. The Gospel reading for the fourth Sunday of

195

Lent in the common lectionary this year was taken from John 9, the story of the man born blind whom Jesus encountered and sent to wash in the pool of Siloam. This set up a confrontation between Jesus and the leaders of the Pharisees. The points of the story are: (1) to drive home that Jesus is the light of the world and we are in darkness if he does not give us sight; and (2) to show that ordinary things like spit, mud, and water become the sacraments whereby we gain sight under the leadership of the Spirit. John's Gospel is one of symbolism and Jewish allegory, a sometimes mystical device that in Latin we used to call the *pars pro toto* — "the part standing for the whole." The man born blind represents all of us if we have not been born again.

The strength of the Evangelical and Pentecostal movements lies in their insistence that a follower of Jesus needs to be born again, although they part company when it comes to deciding what that experience entails. It is my experience that many mainline Protestants and Catholics become embarrassed when talk turns to spiritual rebirth. Yet it is clear that everything in Scripture and the spiritual tradition of the Christian movement should bring us to the realization that some kind of enlightenment and rebirth are required. They are a prerequisite for us to move beyond mere belief to the kind of hope that Paul speaks about in Romans 5. Indeed, faith in the full biblical sense is far more than belief in certain concepts. It is an act of the entire person committing one's self to God, resting in an experience that goes beyond conceptual truth.

The whole of the book of Romans deals with that complex reality. It is probably no accident that more than one renewal movement in Christian history has begun when someone began to appreciate the transformation and new life that God offers those who attend to the burning in their hearts when the gospel is preached. For the gospel, both in its judgment of sin and its promise of grace, presents to us the truth about ourselves. It presents a whole truth about ourselves, one that makes us free.

I suggest that in seeking to discern what shape the church must take in our culture, we need to broaden our horizons and dig more deeply into Christian tradition as a whole. We need to go beyond the normal American cultural approaches to Christianity. There is a peculiarly American temptation to go to sociology and psychology to learn what we can do to make churches appear more attractive and to move them toward becoming institutional success stories. I have nothing against such disciplines, but the church is not merely a tired Rotary Club or Elk's Lodge that needs social-science insights to better appeal to younger business leaders or cocooning baby boomers. The church in its essence is not a voluntary organization, and our cultural experiences ill equip us to grasp this point.

Refounding the church so it can play a part in the mission of Christ and the Spirit to bring all together in reconciliation requires us to contemplate over and over again the words of the hymn: "The Church's One Foundation Is Jesus Christ the Lord." They are more than the words of a popular hymn. They express the nature of church.

Thirsty for God in Consumer Culture

Others can describe the sociological and spiritual situation of the North American people far more eloquently than I. Still, I must take a stab at saying why I think the thirst for union with God is ultimately deeper even than the search for security. Indeed, union with and love of God are ends in themselves and will contribute to security of all kinds. But the eclipse of teaching in the church that God is the end of human life, and is worthy of being loved with one's whole heart, whole mind, and whole being, represents a collapse into moralism and our culture's relentless demand for relevance.[3]

I say this knowing how easy such words can sound coming from a well-paid, well-educated, middle-aged, over-fed white male, with reasonable employment security. I say it knowing too that my own appropriation of and living out of the teaching of Christ is deficient. I am a man who finds it easy to be generous and cheerful when things are going my way, moody and crabby when they are not; magnanimous when I am in the limelight; ill-tempered when my star is eclipsed. I say this, then, fully aware of the flaws in my character and a history of being less than faithful to my undertakings and my God.

This is becoming clearer to me as I grow older and begin to see the world, not as a function of my needs and opportunities for my self-aggrandizement, but as a beautiful world wherein some of the poorest are spiritually rich and some of the richest are spiritually

3. See Edward Collins Vacek, S.J., "The Eclipse of Love for God," *America* 174 (March 9, 1996): 13-16.

poor. The gifts that God seems to be giving me, though I find it easy to close myself off from them, are: gratitude for creation in all its variety and richness; a sense of privilege at being alive; and hope that my egoism can be transformed so I can enjoy the gift.

This gratitude is beginning to result in a profound love for God, not just as giver, but for God himself. It is a gratitude that sees God not as an object to manipulate, but as the fellow sufferer who understands; not only as the stern judge and lawgiver, but as the One in whom we live, move, and take up our being.

Recently, I had the chance to see an old friend, a Cistercian monk who had just celebrated his 80th birthday and who was nearing his 50th anniversary in priesthood. Matt said something to me that he had mentioned in letters and had written in books over the years. It began to make sense in a deeper way than ever before as we talked on that dreary day. "People make a big mistake when they make a big deal about monks," he said. "We're really quite ordinary. But the quiet and the worship give us a chance to realize more deeply than most people what is true for everyone — that God is love."

I may seem to be going a long way from my topic. My intent, however, is to offer reflections that will aid discussion for the following: (1) on the kind of church that will witness confidently to the gospel in a changing world; (2) on the nature and form of witness of churches that believe in the gospel in our social and cultural place; and (3) for identifying approaches and attitudes that will engender such witness in our cultural conditions and historical moment.

I have wrestled with these issues for a long time. I have talked with religious sociologists like John Coleman, Dean Hoge, and David Roozen about what they think is going on in churches today. The insight that made the most impact on me was from David Roozen, in a brief conversation at a recent meeting of the Society for the Scientific Study of Religions in St. Louis. As I recall David's words, they centered around the need of churches to rekindle faith in its most basic dimension, providing the believer with new eyes to see and hear. Calvin, he pointed out, felt that theology was wasted breath if it was not part of a discourse in the context of faith. Of course, that goes back in a straight line through Aquinas and Augustine to Paul.

I propose for consideration the notion that the necessary condition for becoming a church that is confident of the gospel it seeks to witness to, is having the courage to accord primacy to teaching, preaching, and worshiping. These are actions that give space to the Spirit to open hearts for being transformed by God. They are also actions too little appreciated by our dominant, pragmatic culture, with its scant appreciation for liturgy. Liturgy, though, is the primary place where we begin the dance of dialogue with God's Spirit, a dialogue that allows God to transform us.

What I suggest is ultimately this: The kind of church that will confidently witness in our changing world is one that will not be embarrassed by modern-day cultured despisers of religion. Establishment churches have too long sought not to embarrass their enlightened fellow citizens. They've too long hidden from themselves the fact that the gospel is first a message about God and God's partiality for the poor. The idea that Christianity is first of all an assembly of people who listen to, celebrate, and worship God is very radical to the enlightened — including many of us with doctorates from prestigious schools. Since the Enlightenment, indeed, we've been told that the ultimate criteria for being worthwhile are works of charity. And because our works often seem so paltry in contrast to the call to make our world a world of shalom, we've kept establishing committees to try to do it better.

I have no answer to the accusation that after two thousand years of Christianity the world may be worse than it was when Christ came. Nor does perhaps the premier liberation theologian, whose learning and concrete acts for the poor put me and perhaps most of us to shame. Without for a moment saying that the church can give up the struggle to create a just, liberating social order, Gustavo Gutiérrez turns to the Book of Job. He points out that those who talk confidently about the problem of suffering by the innocent are dismissed by Job as irrelevant rationalizers. He shows, too, that it was in the mystical encounter with God and surrendering to God that Job found peace.[4] Those who know Gustavo well are always amazed to hear him accused of being a mere social gospeller. His friends have watched him walk among the poor of the barrios and work in silent prayer. His parish is a place where the gospel is preached, hymns are sung, and bread is broken in worship.

Any opposition between being an inculturated church for others

4. Gustavo Gutiérrez, *On Job: God-Talk and the Suffering of the Innocent* (Maryknoll, N.Y.: Orbis Books, 1987), pp. 27ff., 83-92.

and a church centered on worship, teaching, preaching, and prayer is a false opposition. What seems really important is something that is very straightforward:

1. If refounding is called for, as I think it is, the most important thing is giving people space to hear the gospel and mull it over in places where they're safe, and with persons who honor their struggles;
2. Pastors, pastoral workers, and ordinary people need to listen together to the voice of the Spirit;
3. Church leaders should be wary of giving marching orders on quests to save the world;
4. The primary role in social transformation is for the laity. "Clerics" need always to realize that, in addition to the public witness of the church, more important is the witness of followers of Christ in banks, plumbing supply stores, schools, and kitchens.

What I am driving at is this: a church that gives members space to let the Spirit work will not lack for witnesses. On the contrary, if we too quickly try to move to witness, if the life of faith is not firm and deep, church leaders run two risks. The first risk is being relegated by our culture as well-intended moralists whose vocation it is to urge people to do good and avoid evil. The second risk is irrelevance, where we try to be smarter than God, and where people quickly see our shallowness. How can I possibly know how a bank manager or an intensive-care nurse can concretely act out their vocation? Ultimately, the one who is most fit to lead an evangelizing church is the person who is most capable of quietly discerning the Spirit who blows where he wills. The story of American Christianity is too much one of social reformism that outpaces the genuineness of its proponents and ends up beached on the sands of its own spiritual aridity. The danger of a movement such as GOCN may lie in its failure to realize the primacy of the spiritual and imagine that social analysis can replace the Spirit.

Dimensions of Witness

In conclusion, I want to make four points briefly. First, we live in a culture of "me-ism," a culture in which narcissism is the common cold of mental health. In all likelihood you, like me, are affected by that common malady. If you're not in touch with it, I suspect your ministry will be fruitless because you will be trying to get your own needs met instead of your people's. If you are ministering to baby boomers and their children, then people need: (1) to hear the word preached and see the gospel celebrated *publicly;* and (2) to touch, feel, and experience God *internally.* To do that involves surrendering to God in the negation of self that Jesus spoke about in Matthew 16:24-27.

Second, God speaks to the soul in manners other than verbal. One of the fruits of being contemplative is to remind us that the divine is everywhere and we are one with it. The challenge is to *realize* it. Realizing it requires spiritual exercises. The old scholastic adage was, *nemo dat quod non habet* ("No one gives what he or she doesn't have"). If we are not on the way to liberation from narcissism and me-ism, to a decentering realization of the glory of God in all creation, chances are that God's spoken word in the Scriptures will not touch us.

In a recent conversation with Jürgen Moltmann, he said that he had a hard time dealing with his Reformed church soul in coming to the position he now holds on nature and grace. "What was his new view?" I asked. His response: "Realizing that if people's eyes, hearts, minds, and the very pores of their skin are not open to the sacrament of creation, I doubt if they can hear the Word." Spiritual transformation, in other words, transforms the entire intentionality of a human being. Being fully Christian means having a new heart with which to appreciate things like nature, sexuality, and community. This deepened awareness is also the heart of an ecologically sensitive faith that I think is especially important today.

Third, what I am saying may well sound like a retreat to disembodied spiritualism. It could represent a retreat from one of theology's greatest acquisitions in recent years, a sense of the totality of the transformation indicated by the symbol of God's reign, including the sociopolitical. Although I am willing to be persuaded otherwise, my experience leads me to the judgment that the problem lies not with the theological concept of this kind of transformation, but a truncated awareness: (1) of how badly we need transformation of the heart to accomplish the other goals; and (2) what is especially hard for pragmatic Americans, the depth of the resistance of the world to transformation. Although the term "spiritual warfare" is controversial, the position one takes on its reality will affect deeply one's vision of what is entailed in Christian mission and being the church. Said another way, I doubt that inner renewal will deter anyone from providing bread to the hungry. On the contrary, persons who can still their restless minds and repose in God's love are likely to be compassionate and concerned for justice.

Fourth, in the words of a book by Robert Kegan,[5] one of the characteristics of our time is that we are "in over our heads." People, and I certainly include myself, are in over our heads; we can hardly cope with all that is demanded of us. We are whipsawed by pressures as diverse as job insecurity to the meaninglessness of politics; from the numbing images of a Somalia, a Bosnia, an East Los Angeles, to a bumper-sticker war over abortion; from the desire to be good parents to the near impossibility of doing all that Dr. Spock advises. New Agers seek ways to find rest and make sense in ways I sometimes find quaint and strange. But they often take that path because churches are so spiritually shallow. A church that can witness confidently in a changing world needs to be one that offers a peace the world cannot give, and provides access to a state of mind that can help us cope.

In the final analysis, what everything comes down to this: If we have the patience to wait on the Lord, even if we live in a spiritual desert, surely God will visit us and springs of living water will flow. In that day God will not lack confident witnesses, even in a changing world.

5. Robert Kegan, *In over Our Heads: The Mental Demands of Modern Life* (Cambridge, Mass.: Harvard University Press, 1994).

Witness in the Midst of Religious Plurality: The Model of E. Stanley Jones

MARY LOU CODMAN-WILSON

As temples and mosques are multiplying in North America, North American Christians are faced with an unprecedented dilemma. How are they to witness effectively to those of other world religions? Local churches find people of these religions in their communities. They even face missionaries that have been sent here to evangelize people of other religions. Foreign missions are now on North American soil.

Where is there an adequate model that fits the contemporary pluralistic American culture? One helpful answer can be found in the work of E. Stanley Jones. Jones was a Methodist missionary in India during the first half of the 1900s. He was a personal friend of Mahatma Gandhi and an outspoken political activist. He was also a dedicated evangelist who brought Jesus Christ to the intellectuals and leaders of India. By living his faith in the midst of religious pluralism, he focused on the centrality of Christ.

There was no obscurity to his life and witness. E. Stanley Jones was known on the world stage. His accomplishments include: receiving seven honorary degrees; being chosen as "Methodist of the Year"; being twice nominated in the Norwegian Parliament for the Nobel Peace Prize; being given the Gandhi peace prize; having met emperors, kings, presidents, and prime ministers; and being a prolific writer.

He wrote over twenty-six books, some of them translated into as many as eighteen foreign languages and set in Braille. Two books exceeded sales of one million copies each. He received many honors. Yet, he said, "all these combined do not weigh in the appreciation as much as the honor bestowed on me when I was set apart as the bearer of good news, an evangelist."[1] In the foreword to his autobiography his editors say:[2]

> Jones found the Christian movement largely among the outcastes and left it at the center of India's life, a challenge and an issue to the intellectuals and leaders. He found the Christian movement scattering its energies about the marginal issues of doctrine and denominations and left it centered on Jesus Christ as the one and central issue. He found the Christian movement largely alien and Western and left it more naturalized through the Ashram movement. He found evangelism largely emotional and left it appealing to the total person — mind, spirit and body. He found evangelism largely personal and left it personal and social — a total way of life.

Most of E. Stanley Jones's books are now out of print. But perhaps the time has come to revisit this Christocentric man of wisdom, balance, and missionary zeal. If the North American church can emulate his spirit and methodology, perhaps those of other faiths in our communities will find the gospel relevant and salvific.

There are four elements to Jones's model of evangelism, and when combined together, they provide a timely and relevant approach to evangelism for the twenty-first-century church. These elements include: a broad understanding of evangelism; the centrality of Jesus Christ; a dialogical respect for other religions; and an emphasis on vital Christian experience grounded in Scripture and tradition. Various churches or denominations have often focused on only one or two aspects of this model, missing the interrelationship of all the elements. Evangelism without ministry to those of other religions does not fulfill the Great Commission. Dialogical respect for others without concentrating on the centrality on Christ leads to syncretism. And placing an emphasis on Christian experience, Scripture, and tradition

---

1. E. Stanley Jones, *A Song of Ascents* (Nashville: Abingdon Press, 1968), p. 372.

2. Jones, *A Song of Ascents*, p. 9.

by itself can create doctrinally pure churches, but ones that are irrelevant in a pluralistic age. Jones's genius is in the balanced combination of all four elements. Citations from his works will illustrate his attitudes and the wisdom of his methods.

A Broad Understanding of Evangelism

In the midst of religious plurality, evangelism must fuel the passion for a relevant witness. Jones's definition of evangelism was very broad. It covered renewal, work with nominal Christians, social action, and proclamation. "My evangelistic work had a double objective," he said, "to strengthen and convert the church (to try to Christianize unchristian Christianity wherever found) and to win the educated non-Christian to an allegiance to Christ."[3] He believed that one must see truth lived, not just proclaimed, for there to be a salvific effect.

In India in the early 1900s, the legacy of Christianity was genuine, but it had created a vast nominal church. The lifestyle of nominal Christians often lacked the spirituality that Hindus found in their ascetic practices and in their bhakti forms of devotion, such as prayer, fasting, singing, and dancing to the gods. So Jones worked to convert and strengthen the church. He founded the Ashram movement to "Christianize unchristian Christians."

The Ashram Movement

The Ashrams started as summer "vacations with God." The program combined devotional practice, study, corporate worship, and manual work in an experiment in being the kingdom of God in miniature.[4] The main theme of the Ashram was self-surrender. Jones believed that even if a person made an initial commitment to Christ, the self could remain untouched. This resulted in unchristian Christianity. He explained:[5]

3. Jones, *A Song of Ascents,* p. 111.
4. E. Stanley Jones, *The Divine Yes* (Nashville: Abingdon Press, 1975), p. 144.
5. Jones, *A Song of Ascents,* p. 54.

In conversion a new life is introduced into the conscious mind as we consciously accept Christ as Savior and Lord. . . . The subconscious mind is stunned and subdued by this new dominant loyalty to Christ. Sometimes it lies low for long periods, subdued but not surrendered. It waits for low moments in the conscious mind and then sticks its head up and when it sees an opportunity, takes over the conscious mind. Then we are a house divided against itself. . . . The issue is to give the Holy Spirit total control of all of our life — indwelling our unconscious as well as our conscious mind. It is a matter of surrendering all we know — the conscious mind — and all we don't know — the unconscious — to God's control.

The Ashrams always started with "The Morning of the Open Heart," where people could confess their real needs, answering the questions: "Why have you come? What do you want? What do you really need?" Throughout the week there was a concentration "on people's mental and spiritual attitudes . . . as people surrender to God their wrong attitudes and fear, worries, resentments, hates, self-centeredness, and guilt."[6] On the final day, "the Morning of the Overflowing Heart," there was a service of healing. Jones's experience was that "95-98 per cent will go away transformed and radiant — converted."[7] Hence, one part of Jones's evangelistic strategy was to bring the church into a vital spirituality that was "firsthand, vital and life changing" through the Ashrams and his books.[8]

In the 1990s, the Ashram movement is still renewing the church around the world. Most Ashrams are one week in length, but the goals and program remain the same. The call to self-surrender is still an important agenda for the church today. As Jones warned the church:[9]

When the Cross becomes a mere symbol on churches, or becomes a hard doctrine, or becomes a cheap easy way of salvation . . . leaving the essential self untouched, and not demanding that we face life in the same spirit of self-sacrificial giving, then it has turned to dark-

6. Jones, *A Song of Ascents,* p. 230.
7. E. Stanley Jones, *Conversion* (Nashville: Abingdon Press, 1957), p. 11.
8. Jones, *Conversion,* p. 9.
9. E. Stanley Jones, *The Christ of the Mount* (Nashville: Abingdon Press, 1931), p. 243; and E. Stanley Jones, *The Unshakable Kingdom and the Unchanging Person* (Nashville: Abingdon Press, 1972), p. 244.

ness. . . . The gospel of the Kingdom which can be realized now is a total program of life and Jesus is the pattern of that program.

A Ghost or a Corpse?

Within the gospel of the kingdom Jones found a balance between the individual and a social gospel. With characteristic poignancy he quipped:[10]

> An individual gospel without a social gospel is a soul without a body, and a social gospel without an individual gospel is a body without a soul. One is a ghost and the other a corpse. . . . I want and need one gospel that lays its hand on the individual and says: "Repent, be converted" and that lays its hand on the corporate will and says: "Repent, be converted. . . . Your entrance into the Kingdom is personal by a new birth." But you live it corporately.

In America he demonstrated this commitment by taking a stand for justice. In 1904 he tipped his hat and gave his bus seat to an African-American woman, reasoning: "I had just committed myself as a new Christian to a reverence for people and their possibilities, apart from race and color and status. . . . In the struggles for freedom I am on the side of human rights, for I am bound in every man's bondage; I could only be free in every man's freedom."[11]

Later, in the 1930s, he was asked to preach in Columbia, South Carolina, during a national election. He learned that African-Americans were being disenfranchised at the polls, so he began the sermon with the following words, words that became front-page news the next day.[12]

> I am reading an obituary notice which will come as a shock to the friends of the deceased: 'Today democracy died in the city of Columbia when American citizens were denied the right to vote because of the color of their skin. For those who have eyes to see, the ballot box will henceforth be draped in mourning.' Shall we pray.

10. Jones, *A Song of Ascents*, p. 386.
11. Jones, *A Song of Ascents*, p. 256.
12. Jones, *A Song of Ascents*, p. 256.

Jones's book *Mahatma Gandhi, an Interpretation* also directly influenced Martin Luther King, Jr. King told Jones: "It was your book on Gandhi that gave me my first inkling of nonviolent cooperation. . . . We will turn this whole movement from violence to nonviolence."[13]

Jones modeled an evangelism that transformed the church and its context by its personal, social, and political implications. Evangelism in its totality must balance a personal and a social gospel in the twenty-first century. But Jones's priorities of evangelism are not unique. The significance of his model lies in how he related evangelism to three other components: the centrality of Christ; religious dialogue; and an emphasis on vital Christian experience. This combination creates a synergy needed for a relevant church in the twenty-first century. Let's first consider the centrality of Jesus Christ.

The Centrality of Jesus Christ

In the 1990s, pluralism has created a climate of "alternative absolutes."[14] The term sounds like an oxymoron, a total impossibility theologically, but both Christianity and Islam make mutually exclusive religious claims. This reality is difficult for the church in North America to resolve. In fact, Christianity's claims are being contested by many religions, whether in the marketplace, the neighborhood, or by local religious institutions. How does one present the gospel in the midst of this religious plurality? This is one of the pressing issues of the gospel and culture in contemporary America.

The Problem of Propositional Truth

Traditionally, Western Christian witness has been cognitively based. We have focused on doctrine and have stressed propositional truth. But when there are the doctrinal differences of "alternative absolutes," arguing the validity of an opposing doctrine is an ineffective way to witness to the proponent of another religion. In contrast, both

13. Jones, *A Song of Ascents*, p. 260.
14. Kenneth Cragg, *The Christ and the Faiths* (Philadelphia: Westminster Press, 1986).

Hebraic and Johannine thinking in Scripture emphasized relational truth. John pointed to the relationships within the Trinity and used the incarnational "come and see" approach (John 1:39). Christ himself emphasized the mentoring model. This was the cornerstone of Jones's emphasis in evangelism. He concentrated on the "who" rather than the "what" of Christianity. Why did Jones make the shift?

Jones started his missionary work in India in the traditional style of his day — with outcastes. But some judges and intellectuals had invited him to come to talk to them "if he came in the right way." He soon realized that he could not defend the gospel *and* Western civilization *and* the Christian church *and* the Old Testament before Indian religious folk. As he said, "It was too long a line to defend." He decided, therefore, "to shorten the line and just focus on Christ."[15] He would defend only what related directly to Christ — not the creation stories, or second Isaiah, or other such matters.

> "At the place of Christ dialogue becomes decision, you judge yourself when you look into his face. In him you see what you are and what you might be. . . . In my evangelism among the intellectuals in India, I would not mention the non-Christian religions. I would speak not to Hindus or Muslims but to persons — persons in spiritual need."[16]

The "Who" Must Carry the "What"

Jones was very articulate in explaining the character of God in Jesus Christ. But he was equally careful not to argue for that truth propositionally, such as Paul did in the book of Romans. His explanation illustrates why relational truth, rather than propositional truth, is more relevant to those from other religions:[17]

> In the West our approach tends to be: Jesus was born a supernatural way, he did supernatural things, he arose in a supernatural manner, therefore he was a supernatural person. The what carried the

15. Jones, *A Song of Ascents,* pp. 85 and 111.
16. Jones, *A Song of Ascents,* pp. 85 and 111.
17. E. Stanley Jones, *The Christ of the Indian Road* (Nashville: Abingdon Press, 1925), pp. 167-71.

whom. This is obviously weak. If we were wiser, we would ask men to lay aside the question of birth and miracle until they get under the sway of this Person. Then let them turn from the standpoint of the Person to the question of miracle and miracles become credible in the light of who He is. . . .

The central miracle of Christianity is Christ. The central miracle is not the resurrection or the virgin birth or any of the other miracles. . . . Christ is life's sinless Exception, therefore a miracle. The who carries the what. . . . Don't misunderstand me. The what's of Christianity are important. . . . (But) the strongest way to hold to the inspiration of the Scriptures is to hold to the person. He creates belief. We do not get Jesus from our beliefs, we get our beliefs from Jesus.

And so Jones presented a very concrete Christ. He would tell people:[18]

Although Christ was a mystic, he did not philosophize or discourse about various truths. He demonstrated them. He didn't argue that spiritual life should conquer matter; he walked on water. He didn't argue the worth of womanhood, he treated them with infinite respect and appeared in resurrection first to a woman; he didn't argue that God answers prayers, he prayed. Many teachers have tried to diagnose the disease of humanity — Jesus cures it.

And he kept urging people to experience this Jesus for themselves. His "altar call" was:[19]

I challenge anyone, anywhere to expose his inner life to Jesus Christ in repentance and faith and obedience and . . . such a person will be changed, profoundly changed, in character and life and he will know it in every fiber of his being.

By emphasizing Christ, Jones could also deal with the critical religious questions of others. He was well schooled in the worldviews of Hindus, Muslims, and Buddhists, but handled inquiries comparing religions by concentrating on Christ's uniqueness:[20]

18. Jones, *The Christ of the Indian Road,* pp. 195-97.
19. Jones, *A Song of Ascents,* p. 103.
20. Jones, *A Song of Ascents,* p. 349; and *The Christ of the Indian Road,* p. 160.

Religions are man's search for god — a search upward. The gospel is God's search for men — a search downward. Philosophies and moralism cannot change character and life; they can influence them but not change them. John the Baptist tried to make men better; Jesus made them different. . . . Jesus Christ is the Word become flesh, not the Word become idea. Had it been the Word become idea, it would have been a philosophy, a moralism.

The Cross — Christ's Professorial Chair

He also used the cross to connect to the Hindu and Buddhist doctrines of suffering, karma, and reincarnation. Jones acknowledged other religions' answers to suffering, from the Hindu belief that no suffering is unmerited to the Muslim's acceptance of the divine will of Allah, and then explained:[21]

> Jesus transforms suffering by using it. . . . These answers from Jesus are not easy answers — they are answers from the Cross, which an English poet called Jesus' professorial chair. . . . Jesus answers Yes to life and to the world — and he gave us this final answer from a Cross! . . . The Cross shows us our loving, self-sacrificing God. God becomes immanent, a suffering and an incarnate God. . . . God is self-giving Love. That is the meaning of the universe and it must be the meaning of our lives too.

The Cross is Christ's professorial chair. What a marvelous analogy. It is an example of how Jones took a profound Christian doctrine, that the Cross breaks the pattern of endless suffering through God's love and self-sacrifice, and through emphasizing its incarnation in Christ, communicated it as relational truth. It was a style of witness his hearers could understand.

Why is presenting Christ relationally rather than propositionally so important for the church in the midst of religious pluralism? Because it focuses on Christ alone, not on Christianity as an institutional system or a set of doctrines. It also packages truth in a way that communicates most intimately to non-Western people. It enables those of

21. E. Stanley Jones, *The Divine Yes* (Nashville: Abingdon Press, 1975), pp. 98-105 and 255.

other religions to consider Christ without Western baggage. Many third-world countries have experienced an "oppression psychosis" created by the bonds of Western imperialism.[22] Christianity has been indicted, along with this imperialism, and likewise rejected as a system. Jones recognized that Western civilization and the church were only partly Christianized. He felt free to acknowledge this to his friends from other religions. But he never felt he had to apologize for Jesus Christ: "When it comes to Jesus Christ, there are no apologies on my lips. . . . Jesus has the sum total of reality behind him. . . . Jesus is Word become flesh."[23]

This emphasis provides an important lesson for the contemporary church. The Western church, in particular, must relinquish its dogmatic hold on propositional truth as the basis for witnessing to those of other religions. It must learn to emphasize the "who" rather than the "what" of Christianity. Christians need to concentrate on Christ in sharing the gospel. The other important doctrines of the faith can make sense once the Holy Spirit has brought Christ to life.

A Dialogical Respect for Other Religions

Jones's logic in focusing on Christ was grounded in the third aspect of his model, his understanding of other religions. He used dialogue as an evangelistic strategy that did not demean those he engaged, because he honored their spirituality. In the midst of religious pluralism, it is especially noteworthy that he dialogued with those of other faiths without becoming syncretistic. He said:[24]

> The deepest things of religion need sympathetic atmosphere. In an atmosphere of debate and controversy the deepest things wither and die. In order to discover what is most delicate and fine in religion, there must be an attitude of spiritual openness, of inward sensitiveness to the Divine, a willingness to be led by the beckoning spiritual facts.

22. Jones, *The Christ of the Indian Road*, p. 108.
23. Jones, *A Song of Ascents*, p. 20.
24. E. Stanley Jones, *Christ at the Round Table* (Nashville: Abingdon Press, 1928), p. 15.

Jones sought to avoid the comparative, the controversial, or the dogmatic approach to religion in his witness. Instead, he chose to emphasize each person's religious experience. He believed that a person's openness to the Divine was in direct proportion to one's depth of religious commitment, so he intentionally gathered devout believers of many religions for dialogues throughout India. He called these meetings "Round Table Conferences." During the dialogues he noticed several fundamentals:[25]

1. People who took part had a great deal of intellectual and spiritual culture.
2. No one has a right to teach if they cannot learn from others.
3. We were all called upon to face religion and life in a new way.
4. People are incurably religious.
5. Humanity is fundamentally one, facing the same perplexities and problems.
6. The fundamental need of the human heart is redemption — life is not what it ought to be.

Round Table Dialogues

On the basis of these commonalities, he invited people at the Round Table to share what their religion did for them in experience. The prelude to all discussion was:[26]

> We are all religious people and have been experimenting with religion over a number of years. We have tried it as a working hypothesis of life. As we face the problems of life — its joys and sorrows, its perplexities and its pains, the demands of duty, the moral struggle of sin and evil, the desire to help our fellow men and to be of use, the craving for God, and for redemption — what has religion brought us — of light, of moral dynamic for personal and social life, of inward peace and harmony, of redemption from sin and from the power of this world, of God? What have we and what are we verifying as true in experience?

25. Jones, *Christ at the Round Table*, p. 51.
26. Jones, *Christ at the Round Table*, p. 21.

Then he gave the ground rules for the discussion:[27]

> We suggest that no one argue, no one try to make a case, no one talk abstractly and no one merely discuss religion, but that we simply share what religion is meaning to us as experience. . . . We also suggest that we don't want people to feel that the friendliness of the atmosphere will iron out differences in our viewpoints — to reduce everything to a least common denominator; that if religion centers for them in Rama or Krishna or Buddha or the Vedanta or the Koran or Christ, to say so. Let everyone be perfectly free, for we are a family circle; we want each one to feel at home and we will listen with reverence and respect to what each one has to share.

Because of the attitudes of openness and appreciation that he modeled, he found that religious leaders in city after city thronged to participate in these conferences. After using this methodology for years, he observed:[28]

> There was not a single instance I can remember where Christ was not in moral and spiritual control of the situation by the end — those who knew Christ were testifying to something redemptively at work at the heart of life, redeeming them from themselves, and from sin, putting worth and meaning into life, giving an unquenchable hope to men, lighting up the inward depths of life, bringing them into fellowship with God in beautiful intimacy and furnishing a dynamic for human service.

It would amaze the modern evangelical church to realize that dialogue was a successful evangelistic strategy for Jones. The conservative church in the West has been reluctant to use dialogue, and perhaps for legitimate reasons. Dialogue can lead to syncretism; it can reinforce a belief that all religions are the same and all paths lead to salvation. Some people have even approached dialogue with a dogmatic, confrontational attitude. It has been a browbeating witnessing experience on more than one side. Others have avoided dialogue because it is uncomfortable. C. S. Song explains this discomfort as an allergic reaction:[29]

27. Jones, *Christ at the Round Table*, pp. 21-22.
28. Jones, *Christ at the Round Table*, p. 51.
29. C. S. Song, *Tell Us Our Names, Story Theology from an Asian Perspective* (Maryknoll, N.Y.: Orbis Books, 1987), p. 146.

Nurtured in our long religious tradition, the spiritual constitution of most of us has become delicate and weakened. We can breathe only the spiritual air purified by our own rituals and liturgies. All this makes us very sensitive to "pollens" coming from other religious quarters. Our nose becomes stuffed and cannot smell the fragrance of truth emanating from the minds of other religious teachers. Our watery eyes fail to see the beauty that the hearts of other religious devotees may display.

But this was not Jones's experience. He testified: "The round table conferences have not only confirmed my faith in Christ, they have enriched my faith by adding new insights."[30] At the round tables dialogue was neither offensive to those of other faiths nor universalistic in its theology. Jones was able to combine the uniqueness of his emphasis on Christ with his respect and ability to listen to and learn from those of other religions. They repaid the courtesy, and many came to Christ as a result.

The Balance of Vital Christian Experience, Scripture, and Tradition

Jones emphasized vital Christian experience in his dialogues with those of other faiths. This is the fourth necessary component of his model. The emphasis was on personal experience grounded in Scripture. It was not merely existential relativism. He declared:[31]

That place of final certainty and authority is at the junction where the Jesus of history becomes the Christ of experience and where the resultant individual experience is corroborated and corrected by the collective experience. . . . [He believed that] everything Jesus said in history was verified in experience. The two kinds of reality, objective and subjective, were coming together and verifying each other in Him.

In a country like India, where religions define life, the voice of experience was a powerful witness. Jones recognized this. He also recognized the need for humility in that witness:[32]

30. Jones, *A Song of Ascents*, p. 242.
31. Jones, *Christ at the Round Table*, p. 169; and *A Song of Ascents*, p. 103.
32. Jones, *The Christ of the Indian Road*, pp. 147-53.

215

India wants to know: What have you found? When people have a deep faith in their own religion (but still unmet spiritual need), can we come to them with an argument, a doctrine, a superior Book? Unless we can gently and quietly but with a radiant positiveness share our own deliverance and victory, we had better not come.

"India wants to know: What have you found?" And what had he found? Jones's witness was that he had found God. This was an amazing revelation. Even Gandhi, the most beloved of India's spiritual and moral leaders had said:[33]

He who would find God must have as much patience as the man who would sit on the ocean beach and take up a drop of water on a straw and put it aside and thus empty the ocean by carrying away one drop of water at a time.

Religion on the Experiential Level

This fourth part of Jones's model is valuable to the contemporary church for two reasons. First, the power of a transformed life and encounter with God is significant to all religious people. This is not just propositional truth. This is lived truth that can be shared relationally. Second, focusing on a personal experience with Christ deals with religion on the experiential level — the level on which people live their faith. In witness there is a vast difference between relating to people's formal religious allegiance, or relating to their actual religious experience. It is the difference between the Great and Little Tradition.

In all religious traditions the Great Tradition includes the sacred texts, the religious professionals, certain traditional religious rituals, and a religion's history. In many cultures, it is associated with culture and therefore is linked to a person's national identity. The Great Tradition is the embodiment of religion we usually think of when we hear someone is of another faith.

Most people, however, practice the Little Tradition within their religion, which may have very little resemblance to the Great Tradition. The Little Tradition includes the local deities and popular religious culture. It is the behavioral dimension of religious practice that

33. Jones, *Christ at the Round Table*, p. 69.

affects how an individual deals with money, health, happiness, and family. The Little Tradition defines how a person experiences religion. It is the heart of a person's faith.

When Christians focus on a vital experience with Christ, they emphasize how their faith is lived out — the Little Tradition. But if Christians focus on propositional truth and seem to "attack" another's Great Tradition (arguing with its doctrines, its history, or its religious professionals), this can be perceived as an attack on one's country and culture. People will become defensive in order to protect their identity and their Great Tradition even if they don't practice it. In contrast, sharing what has worked in one's own daily religious experience, the Little Tradition, invites a mutuality and openness. Jones's success in his witness reflects an understanding of this distinction.

Lessons from the 1980s

The applicability of Jones's model for the twenty-first-century church relates to the synergism of his model as a whole. My experience as the Associate Director of the Chicago Ashram of Jesus Christ in the 1980s confirms the need for applying all four elements of his methodology.

We called our outreach ministry in Chicago the Ashram because "Ashram" was a Hindi word that Hindus understood and felt more comfortable with than "church." Ashram means a place of refuge, a coming together to dialogue. Gandhi and many Hindu religious gurus had ashrams in India. E. Stanley Jones had *Christian* ashrams. It was an attractive concept to southeast Asians.

At the Chicago Ashram, we used dialogue to reach out to Buddhists and Hindus in our area. Although we did not have Round Table Conferences, we had spiritual growth groups and studied many texts, such as the Sermon on the Mount, James Fowler's *Stages of Faith,* and Herman Hesse's *Siddhartha.* People of many faiths joined Christians in these groups. But in our efforts to build relationships and convey respect and openness to others, I believe now we failed to heed two of Jones's strengths. These were a passionate focus on Christ and dialogue based on religious experience. In the spiritual growth groups, people could discuss the books objectively as members of a Great Tradition culture and still not deal with the limits and benefits of their own religious experience. Thus, many discussions did not deal with issues of the heart. They were a form of dialogue, but not the kind of dialogue Jones modeled. Plus we did not sufficiently emphasize Christian self-surrender and the experiential witness of deliverance and victory shared with "radiant positiveness." We did see some people come to faith in Christ, and we made many appropriate efforts at contextualizing the gospel for Hindus and Buddhists. But we followed Jones's model only partially and lacked the synergism brought by using the model as a whole.

As I have researched Jones's work in depth since the Ashram disbanded, I have reaffirmed the wisdom of his balance and his zeal. One part of the methodology alone is not sufficient to address religious pluralism today. Only when we have combined a broad evangelism with dialogical respect, a fervent commitment to Christ, and vital Christian experience, will we be able to bring those of other faiths to Christ.

At the end of over forty-five years of ministry Jones was able to testify:[34]

> You don't know the worth of your Christian faith until you have compared it with others and subjected it to life. . . . I've put my faith out before the non-Christian world and have said: 'There it is . . . if you can break it, break it. For I cannot live in a paradise if it turns out to be a fool's paradise'. . . . So the keenest minds and the most philosophical of the world have smitten upon my faith, night and day for over half a century. Result? Broken? There are scars on my faith but underneath those scars there are no doubts. The song I sing is a life-song. Not the temporary exuberance of youth that often fades when middle and old age set in with their disillusionments and cynicisms. No, I'm eighty-three and more excited today about being a Christian than I was at eighteen when I put my feet upon the Way. . . . Now by seasoned, tested, corroborated experience I know that this is not a way, but the Way.

We could do as well in the church of the twenty-first century.

---

34. Jones, *Christ at the Round Table*, p. 108; and *A Song of Ascents*, p. 20.

The Prophetic Voice of Poverty

GEORGE D. BEUKEMA

The Church of the Good News is a ministry of the Reformed Church in America, which serves in the Lathrop Homes community in the City of Chicago. The following article is designed to introduce the reader to the unique ministry of this church in three ways: (1) by providing some background on the church: (2) by listening to the voices of a number of persons who are directly involved in the ministry; and (3) by offering some theological reflections on this ministry.

Introduction to the Church of the Good News

The history of our church began with a risk. The Reformed Church in America (RCA) commissioned a seminary intern to live in the Lathrop Homes community, to listen for a call to ministry. This community is a north-side Chicago low-income public housing development. The call resounded with clarity as a group of residents began gathering regularly in Lathrop Homes apartments for worship, Bible study, and prayer. As natural as breath leads to movement, worship led to action. For example, many in Lathrop were hungry and so food was provided; many youth were in need of a safe haven amidst the pressures of gangs, and a Coffee House was established; many of Lathrop's elderly lived alone, without family, and so they were visited and cared for. Soon a full-time pastor was commissioned to live and work in Lathrop Homes. This established a formal partnership between the RCA denomination and a body of believers who became organized as "The Church of the Good News."

To understand something of the unique character of this church, it is helpful to review the mission and vision statements that have been forged over the years.

Church of the Good News Mission Statement
BLESSED TO BE A BLESSING

We are one people mindful of our common need for healing
and rooted in God's grace.
We believe that God gives us healing and endurance for both
happiness and distress.
In worship and celebration we will share the Good News that
Jesus is Lord.
We accept the challenge to create an inclusive family.
Therefore we will . . .
Equip each member for growth and service.
Invite our children and youth in full participation.
Welcome visitors with fellowship and love.
Respond to human need in Lathrop and its surrounding community.
Be conscious of need and opportunity everywhere in the world.
Link people of many cultures and economic backgrounds, all as part
of God's diverse kingdom.
Serve as ministers with and to the Reformed Church in America.

Church of the Good News Vision Statement

Our vision is always for wholeness and shalom
. . . within our individual selves,
. . . our own church,
. . . the Lathrop community,
. . . the surrounding communities,
. . . and around the globe.

Currently, we have a membership roll of around sixty communicant members and nearly two thousand adherents — the approximate number of persons living in Lathrop Homes. In other words, we are the church of Lathrop Homes. Many residents of Lathrop may never darken our doors, yet they are likely to find support and strength through the ministry of Good News. Ours are a people who struggle daily with gang warfare, street-corner drug dealing, prostitution, child neglect and child abuse, substance abuse, and other forms of violence that often arise from places of economic poverty. Underlying these symptoms of distress remains a problem that keeps the stage set for violence in our community — the unavailability of living-wage jobs.

In 1990, we moved out of the storefront space that had housed our ministry for over twenty years, and into a new building. This marked a new era for the church and community. The new facility stands as a concrete symbol of God's Kingdom, which is "at hand" in our neighborhood. Designed with and for the people of Lathrop, we view the building as belonging to the community. One example is the basement, built "to code" for housing the community's Head-Start program that every weekday brings numerous children and parents into the church.

To design the church building with and for the community was considered only natural. We believe the church and its community belong together in the same way the Word belongs with the flesh as witnessed in Jesus Christ. Good News isn't about the business of creating its own spiritual community apart from Lathrop Homes. Although we worship, study the Bible, organize youth groups, and provide other faith-nurturing activities, these are not considered "in-house" activities. All that is done is done with and for our community. A few examples may help illustrate this point:

- We have a choir that practices and performs in the church, but it is not a church choir. Its name is "The Lathrop Community Choir." There are some in Lathrop who want to sing, but either may not feel worthy to sing in a church choir, or simply are leery of churches in general. They will sing in our choir.
- We are concerned about the health of those in our community who are hungry. We did not create a church food pantry, but rather "The Lathrop Community Food Pantry." It is run by those in and out of the formal structure of the church.
- We believe the arts can play a positive role in the education of our people. So we offer high-quality music instruction for children and adults at an affordable rate through a music school. We did not create a church music school, but rather "The Lathrop Community Music Center."

221

Ours is a vision that calls forth the best from the people of our community toward Kingdom goals. Often, this vision is not understood or accepted by more traditional churches. For example, a large, wealthy, suburban church once showed interest in providing the music center with major financial support, the kind of support that would have relieved a huge financial burden from our shoulders. The suburban church decided the money would be granted only if it was agreed that the music instructors pray with the students before every lesson. We sadly said "No, thank you" to the money — not because we don't believe in prayer, but because we believe music doesn't require prayer to make it a spiritual activity. Further, and perhaps more important, the instructors of the music center come from all walks of life to offer their gifts of music, but not all would be prepared to offer the gift of prayer. We were concerned that such a policy might hinder, rather than help, the Holy Spirit already at work in the lives of the instructors and students.

Our church's concern for our community is clearly evident to many, even to those outside our immediate community. Recently, hundreds gathered in our sanctuary for a jobs rally organized by church and community leaders. We gathered to voice our concern over a piece of land in our neighborhood that was in process of being rezoned for the building of a wealthy residential development. Our concern was simple. We wanted the land to remain industrial so the people of Lathrop would have a better chance of securing living-wage jobs. Our voice was loud enough to be heard by the mayor, who gave us the opportunity to do what we seldom have reason to do — celebrate a political, indeed a spiritual, victory.

It is our hope and prayer that those who walk through our church's doors will be moved to stay and more fully become a part of our life and body. But new members are viewed as only one of the many kinds of fruit we are called to cultivate. Such fruit is wonderful and much needed (there is much work that needs to be done!), but our mission is to cultivate all the fruits that come from being followers of Christ. Our focus is on love, justice, acceptance, and humility — all in a neighborhood for which Christ has died. Our neighborhood belongs to God. We claim it for God. Our business is not to create "church," but to *be* the church.

Listening to Voices from the Church of the Good News

Ray

I moved into the neighborhood a few years ago. At the time I was dealing with life single-handedly. I would see Pastor Liala on her porch and we'd talk and before I knew it, we were good friends and good neighbors. Being disabled, I was unable to hold a job. I needed to do something with my time. My involvement with Good News started when Liala asked for my help in carrying some books and items to the church. My life has not been the same since.

I would see Liala most every day with a smile on her face. I needed the joy she had. I told her that if she ever needed help at the church — answering phones, washing windows, or whatever — I'd be happy to help out. Last summer the challenge came when she asked me to teach in the summer Bible School program. I said, "Now wait a minute. I don't know that I can handle kids!" I don't have children of my own, and I thought Liala had lost her mind. But I took the challenge, and it became the most rewarding week of my life. Seeing those children look up to me, asking me questions, and just inviting me into their lives — it was overwhelming. Since then I've become a member just a few months ago.

As far as community involvement is concerned, just about all my time goes to the community. I'm on the board of the Lathrop Community Music Center, involved in the choir, and recently joined the Logan Square Neighborhood Association which helps our neighborhood organize around community issues like jobs and safety. That people need work goes without saying. Our neighborhood has lost a lot of factories over the last few years. But safety is also a big concern of ours. We have a lot of gangs and drug activity around here. It's just not safe.

I guess I've always felt I had God inside me, but didn't think a church could ever hold me. But I found in this church people who love me and accept me as I am. I don't think I could find this anywhere else. If there is a place, I want you to tell me because I want to see it again and again.

223

Sharon

I don't know what to say. There's so much to say. I guess I'll start by saying this church is my family. One of the most meaningful things about the Church of the Good News is the recognition given to the gifts of its people. This community is so often overlooked in that respect. The church offers what most social service organizations do not. People are just numbers to them. We don't assign numbers here. People know this.

This is a place where you have a name. You are recognized for what you have and not for what you don't have. I'm doing things now that if someone seven or eight years ago told me I'd being doing I'd say, "Yeah, right." George was the first one who approached me and asked me to help in leading worship. I've never had that experience with the church. I mean, you just don't participate, you know? And so I started doing parts of the liturgy, and before I knew it Liala had me teaching Sunday School! I'm learning so much about myself and God. And now I'm learning how to seek out the gifts in others. We have very talented people in this community.

Zsame

When I was a kid, I used to run into the church when it was in the storefront on George Street. I'd run in, mess with Liala, and then run out. One evening I was gonna go to a party. I said, "I can't go to the party, I gotta go to church." So I went to the church but didn't stay too long. I would join other churches, churches that would sing, you know? I mean, if the church ain't singing, I figured I ain't in church! Then Liala says to me, "We're gonna have a choir." I said, "Alright!" And she said, "It's gonna be a community choir. And you don't have to be a member of the church to sing in it." I said, "Great!" I had tried singing in other church choirs, but there was always arguing. Everyone was concerned about who was gonna sing this, or who was gonna sing that, or saying stuff like that. I started going here more and more. A couple months ago I joined the church.

A lot of my friends in the neighborhood ask me what church I go to, and I say "Church of Good News." And they say, "They don't have a choir, do they?" I'd say, "Yeah, come check it out." And they'd say, "We can't go down there, they have white folk there, and the pastor, she's a lady!" Which reminds me, I was walking down the street one day and I saw this guy talking to Liala. After he finished the conversation with Liala he came over to me and said, "I was talking to her over there. Do you know her?" I said, "Yeah, that's my minister! She's pastor at the Church of Good News." He couldn't believe me! He said, "You're kidding! She's so cool! She can't be a pastor!"

So I learned that I don't have to search for a choir any more. I can just come here and be myself. In our choir, we just have to be ourselves. We don't have to sing perfect. If we hit a note wrong, in our choir everybody joins you and it just sounds good! My kids love it here. My youngest son sees George playing the guitar and he goes around the house all day strummin' and stuff! I'm not gonna lead any Bible study like Sharon, that's just not my gift. But I am helping to start a Food Co-op in our neighborhood. The food pantry's okay, but it makes people feel ashamed sometimes. So we're gonna buy a bunch a food cheap so folks can come, volunteer some time, and get a discount on some good food. Of course, a lot of people are gonna want the food and they ain't gonna want to work for it. So they've got some learnin' to do!

Some people don't come to the church because they're afraid. I tell 'em to just walk in. I say, "Hey, if they let me in, they'll let you in!" My mother joined, and my brother too. My sister's trying, but I don't know. A lot of people are just afraid. But I tell 'em that here you don't have to do nothin' you don't wanna do. I just tell them "God will work it out for you." I hope more of my friends come.

Maynard

I've been associated with the Church of the Good News since its inception. My family was one of the first black families to move into Lathrop in the sixties. This church has always been an integral part of the community. It's always been inclusive. We have black folk, Hispanic folk, white folk, and all kinds of folk. You don't have to be a member to belong here. People who have never attended a service claim this church as their church. There are no strings here. And we don't care whether you have fine clothes or "raggedy" clothes. I've lived here for forty years. I've raised seven children here, and I don't know of any other place I'd rather be. Because Lathrop is low-income housing, it has, like, an invisible wall around it. This church breaks down those barriers. People who live in the townhouses near here struggle just as much as the people living in Lathrop. The struggles may be different, but they're still struggles. Even rich folk can find a home here. And some have.

Sandra

I come here because this is my family. I feel welcome here. We got people with AIDS, people with mental problems, we got everybody here! I don't care what you have, at Good News you have family. I had to leave Lathrop because of my boy. I was afraid of the gangs. Now I live on the West Side. I'm still afraid, but you have to do what you have to do. But now I'm trying to come back. I miss it too much. So I'm comin' back as soon as an apartment opens up.

Listening to the Pastor of the Church of the Good News

My name is Liala Ritsema Beukema. I serve as pastor of the Church of the Good News. I just want to say that loving people just as they are doesn't mean that we don't push each other. To be family means not only that you are accepted, but also that you are supported and disciplined in ways that help you more fully reflect the image of God. The sadness of our community, our city, and even the church at large is that we forget that people who lack financial resources are still people who belong to God. If people aren't viewed this way, we're cheating the Kingdom of God. Those like me, who have been trained professionally in the church, often find it difficult to give up the reins of control so that people can stumble and make mistakes and simply be the people of God.

We have people in this church who are mentally ill. Sometimes they like to talk during the worship service. But they are worshiping! Who are we to say that they don't belong here, or that they should get themselves together before they come here? They need a place to worship too. The fact is, they have much to give to us. Like Gregory.

He's an adorable person. But Gregory is goofy! And I tell him, "Gregory, you are goofy!" He has this idea in his head that it's his job to pass out information to the community. And so he comes to the church and picks up literature, any literature that's lying around, and passes it out in the neighborhood. Once he cleared off my desk and passed out all my stuff to the neighborhood! My sermon notes were being read before I had the chance to preach them! If we claim all are welcome in the church, it's not our business to exclude Gregory. It's not even our business to put up with him. It's our business to see in him what God sees in him and to let him be in our lives.

When we built this new building four years ago there was a lot of gentrification [upscale housing] going on in our community. I can't tell you how many people said to us things like, "Oh, now that you have a nice building you should try to get those young wealthy families to come to your church." What's that all about? Does having a new building now mean we should focus on the affluent in our community? That just makes me mad. I don't mean they shouldn't come here. Of course they can come here. If they're in our neighborhood, they belong here. God knows they need the church to help them deal with their wealth and all the problems it will bring them. Coming here might be the best thing they could do. But I think I know what's behind comments like these.

They seem to suggest that we should try to get rich folk into our doors so we can become financially self-sufficient. But we think it's wrong to look at people in terms of what they earn. It's dehumanizing. It's dehumanizing if we do it to people who are economically poor, and it's dehumanizing if we do it to people who are economically affluent. It's simply not Christian. This is not to say we don't desire to be financially self-sufficient. We do. But we understand this in a different way. Our concern is for the financial well-being of our community. If we take care of this, the rest will take care of itself.

Considering Some Theological Reflection on the Church of the Good News

As the author of this article, it is important to me to share another dimension of the ministry of this church. You have read the comments of my friends and wife, who are all participants in this church. Their voices speak collectively to the individuals of this community, to the families of this community, and to the broader systems and structures that impact this community. But theirs is also a voice that speaks to the greater church. This is a topic close to my heart and vocation. I left my role as pastor at Good News about six years ago when I felt a call to work with Christian college students at the Chicago Metropolitan Center (CMC), which is a Christian college urban work-study program. There is much I could share concerning how CMC utilizes the voice of the poor in educating Christian college students,[1] but I will focus on the Good News workcamp ministry that reaches out to non-urban and non-poor congregations.

During my eight years as copastor at Good News, one of the most meaningful aspects of my work was organizing the workcamp program. Youth groups, young adult groups, and family groups from churches in Iowa, Wisconsin, Nebraska, Oklahoma, Michigan, and many other places come to Good News to work and learn in our community. Although the churches who come are not always aware of our educational, or perhaps you could say "missiological," agenda, this agenda is the primary reason we dedicate so much time and energy to the greater church. As Sharon said earlier, many people on the outside tend to look at communities like ours in terms of deficiencies. We know better. Yes, we have our deficiencies, but we also have our capacities. An excerpt from a letter I received from a workcamper following his summer visit gives testimony to this reality:

> When I left for Chicago I felt like I was really going to do some good. You know, doing my good deed for the year. At first I thought we would be doing all of the giving by spending our time helping others. However, totally the opposite proved to be true. Many of the people we met in Chicago were far worse off financially than any of us had ever dreamed of. Some practically survive from one meal to the next. Everyday they live with garbage left in the street, landlords who do not maintain facilities, poor public education, few job opportunities, and at times abuse. I expected to see them bitter and hateful due to their living conditions. Yet the kids and the adults we met were full of love and life. They would give us hugs, hold our

1. See George D. Beukema, "Bicultural Liberative Education: Educating the Non-Poor in an Urban Work-Study Program," Doctor of Ministry Dissertation, Western Theological Seminary, 1992.

hands, smile and laugh so much that we knew we were getting more than we gave. Our friends in Chicago showed us that there is more to life than money. My eyes have been opened.

It is very fulfilling to bring non-urban, non-poor folk into our community and see them witness the deeper dimensions of the life and spirituality of our community, while at the same time expanding their understanding concerning the causes of poverty. Our Christian brothers and sisters come with preconceptions about poverty that are not based in reality. They have misguided conceptions of poor folk. It is important to the Church of the Good News that the greater church discover what is true and what is not true concerning their brothers and sisters in Christ who happen to be poor.

I remember hosting a large youth group from Oklahoma one summer. We began the week by asking the group to brainstorm a list of words and phrases that describe the ways they believe the people in their church think about poor people. They created a list that included the words *dirty, lazy, loud, violent, bad parents,* and *welfare cheaters.* We didn't talk much more about the list. I simply put the list away and closed the session with prayer, asking God to help them see what God sees in our neighborhood.

Throughout the week the group shed some blood, sweat, and tears working on rehabbing a number of Lathrop Homes apartments. In addition to the work, we structured a number of activities where the group had the opportunity to interact with the people of our church community. For example, one evening I asked Gladys, a long-time church member, to come and share a bit of her life story with the group. The following is a close rendition of the story she told:

> I really don't like being on welfare. I want to work. I've always wanted to work. There are some [mothers in Lathrop] that don't want to work, but most of us do. Well, I heard about a job at a box factory down the street. I applied and I couldn't believe it. . . . I got the job! I was so excited. The next Sunday I came to church and shared the good news with everyone during prayer time. I was so happy. It's not the best job . . . just folding boxes, but the boxes are being made to ship Christian books! I feel like I'm really working for the Lord! Everything was fine until a few weeks ago.
>
> My little girl gets nose bleeds and I have to take her to the hospital because the bleeding won't stop. She used to get these a lot, but lately

it's been getting better. I was just praying that she wouldn't get sick anymore because when I took the job I had to give up my green card [a green card provides people on public assistance with medical coverage]. My job only pays minimum wage with no benefits, so I knew I'd be in trouble if my daughter got sick again. But I had to risk it. I just hate being on welfare and not working. Well, a week after I got my new job my daughter got a nose bleed. I had to take her to the hospital and I got a bill for $1,500! I couldn't pay it. I was all upset because I knew I had to quit my job so I could get my green card back.

On the last day of the group's visit, I hauled out the newsprint from our earlier brainstorming session. They stared in disbelief at their own ignorance.

We believe in the power of story at Good News.[2] It is in sharing our stories that we come to know each other and learn to love each other more deeply. It's a way for folks who are not poor to understand the kinds of obstacles that our people face. Its a way for them to see their own cultural blinders which prevent them from acting justly and compassionately on behalf of their poor sisters and brothers. Our purpose is not to convert them into urban ministers, or to have them give us lots of money, but to go back home and work to change the systems and structures of our society that hurt our people.[3] This is important because our people have limited power to change the systems and structures of our society or to change the negative attitudes and thinking, all of which hurt the families of our community.

Paulo Friere is an educator in Brazil who has influenced the way we understand our educational mission to the greater church.[4] He

2. To explore the biblical foundations for educating through story, see Walter Brueggemann, *The Creative Word: Canon as Model for Biblical Education* (Philadelphia: Fortress Press, 1982); Thomas Groom, *Christian Religious Education* San Francisco: Harper & Row, 1980); Parker Palmer, *To Know As We Are Known: A Spirituality of Education* (San Francisco: Harper & Row, 1983); Daniel Schipani, *Religious Education Encounters Liberation Theology* (Birmingham, Ala.: Religious Education Press, 1988); and Robert Alter, *The Art of Biblical Narrative* (New York: Basic Books, 1981).

3. See Walter Wink, *Engaging the Powers: Discernment and Resistance in the World of Domination* (Philadelphia: Fortress Press, 1992).

4. Paulo Friere, *Pedagogy of the Oppressed* (New York: Seabury Press, 1974). See also Schipani; and Evans, Evans, and Kennedy, eds., *Pedagogies for the Non-Poor* (Maryknoll, N.Y.: Orbis Books, 1987).

talks about the power of ideology in our culture. Ideologies are the thought patterns and belief structures that reinforce the social systems that oppress people in communities like ours, like the welfare system about which Gladys spoke.[5] I agree with Friere that it is very important to help Christians examine these thought structures and systems because they often do not reflect the purposes of God.

People for whom the realities of poverty remain outside their experience do not understand what our people are up against. But it is in the interest of our neighborhood to be about this kind of education. Most churches that do a workcamp with us come in order to meet a need in their lives — the need to serve. We allow them to meet that need, but not without meeting our need as well — our need for them to listen to our story and to be challenged to find ways to respond to our story with loving and just action after they leave.

A few years ago our teen youth group went to visit the church of a youth group that participated in one of our workcamp experiences. Following the Sunday morning worship service, the father of one of the workcamp youths asked for a moment of my time. It seems that when his daughter returned from Chicago, she called a family meeting. She told them of her experience at our church — in particular, her experience of the wealth of our people. She then shared about one of our Bible reflection sessions where the biblical notion of shalom was connected to the notion of justice — how peace is possible when all people share the resources of the earth.

She also told them of another Bible study where we discussed Christ's warning to the rich man about the deadly power of money. Explaining how she wanted her family and the world to experience a greater sense of shalom, she pulled out a piece of paper listing various household items: three television sets, two stereos, two VCRs, two automobiles, three snowmobiles, skis, . . . and the list went on. She placed the list on the table in front of them and asked that they consider ridding themselves of some of these items that she feared were getting in the way of shalom. At this point in the father's story, I wasn't sure whether to smile or run! But his response was warm. He simply said, "Well, today we have two less television sets. I guess that's a start." I smiled and said, "Yes, it's a start."

---

5. See Paul Hiebert, "The Gospel in Our Culture: Methods of Social and Cultural Analysis," in Hunsberger and Van Gelder, eds., *The Church between Gospel and Culture* (Grand Rapids: Eerdmans, 1996).

Gifts from the Global Church

ISAAC K. FOKUO AND
PATRICIA LLOYD-SIDLE

My name is Patricia Lloyd-Sidle. I am a Presbyterian Church (USA) minister who spent seven years as a missionary in Latin America. What a privilege that was! I learned so much and received so much from my Latin American colleagues. I returned to the United States convinced that Latin American Christians have a great deal to teach Christians in this country. I longed for others here to have the same experience of receiving the gospel witness from Christians whose difficult life circumstances have shaped their faith in profoundly moving ways. Aware of the spiritual poverty that too often characterizes our churches, I know that hearing the gospel message afresh from a different perspective can bring great renewal.

Leslie Newbigin once said, "It belongs to the very essence of the Gospel that we need to hear it from someone else."[1] Similar in thought, Jose Comblin has noted, "The light of Christ does not come to us from others as an echo of our own thoughts; it comes in alien guise and speaks with a foreign accent, and it shatters the barricades of our selves, leaving us open to others so that Christ's light can pass through us to others."[2]

---

1. In an informal presentation at the World Conference on Mission and Evangelism, San Antonio, 1989.

2. Jose Comblin, *Sent from the Father: Meditations on the Fourth Gospel* (Maryknoll, N.Y.: Orbis Books, 1979).

The Presbyterian Church (USA) invites Christian colleagues from around the world to minister in our midst through a program called "Mission to the U.S.A." Other churches have similar programs. For one month or longer, local churches have the privilege of being on the receiving end of mission as a pastor or lay leader from abroad preaches, teaches, and ministers in a variety of ways in their midst.

On occasion a missionary to the United States stays for a year or more. Isaac Fokuo is one such missionary to the United States. He is spending one year with the Presbyterian Church (USA). His faith story which follows, and his reflections on mission and on the church in the United States, provide an example of how we can experience "gifts from the global church."

Background on Isaac Fokuo

My name is Isaac Kwaku Fokuo. I am a minister of the Presbyterian Church of Ghana, and am pursuing an advanced degree at the Louisville Presbyterian Theological Seminary. During 1995, I served as the Mission Partner in Residence for the PC (USA). My father and his junior brother were among the first converts of the Salvation Army Church in my village. When my father decided to embrace the gospel, my mother decided otherwise. When she finally made a decision to trust Christ, a miracle happened to her. She was cured instantly, soon after her baptism, of a disease that had previously proved incurable. The story is that on one Sunday morning during worship, my mother, to the surprise of the worshipers, appeared at the entrance of the sanctuary and declared her intention to the pastor to become a Christian. She was baptized, and to the surprise of the church, my mother was completely cured of her disease. Whenever I read the gospel story of the woman in Matthew 9:20-22 who had a flow of blood for twelve years, I am reminded of my mother.

At an early age of about seven, I went to stay with my uncle, who was a trader in the northeastern part of the country. In this new environment I was introduced to people whose culture was different from mine. I learned to speak the languages of some of these tribes, and came to appreciate many of their customs. This was the beginning of my cross-cultural experience, an experience that played a significant role in shaping my life. After I left my home village at the age of seven,

I never went back to live among my own people. I realize now that each time I visit my village I feel like a stranger.

I had a conversion experience when I was in high school. God used a senior student, a member of the Scripture Union, to challenge me about the spiritual dimension of life. For some months after this encounter I read my Bible, and the more I read, the more I came to enjoy reading it. I also fellowshiped with members of the Scripture Union in my high school. As time went by, my love for Jesus and his word increased and surpassed my love for any other thing in the world. One of my favorite passages was Philippians 3:8-11.

A significant aspect of my conversion experience was the realization that God was not just "up there," but was a present Father — a friend. During my senior year in high school, I became convinced that God was calling me into a full-time ministry. I tried to defer this call, but never succeeded. Finally I gave up and said "yes Sir," to God, and went to seminary to be trained as a pastor of the Presbyterian Church of Ghana (PCG). I graduated from seminary in 1973, and I have since served the Presbyterian Church of Ghana as a minister of the gospel.

The PCG owes its beginnings to the Evangelical Missionary Society in Basel (Basel Mission) and the United Free Church of Scotland (Church of Scotland). The Basel Mission work started in 1828. During the First and Second World Wars, the German missionaries were deported from what was then the Gold Coast. The Free Church of Scotland, with the permission of the British Government, decided to fill the gap created by the departure of the Germans. They provided the infant church with much-needed spiritual leadership. Today the PCG is the second largest denomination in Ghana, with congregations spread throughout the whole of the country. It works in partnership with churches both in Europe and the United States.

An Experience as a Missionary to the United States

The topic given to me by the Moderator sounded distasteful in my ears. At the same time, I knew that she did not mean to be offensive. Some friends suggested that I change the topic, but I decided not to change it. I decided not to change it because this was a topic from the Moderator of the PC (USA). I saw her as a senior member of the Christian Community, a person who was worthy of my obedience.

My traditional upbringing did not permit me to say "no" to my elders. But I struggled with how to present my views in such a way that I would not appear to be rude to her.

I turned to God and asked the Holy Spirit to give me wisdom in my preparation. The following is the text of that presentation.

Madam Moderator, fellow sisters and brothers, I deem it a singular honor to be called to address this Conference. My topic is "I am a result of Mission Overseas." To tackle this topic with a clear conscience I wish to state two assumptions. These are:

(1) That this topic is a general statement referring to no particular achievement of any person or group of persons.

(2) That I am to comment on the statement briefly, and possibly the mission paradigm it represents.

First, I want to say that, looking at the statement broadly, it is a statement of fact, one which is a reaffirmation of what we are as Christians. We here assembled are all the results of God's missionary activity on the planet earth. Nearly two thousand years ago God in the person of his son Jesus Christ crossed the ocean of sin that separated humanity from its creator, and visited us. Angels were the first announcers of the Good News, and shepherds were the first recipients of the Glad Tidings. None of us sitting here was present when the angels announced the birth of the baby Jesus. We have all received the gospel message from someone else. Through the cross, God dealt a final blow to sin and death which had held humanity captive. Through the resurrection, Jesus has given us access to the very presence of God, and has made us children of God. Mission is God's activity. We are only privileged to be partners with this gracious God in his mission.

Second, I want to note that it was in the early twentieth century, the great century for Protestant missions, that many mission societies from the Western world went to Africa, Asia, and other parts of the non-Western world. They went to spread the gospel, as well as Western civilization, to the then "pagan" world. Africa was called the "dark" continent. These nations, which the missionaries from the West visited, were the targets and objects of missions. The spread of the gospel, which went side by side with the spread of Western civilization, has left very negative results in many lands, results with which many churches are continuing to wrestle.

Third, I want to acknowledge that after the First and Second

World Wars, many mission societies and churches became convinced that the whole world had become a mission field. Africa and Asia were not the only mission lands. The West had also become a mission field. Lesslie Newbigin, in his book *One Body, One Gospel, One World,* asked the question, "What is the precise differentium that made an activity missionary?" His answer was, "The differentium lies in the crossing of the frontier, between faith in Christ as Lord and unbelief."[3] By this statement Newbigin is saying mission is everywhere. We can no longer call any geographically identifiable location either a pagan land, or Christendom. Mission is now to the six continents.

At various meetings of the International Missionary Council, it became clear that fulfilling the Lord's command, "Go into all the world and proclaim the gospel," requires all hands on deck. By the 1960s, it was evident that churches in the former mission lands were no longer daughter churches. They had produced mature leadership and resisted being called sons and daughters. They were involved in missions in their own lands, often with spectacular results. They were no longer targets and objects of Western Missions; they had become partners in God's mission. The PC (USA) has embraced this new paradigm in missions; hence we see such units as Ecumenical Partnerships and People in Mutual Mission, in addition to programs such as "Mission to the U.S.A." All these express the new paradigm for mission.

My sisters and brothers, if we want to be faithful to the God who has called us to participate in His mission, then let us put aside all the walls of division that separate us, and let us see ourselves as the one people of God. Let us all seek to be obedient to the Initiator, Sustainer, and final Lord of our calling, Jesus Christ, who has qualified us to be members of God's kingdom.

Reflections on PC (USA) Churches in North America

There are both positive and negative aspects to the ministries of PC (USA) churches in North America, which I have been privileged to

---

3. Lesslie Newbigin, *One Body, One Gospel, One World* (London: Wm. Carling & Co. Ltd., 1958), p. 29.

observe. One positive thing I have observed is the openness to embrace the diversity that exists in the denomination. I am aware of the risks involved in this, but believe that they are worth taking. Each congregation needs to be free to pursue ministry in its own way. A second positive thing I have found is the search for new ways of doing and speaking the gospel so that it will be relevant to people of this age.

There are, however, some negative things, which I have also observed. First of all, there have been times when I have felt that the church in the United States is handled just like a business organization. In some cases the spiritual dimension seems to be given a low profile. Long-range planning and focusing on management methods, with little or no prayer, seem to be taken to be the answer for both spiritual and material needs.

Second, there is very little mention of the Holy Spirit in most of the congregations I have visited. There is a tendency to depend on our intelligence and ability. I remember asking a minister why he had not preached on the Holy Spirit on the day of Pentecost. His simple answer was that he had spoken about the Holy Spirit during Pentecost the previous year.

A third issue I have observed concerns a tendency to compromise on our prophetic role in order to please people. This sometimes leads to the preaching of sweet-sounding messages, the aim of which seems to be to hurt or offend no one. The word "sin" appears to be in the rear of the vocabulary used by most preachers that I have come across.

Conclusion

In light of the positive things I have observed, and despite the negative ones, I strongly believe that God is doing something new in the various denominations in this country. We need to keep our ears and eyes open and be ready to move when God commands.

SECTION V

Rethinking the Church in the North American Mission Context

As the church continues to adjust to a changed context, it must not only refocus its witness to its community but also rethink its own life. It needs to redefine the essential character of both its life and its ministry. This is not an easy task, especially given the embeddedness that many forms and practices of the church have in our present culture. This final section provides an overview on the task of rethinking the church in the emerging postmodern mission context, and relates some practical ways to readjust the life and ministry of the church.

The opening article by Alan Roxburgh introduces the challenge of rethinking the church by critiquing the church's fascination today with the "new and the next." While the new and the next appear to be on the cutting edge of keeping the church relevant, Alan suggests that, in effect, many of these efforts end up capitulating to the ideology of postmodern culture. In contrast to this approach, he suggests that it is critical for the church to go back to its beginnings, to once more root itself in the story of God's people throughout the ages. Such a rooting requires a certain discipline, for the church that is being increasingly marginalized has much to let go of, and much to learn, about being shaped by God's story. Alan draws on his years of experience of pastoring a congregation that lives within a postmodern context to make this journey come alive with inspiration and practical advice.

Many of the articles in this book have pointed to the need of the church to rediscover its essential nature as a community of God's people. The challenge and practice of shaping biblical community is the theme of the second article in this section, by Paul Dinolfo. He draws on his personal experience in the Work of Christ Community to develop the importance of covenant in shaping community, and suggests practical ways to apply the notion of covenant within a variety of organizational structures. Covenantal commitments, he suggests, are at the heart of the church's rediscovering the essential character of Christian community in our postmodern context.

Worship is without question the most central and important of the functions in which Christian communities engage. In the third article in this section, Marva Dawn provides some practical suggestions for shaping a theology of worship in postmodern times. She notes that the postmodern condition brings some new challenges to the church as it rethinks its worship life. But this new context also presents some new opportunities for Christian faithfulness and fruitfulness. She applies her insights to what worship might look like in a church that takes seriously its missional nature in the midst of its parallel existence as a marginalized community in a postmodern context.

It is not possible to rethink the church without the church going through some fundamental change. Missional churches that live as marginalized communities need to learn both the theory and practice of organizational change. In the final article in this section, Jon Huegli provides the reader with an understanding of this theory and practice. He does this by drawing on the best of what is available from the social sciences and integrating this into a missional understanding of the church. Leaders of congregations will be well served to give careful attention to this material if they want to help guide the change that is inevitable when congregations choose to be missional. This is especially true for those who seek to make the experience of change more redemptive and effective for the congregation's ministry.

The Church in a Postmodern Context

ALAN J. ROXBURGH

A key issue that has guided the Gospel and Our Culture Network (GOCN) conversation concerns the church's identity in North America. The task of articulating a missionary ecclesiology for this context has shaped much of the Network's discussions. The tension resident in the title of this paper goes to the heart of this discussion. What are the narratives that currently shape our lives as churches? Will they be formed primarily by the particular intellectual and social narratives of our emerging postmodern context, or will churches interact with this context in ways consistent with their own gospel-shaped narrative?

The church always exists in particular contexts. These contexts help define the church's identity and shape its narrative. One of the gifts of the postmodern turn is the shedding of any illusions that the church can be defined apart from its embeddedness in context. But this represents only the background of this conversation. The GOCN has always taken seriously the fact that the gospel is expressed and lived in *our* culture. The critical issue to address is the relationship between the narratives of our context and the uniqueness of the biblical narrative.

This paper argues that much of what currently passes as ecclesial engagement with our culture represents what might be described as a *postmodern church*. The current literature being read by pastors about the ministry of the church in our culture offers descriptions of churches such as: "Next Church";[1] *A Church for the 21st Century;*[2] *The Purpose Driven Church;*[3] or *The Church for the Unchurched.*[4] In these materials I find a stunning absence of serious biblical and theological reflection on the nature of the church. What I do find is a clear focus on what can only be described as "the new and the next." Both the content of the gospel and the nature of the church are simply assumed. What results from these conceptions of the church is a reductionism in which our understanding of the church is shaped primarily by the categories of a postmodern context. By trying to understand something of what is shaping these forms of the church, we may discover the contours of a church in postmodernity.

The Postmodern Context

Many of the articles in the present volume refer to the postmodern context. This is currently a major theme in the literature about a gospel encounter with our North American culture. In responding to the question posed by the title of this paper, I must begin with my own situation. I am a pastor working in a particular context, struggling to engage the gospel with *our* culture. What I would like to do in this paper is use myself as a kind of laboratory. I want to share with you the ways in which *this* pastor, *as a pastor,* is trying to think, feel, and work his way into the issues of how a church might be formed with both integrity and missional identity in a postmodern context. I will begin by sharing several recent encounters and experiences in my life as a pastor. One involves a brief meeting in a local coffee shop; another, a lunch with a woman whose third husband, from whom she just separated, is dying of cancer; a third, insights gained while preparing for a teaching session with a Bible study group; and the fourth, being en-

1. Charles Trueheart, "Welcome to the Next Church," *The Atlantic Monthly,* August 1996, pp. 37-58.
2. Leith Anderson, *A Church for the 21st Century* (Minneapolis: Bethany House Publishers, 1992).
3. Rick Warren, *The Purpose Driven Church* (Grand Rapids: Zondervan, 1995).
4. George Hunter III, *Church for the Unchurched* (Nashville: Abingdon Press, 1996).

gaged by a recent TV ad. These represent the people and events where I live in engaging the issues of gospel and culture.

Jim in the Coffee Shop

I was sitting in my favorite coffee shop early Monday morning enjoying the taste of coffee, listening to the buzz of the Boomers getting their lattes before tackling the bridge to downtown Vancouver. This is my little missional context. I sit with lawyers, real estate salespersons, builders — persons who are all making a great deal of money. The coffee shop is a local community gathering spot, as well as a place for networking and business. As I sat drinking coffee and reading the morning paper, in walked another regular, Jim, who happens to be a member of our church. Jim is a high-powered stockbroker with an office in prestigious West Vancouver. Most of his clients are offshore. He has found his niche in life. I had not seen him the previous day in worship, so inquired about him, Ann, and their two kids. My inquiry about not seeing them the day before elicited a spirited description of his weekend.

He was returning to the office Monday morning to rest, he told me with some passion. The weekend had been one long series of coaching events and meetings with and for the kids. It was a nonstop two days, with no rest built in. Sunday morning, he and Ann had "done their turn" at our West Van church. They had volunteered to teach kids during the second service. After the service, they had rushed out for another soccer game somewhere. The last lines of his conversation were the most revealing. He said that he and Ann nurture their own Christian life at home. The church, when they can get to a service, is a plus, but they really don't need that to continue growing in their Christian life.

With that, Jim was off to get some rest with all his stocks and clients, before another mad weekend descended on him. Jim and Ann are immersed in the postmodern condition. They are strapped to their watches, rushing around their nuclear family and using little bits of this and that to tape together a lifestyle that is peculiarly their own. The stockbroker office, the coffee shop, the soccer field, the private school in the British Properties, and the Sunday mornings at West Van Church are all very separate pieces of their world that never connect. Jim and Ann move through these experiences like a Star Trek ship going into warp drive. They represent typical members of my church, a church that is deeply postmodern in the ethos of the context it engages and the people it serves.

Lunch with Carol

Carol and I met for lunch. We had tried to set this up on several other occasions, but now she needed to talk. Carol is forty-nine, a professional fund-raiser, a consummate Boomer with a Saab, a house in the Gulf Islands, and a sailboat in the yacht club. Newly separated from her third husband, whose cancer has come out of remission, she is concerned about their ten-year-old son. Carol is a physically beautiful woman who has no center to her life. After an hour of conversation, she summed herself up by saying that her ten-year-old son was the "X" mark on the map of her life, her reference point, her anchor of meaning. There were tears in her eyes and a lot of pain in her story. Toward the end of our conversation I said to her: "Carol, you have talked to me for over an hour, but I have no sense of who Carol is, of where your center lies, of who are you?" In tears, at age forty-nine, she said: "I don't know!" She too is a part of my church — a thoroughly postmodern individual with no sense of who she actually is as a person.

I struggle with this. What does it mean to be the church for the Carols and Jims? Do I start a separation recovery group? Would a twelve-step program be the right approach? What do I do as a pastor to help these individuals understand what it means to be church on the North Shore of Vancouver?

Preparing for a Teaching Session

Answers to such questions often seem to come along while you're doing other things. As you struggle with the ambiguities of the questions, you encounter Scripture and something starts to happen inside your mind. In the midst of my questions, I was encountered by the Word. Several weeks before, I had been asked to introduce the book of Genesis to a study group. "Not a problem," I told leaders. "I can do it in my sleep." As I thumbed through Genesis making notes in preparation, these earlier conversations were running through my head. I had been reading books about the church at the end of the twentieth century, books that talked about the necessity of the church being relevant to the culture, purpose driven, and focused on the lost. As I reconnected with Genesis, the book of beginnings, the story of the generations, its message began to peel back the questions running through my head about being the church. Here's what started to unfold and connect.

It seems to me that the writer of Genesis was doing something quite risky in putting this account of beginnings before Israel. He was offering a counter-story to the one pervading the nation in its settled place within the land. This counter-story represented a different narrative about what it meant to be God's people. Let me explain. Stuart Blanch, in his wonderful little book *For All Mankind: A New Approach to the Old Testament,* visualizes the book of *Exodus* coming to Israel in the early part of the monarchy.[5] The people have their king, their Temple on the holy hill of Zion, their priesthood, and the sacrificial system. They had the Law as a means of regulating their common life, along with an elementary judicial system. In addition, they had prophets and judges and singers and psalmists.

Israel was to play her part within a complex, multi-ethnic social system that took into account Canaanites who worshiped other gods and who lived by other laws. There was a thriving commercial relationship with Phoenicia and Tyre. All the moving, mixed populations of this period shifted back and forth through that area. If an ancient demographer or sociologist were to have settled in the area and plied her trade, she may have reported that Israel had numerous idiosyncracies, but for all intents and purposes, this little group of "wanna-be's" were not significantly different from those amongst whom they lived. They looked like them, they spoke not altogether dissimilar languages, they married, they got sick, and they died. They did not live in a ghetto, but were part and parcel of that ancient world.

The question the compiler of Genesis was grappling with was, "What did it mean to be God's particular people in that particular context?" How was their identity to be formed? What were the sto-

---

5. Stuart Blanch, *For All Mankind: A New Approach to the Old Testament* (New York: Oxford University Press, 1978), pp. 78-84.

ries and narratives that would give life and shape to them as a people? The nature of those choices was not difficult to describe. Would God's people be shaped primarily by the narratives of their surroundings, or would they live by another kind of story? And if the latter, what was that story and where did it come from? What would be the sources of the distinctiveness of Israel, and how would that be preserved in the land? The argument can be made that Genesis was written to answer these questions and provide precisely the narrative required to sustain Israel's identity in the land. Genesis challenged the drift that was occurring within Israel toward an accommodation of their ways to the larger culture. It confronted the reductionism of their identity as God's people to the categories of their surroundings.

After reflecting on the "new and next" futures of North American churches,[6] I was struck by the obvious. Genesis does not celebrate the novel, or the new, or the contemporary, or the next. Rather, it compels Israel to measure her immersion in the land by the standard of a different narrative of beginnings. If it was to be followed, this narrative required the formation and continuation of a peculiar people in the midst of many other peoples. I believe that the intentions of this compiler to reconnect Israel with an alternative tradition provides clues about ways we might be a church in the postmodern condition. As I introduced Genesis to the Bible study group of seeking Boomers, persons shaped by the worlds of Jim and Carol, I was struck by how much I, and they, needed to reconnect with this alternative narrative. Here was a clue to being the church in a postmodern culture.

Recent TV Ad

A final image helped me, as a pastor, to assemble the pieces of this puzzle in ways that begin to answer the question posed in this article. This image came across the television screen. It is an advertising piece created by the Bank of Montreal, one of Canada's four largest banks. The video depicts a group of children walking through a beautiful, idyllic countryside, singing, as they come together in one great pilgrim-like throng, the old Bob Dylan song, *The Times They Are a*

6. Trueheart, "Welcome to the Next Church."

Changin'. The Bank of Montreal did not simply get permission from Dylan to use this song, they actually *bought the rights* to the song. One can only guess what the dollar figure was, but estimates put it at over a million. It represents a major advertising commitment. As I watched the ad over and over, the questions going through my mind were these: What does a bank ad using a Bob Dylan song have to do with all these excited, committed children marching through the countryside? What does it have to do with the Jims and Carols in my life? What underlying message is it portraying about being a part of this culture? But most importantly, the question that came to mind was: What would the compiler of Genesis have to say to this narrative about the meaning of living in this postmodern land?

Children, joyfully singing with great conviction and energy: *The times, they are a changin'.* As they march by on this great pilgrimage to who knows where, they pass an old man sitting in a chair. In the background stands a countryside church. These two images, however, serve only as backdrops. The flow of the future is passing them by. They are only brief life gestalts of what was once important, but what must now move out of the way, because, after all, *the times, they are a changin'.* It is important to note that this advertising image is not directed at the children of our society. It is aimed at Boomers, the children's parents, the people with all the money to bank and invest. Boomers easily recognize where this song comes from — Bob Dylan and the heyday of the protest movement in the 1960s and 1970s. The message is plain and simple. The new is the answer to all our problems, anything that doesn't support the convictions and emotions of our generation belongs to the old. It is reactionary and has to be removed. "Come, fathers and mothers, throughout this ol' land, and don't criticize what you can't understand. If you can't lend a hand, then get out of the way, for the times, they are a changin'."

Uniquely, the Bank of Montreal has captured a major theme of Boomers living in a postmodern, post-industrial world. The answer to any malady or problem always lies ahead in the new and the next; in the assimilation of the latest; in reading, crystal ball-like, the next wave that is coming; and, in the spirit of Faith Popcorn, clicking into the next wave without losing a beat. What is continually driving the Boomers is the need to stay ahead, grab the new, be relevant and contemporary, and ever change to stay on track. This impetus of the postmodern culture moves in two directions. First, it is "rooted in the modernist ideal of individuals emancipated from convention,"[7] and in the postmodern turn toward the novel and the new, where individuals are free to continually construct their identities as they choose, over and over again. Words like *new* and *next* are encoded signals of this worldview. A pantheon of technologies and methodologies lie before anyone who dares to go boldly where no one has gone before, to help them stay on the curve of the new and the next which lie ahead. We are thus immersed more and more in a world that propels us toward some future that is next, while denying any validity or power to all that has gone before. In the words of Eric Hobsbawm, "The destruction of the past, or rather of the social mechanisms that link one's contemporary experience to that of earlier generations, is one of the most characteristic and eerie phenomena of the late twentieth century."[8]

What this ad from the Bank of Montreal did for me was to help me coalesce a lot of the experiences and conversations I had been having. It helped me understand some of the forces that are shaping our postmodern context and the church's identity in that setting. The video expressed in powerful images the ways in which our present time disintegrates old patterns of human relationship, snaps the links between the generations, and rests its whole identity on some image of the new and the next. It seems to me, however, that the more we have lived by this mythology of the new and the next, the more we have lost a sense of our own identity. When one is continually making oneself over anew, one "disappears," if you will. There is no longer an "I" at the center of the process. But what is true of the individual in this postmodern culture is just as true of institutions. It was Marshal McLuhan who suggested that we become what we behold. When we are continually beholding the new, the next, the future, the contemporary, that is what we become. This kind of process, this disembedding from any larger narrative, and being continually shaped by the new and the next, represents the character of both North American society and its churches. As a consequence, the church's self-identity is disappearing as it is con-

7. Christopher Lasch, *Revolt of the Elites* (New York: W. W. Norton & Company, 1995), p. 234.

8. Eric Hobsbawm, *The Age of Extremes* (London: Abacus, Little, Brown and Company, 1994), p. 3.

stantly being made over anew in terms of the new and the next. This is what I would mean by a postmodern church.

This is where my pastoral engagement and networking have led me to reflect on being the church today. I have begun to think in some other directions. Might it be that the notion of a church *in* postmodernity would somehow mean a church reconnected and shaped by the beginnings — by a tradition, by a narrative that comes from the past and moves toward a future? It's not that our churches would deny as essential the need for these kinds of beginnings. The issue is more complex than that. Rather, what happens is that in the kind of postmodern churches that are driven by the new and the next, the "narrative" of the gospel's content and meaning is often assumed but never inhabited. Consequently, the narrative of the tradition is re-shaped by what the postmodern church actually beholds. The meaning of the "beginnings" or the "foundations" of the "gospel," if you will, becomes invisible because those who still carry the words of the tradition have crossed into another land — the land of the image, the land of the new and the next. In this land, the language of the "beginnings," and its power to shape our present life, becomes invisible. In the postmodern church, there is no essential connection between the word used and what, in fact, it was intended to denote. Language that should shape and give meaning out of the richness of the tradition is disconnected from the objective particularity of its origins, its *genesis*.

My argument is not that this has happened with deliberateness. It is that the narrative of postmodernity has come to indwell the way in which the postmodern church reuses the language of the tradition. In doing so, the larger meaning disappears while the words are still used as if they represent the power of the tradition. The overpowering presence of the new and the next is itself a sign of a devastating loss of confidence in the objective power of the beginnings. This confidence has moved on to the shifting image of the new and the next. In the competitiveness of the postmodern narratives, the winners are always those who have the newest and best images to offer the individuals who are "seekers" looking for ways to re-create and remake themselves. "Come, fathers and mothers, throughout this land, and don't criticize what you can't understand. If you can't lend a hand, then get out of the way, for the times they are a changin'."

Detachment from the given and a disappearance of the beginnings — the result is disconnected, atomized individuals. Pulitzer prize–winning novelist Carol Shields expresses this reality most poignantly in her book *The Republic of Love*. Set in Winnipeg, it is the story of two adults trying to find a relationship that connects them, one that lasts and holds things together. One of the main characters is a thirty-five-year-old woman named Fay. She has just left her live-in relationship of three years. No reason is given for her leaving him. It has just lost its meaning. Something, someone else will emerge; they always do. This is how Shields describes her character:[9]

> Fay is gregarious by nature. She's even wondered from time to time — and idly worried — about being perhaps overly sociable, too dependent on the response of others and incapable of sustaining any kind of interior life for more than a few seconds at a time. Who is she anyway but a jumble of other people's impressions? A receptor of external stimulation. A blank lake.

At the other side of these bright, wonderful children, coming together to sing their hymn to the new, lies not a bright new world connecting them together, but a blank lake — Carol and Jim and Fay. Unfortunately, the postmodern church has built its future on meeting the needs of these people.

A Postmodern Church

Let me explore some of these issues a little further by looking at two examples of the church in postmodernity. The first is located in an article in the August 1996 issue of *The Atlantic Monthly*, titled "Welcome to the Next Church." Its subtitle was:[10]

> "Seamless multimedia worship, round-the-clock niches of work and service, spiritual guidance, and a place to belong: in communities around the country the old order gives way to the new."

We are told that for years its author, Charles Trueheart, traveled across America visiting churches, interviewing pastors, reading

9. Carol Shields, *The Republic of Love* (Toronto: Random House, 1992), p. 80.
10. Trueheart, "Welcome to the Next Church."

250

books, and talking on the telephone to church consultants. Trueheart claims to have identified the characteristics of a church form that is reshaping the American religious landscape. The names of these churches are familiar: Willow Creek in suburban Chicago, Saddleback in suburban Los Angeles, Mariners Church in Newport Beach, California. They are characterized chiefly by their size. The statistics are impressive. There are thousands of people in attendance at any one of these churches. Half of all churchgoing Americans are attending only 12 percent of the nation's churches. The "Next" church is a new social formation in an impersonal, transient nation. It is a church of options, restlessly creative about developing forms of worship.

What I want to look at in this conversation is the language at work in Trueheart's account of these churches. The details of what they are doing is secondary to the underlying assumptions buried in the language that shapes their reality. This is where we see why they are postmodern churches. My point is not to critique the skill, ingenuity, creativity, or energy that has gone into forming these churches. This is not even a critique of bigness or growth, both of which have their own inherent value. Rather, it is a question of how they betray the "beginnings" by reshaping themselves into the categories of our postmodern context, and therefore cause the gospel to disappear even as they work hard to proclaim that very gospel.

The language suggests the problem, as noted in the very name of the article, "The 'Next' Church." It is described by what is not — what is not traditional and what is not formed by centuries of tradition and Christian habit. These "are deliberately being abandoned, clearing the way for new, contemporary forms of worship and belonging."[11] Again, don't misunderstand my point; I am not a proponent of the past for the sake of the past. What I want to get at is the underlying narrative forming these churches. That narrative is revealed in the words: "next," "new," "future," "contemporary," and "new tribe." There is nothing in the article that indicates any reflection on the meaning or nature of the "beginnings," or the truth of the tradition in relation to this juggernaut into the new and the next. The meaning and content of the gospel are simply assumed, but they are not encountered or indwelt. What is indwelt are vague notions of new, future, next, and the unchurched.

11. Trueheart, "Welcome to the Next Church," p. 37.

What is happening is that the "beginnings" are disappearing in the constant work of rewriting the script for every new moment, since the last moment will not do for the new. We need to distinguish between the need for a contextualized church and a theological critique of the context that is grounded in a different narrative. The postmodern context is forever rewriting the script, so that it is continually being born again in ever newer forms. A proper contextuality is one that brings the power of an alternative narrative into an encounter with this reality. This is what is not happening. The postmodern church is forever embracing the new in the name of reaching the unchurched, and therefore is in danger of losing the gospel.

Let me move briefly to a second example of the problem. George Hunter III has recently written a book about the next church called *Church for the Unchurched*.[12] What troubles me most about this book is its underlying claim to certainty, based again on lots of interviews and statistics. There is an air that it has gained clarity on just what the church needs to be like, and here it is. I find it hard to digest or accept this position: this self-possessing certitude about what is right; this endless modern susceptibility to have certainty because you have the data and the definitions. My own pastoral impression is that we struggle to understand the meaning of all the changes happening about us as Christians. Certainty about what we ought to be about is far down the list. As a pastor, I experience not certainty about the way ahead, but a continual struggle to understand, to engage, to see what it might mean to form a faithful, witnessing community in the postmodern setting. This is a consistently difficult task. I think we need to operate by this rule of thumb: When we hear a claim to clarity about what the church should do, the opposite is probably the case.

Hunter's book again identifies a "new" paradigm for being the church in North America. His newly discovered paradigm is the result of extensive research into an emerging topology of church. Like the *Atlantic Monthly* article, it is pretty much the "Next" church group. Only Hunter has his own term for this paradigm. He calls it the "apostolic congregation."[13] Note the fundamentally biblical nature of this word. Here is language rooted in a narrative that goes back to the beginnings. But how is it used? Hunter presents nine churches as rep-

12. Hunter, *Church for the Unchurched.*
13. Hunter, *Church for the Unchurched,* p. 12.

resentative of this "apostolic congregation." The operative meaning of this concept, based on his description of these nine churches, is that they are structured to be churches for the unchurched. But is this what the word *apostolic* actually means?

Hunter's use of this language highlights the point I want to make about the character of the postmodern church. This is not to diminish the importance of the skill and creativity exhibited by the leadership of these nine churches. But the book is a prime example of the problematic, namely, the lack of rootedness in the "beginnings." We find the transmutation of the biblical narrative into a gospel reduced to the categories of the new and the next. The two words, *apostolic* and *mission,* are central to the book's thesis. But their meaning is not determined by the tradition. It is created anew out of the overarching postmodern narrative. *Mission,* for example, is reduced to images of numerical growth. What is it about these nine churches that makes them missional? It is their size. Further, *mission* is reaching the *unchurched,* hence the title of the book: *A Church for the Unchurched.* Thus, *mission* is the growth of the church through the reaching of the unchurched. The new paradigm of the *apostolic congregation* is churches characterized by outstanding skills in growth through reaching the unchurched.

The point is that in this definition of *apostolic congregation* the operative definition comes from the categories of the new and the next, so that the actual meaning of the terms *apostolic* and *mission* disappear. Consequently, the potential of these words to confront and transform the church through an alternative narrative disappears in the move toward the new and the next. The gnosticism of the new displaces the givenness of the tradition, of the beginnings. The myth of the next continually reshapes the meaning of words even while the actual symbols remain the same. Both the tradition and its symbols are thus emptied of their meaning and power.

In the new vocabulary, the word *apostolic* comes to mean churches that grow large because they reach the unchurched. The meaning of the word, in the historical Christian tradition, disappears as it is reshaped to the categories of the postmodern. The book's definition of *apostolic* illustrates the point. In the first chapter, the idea of a new *apostolic age* is linked to two events: the end of Christendom and the demise of the modern (*sic* — the Enlightenment worldview).[14]

14. Hunter, *Church for the Unchurched,* p. 23.

These two events mean that we are, once again, in an "apostolic age," like that of the early church. Somehow, nothing in the last several hundred years of the church's life in Europe or North America could be understood as "apostolic."

Don't misunderstand, I know what Hunter means by using the word in this way. He is describing the *opportunity* the church now has to reach all the non-churched, secular people who are now out there and who need to be reached. The point is not lost, and this passion for people is essential. But, is this what the "beginnings" mean by "apostolic?" Does the narrative of the New Testament permit us to make this argument? I am not trying to split hairs, but rather ask a fundamental question about which narrative shapes our views and our actions. In the postmodern church, exemplified in Hunter's book, the "apostolic" congregations are contemporary, high expectation, innovative, purpose driven, and user friendly.[15]

Hunter then offers a definition of this "apostolic" church. There are three elements to the definition: (1) a belief that the church is sent to reach an unchurched, pre-Christian generation; (2) that its message centers on the gospel of early apostolic Christianity; and (3) that such a church is contextual. Nowhere in the book is there any sustained discussion about the critical meaning of the second point. Everywhere one finds descriptions of what these large churches look like that are reaching the unchurched. Again, my point is that the postmodern church is reductionistic; it collapses the meaning of the gospel into the categories of the new and the next. Such churches may grow, but they do not necessarily function as a demonstration, or as a sign and foretaste of the older narrative about the in-breaking of God's kingdom. It is hard to identify any notion of the social reality of the people of God. Lost is the church as a city set on a hill existing as an alternative community. Baptist theologian James McClendon, in his *Ethics,* put the point in this way:[16]

> . . . the theology of the church is not the standpoint, basic point of view, theology of the world. The church's story will not interpret the world to the world's satisfaction. Hence there is a temptation . . . for the church to deny her "counter, original, spare, strange" start-

15. Hunter, *Church for the Unchurched,* p. 27.
16. James Wm. McClendon, Jr., *Systematic Theology: Ethics* (Nashville: Abingdon Press, 1986), pp. 17-18.

ing point in Abraham and Jesus and to give instead a self-account of theology that will seem true to the world on the world's own present terms. . . . If we yield this point, conspiring to conceal the difference between the church and the world, we may in the short run entice the world, but we will do so only by betraying the church.

So, what of a church in postmodernity as opposed to a postmodern church?

A Church in Postmodernity

I struggle in these times with the Jims and Carols, to give shape to a church that resists the temptation of the new and the next while seeking to be formed by a alternative story. I am a child of my generation. When those children begin singing "the times they are a changin'," a shiver goes up and down my spine. I feel the words. A part of me wants to rush out and join the march. I have been a changer of the old, turning churches around and upside down. I have made them new and next, but now I wonder. Where in all of this is that other Word, the beginnings?

Trying to describe the contours of a church in postmodernity is a risky business. But once the critique has been made, it is incumbent to put one's cards on the table and at least try to express what one, as the leader of a church, thinks it needs to become. I lead what can only be described as one of these eminently postmodern churches. I confess my struggle in trying to articulate the shape such a church should take. The pressure and appeal of being relevant, of living deeply into the individualizing power of my context, are very great. The demands of the new and next are continually at my door. And in the midst of all the conflicting demands of my *Starbucks* church, the images of the "Next" church outlined in *The Atlantic Monthly* are very tempting. I live and lead in a context where, at one level, what is being expressed in that article makes a whole lot of sense. And yet, I struggle with a set of very different images of the church. I wrestle with notions that take me in an alternative direction. But this direction is not popular. It will not win me accolades in the denominational press for my brilliant leadership in multiplying the congregation.

My first response to a church in postmodernity is about the nature of its leadership. What I mean is that beyond the context of the local parish, I need to be part of a community of pastors/priests who are bound in a covenant to walk in a certain direction and be accountable to one another. Without this form of intentional, nonlocal order of apostolic leaders, it will be extremely difficult to indwell a congregation with the life resources needed for this journey. For the kind of journey we need to go on is a long journey in a direction that is not amenable to the fixes of technical rationality.

This leads to a second point about the nature of this leadership. Within the context of such apostolic orders, there need to be disciplines such as being shaped by prayer; wisely using money; and being immersed in Scripture. But, equally important, the heart of this leadership commitment involves a deep immersion in the task of doing theology. My own experience is that the church in postmodernity needs to be comprised of leaders who take the time to drink long and deeply at the intellectual and theological well. This is why I have found the GOCN so crucial for my own formation and journey over these past several years. Without this community of fellow travelers, I would have been tempted to return to the new and the next.

The church in our postmodern context must move in directions fundamentally different from the new and the next as suggested by the "Next" church article or by Hunter's book. This is not to deny their skills, passions, or insights. But their beginning points are basically wrong because they have disconnected the church from the traditions. What then might a church in postmodernity look like? I want to return to the word at the center of Hunter's book: *apostolic*. He reduces this word to describe the actions of churches effectively reaching the unchurched. This is a truncated understanding reduced to the narrative of the new and the next. Its power to address our context is lost.

The idea of the *apostolic* refers primarily to one who is *sent* bearing and announcing a message. So at a basic level *apostolic* means *sent*. This far Hunter is correct. But there is a multilayered meaning to this being *sent*. *Apostolic* implies a focus on the original witness, on the foundational content and proclamation. In other words, the determinative factor is the witness, the content of the message. It is *the faith* of the apostles that makes them apostles and causes them to be sent. Just because some person or group go to encounter, engage, or take a message to another group does not make them apostolic. Scudieri states, "*Apostolic church* refers to the nature of the church as continuously embodying the mission of the Savior of the world. . . . It is really not possible, and it certainly is not beneficial, to separate faith content and missionary action in the term *apostolic church*. Both are necessary."[17]

What legitimizes those who are sent is not, primarily, the methodologies of communication or the needs of the context. It is rather their faithfulness to the unique nature of the message that has been handed on and that needs to be delivered. This is where, I believe, the "Next" church people make the turn toward postmodernity. They assume the words can simply be taken up into the categories of the new and the next. As was said above, when that happens the meaning is reduced to the narratives of postmodernity.

What then is the context that makes the apostle *apostolic?* That context is based on a Word that has been given, located historically in a contextuality that cannot be dismissed or removed. The key to understanding this Word is the Incarnation of Jesus Christ. Minimally this requires a church to find its fundamental grounding and reference point in the Incarnation. Therefore, when we talk about an *apostolic congregation*, we are confessing that the contours and meaning of our existence as such a congregation are rooted in a tradition.

The beginnings are the crucial reference point that cannot be stepped over if there is to be faithfulness to our apostolic nature. First and foremost, this is a church grounded in and based on the Incarnation. The ontological reality of this narrative shapes everything else. It is this narrative that informs and interacts with the context. But it can never be reduced to the categories of the context. The Logos has been revealed (John 1:1-5). Therefore, ecclesial practice in a postmodern context is first shaped by the givenness of the Logos. The new and the next within this context must be intrinsically related and interpreted in relation to this Logos. Practically speaking, and this sounds like strange and irresponsible language in our time, the first concern of the *apostolic congregation* is not the unchurched or the needs of the people who are in the community. The primary focus of the *apostolic*

17. Robert Scudieri, *The Apostolic Church* (Fullerton, Calif.: Lutheran Society of Missiology with R. C. Law & Co., Inc., 1995), p. 73.

congregation is the formation of a people whose life witnesses to the apostolic message.

The formation of such an *apostolic congregation* is grounded in the reality that the message announced and lived by Jesus is not about individualistic salvation. It does not focus on an anthropocentric, needs-oriented, subjective experience. Instead, it is the radical call to enter a new social order. The new birth is the way one moves into this new social reality. Becoming the children of God is a not a "king's kids" good feeling experience, it is citizenship in God's new society. Baptism is the initiatory rite into the vocation of citizenship. The gift of the Spirit is the empowering presence of God living within this new society. What Jesus came to announce and evoke was put in graphic social and political language: the city set on a hill is about a people-hood, about having an identity as a community that is distinct from the established order of things.

Vigen Guroian comments on the way George Meilaender, in his book *Faith and Faithfulness,* takes us back to Basil of Caesarea to make a critical point about the way we shape and direct the church's life. Guroian states that "it was not Basil's first concern to find some common morality grounded in human nature or reason between Christians and non-Christians. He was more interested in exploring the forms of community and discipline that would enable Christians to live the Gospel and show others the way of the kingdom of God. . . . This is the point on which a new *modus vivendi* of the churches in North America must turn in our time as well."[18] I believe this is what it means to be an *apostolic congregation*. If this is so, it will take us in quite a different direction from those offered by the new and the next.

Being *apostolic* does not primarily mean being able to effectively reach the unchurched. Being *missional* does not mean primarily being in a situation so secular that the unchurched are now ready to reconsider the church, if only it will embrace the new and the next. Being *apostolic* and *missional* means embodying a particular way of life that exemplifies the ontological reality of the eschatological future brought into the present by the incarnational reality of Jesus Christ. This requires a church that rather than being "unchurched centered" or "seeker centered," is to be "ecclesially centered." A meaningful

18. Vigen Guroian, *Ethics after Christendom* (Grand Rapids: Eerdmans, 1994), p. 25.

contextuality that has grasped the language and narrative of a postmodern North America will call forth a church that disconnects itself from the need always to seek the new and the next of the culture. Such a contextuality will, instead, seek to recover the call to form a pilgrim people who are strangers and aliens in the land. What this means for the church in postmodernity is best put by Vigen Guroian, ". . . Christians must keep clear in their own minds the difference between the culture's language and their primary language. . . ."[19] This is a call to live into the tradition in a new setting as a pilgrim people being formed as the people of God.

Being an *apostolic* leader involves living like a gardener who is forming a demonstration plot. Such a gardener carves out in the middle of the land a people who are living a distinctively Christian life. But such leadership must begin in confession. The confession is that, beyond some intellectual and theological ideas, most of us who are pastors haven't got a clue how to do this. We have rarely seen it modeled, we have not been schooled in the way of this leadership, and we feel quite alone in the midst of this strange land to which God has taken us. We need to settle in the land and live into our disconnectedness. But we can't do it without becoming part of an intentional order of novices who are committed to apprenticing in the school of the Spirit's work in Babylon.

This is the call to announce by demonstration the existence of a distinctive and alternative community of Jesus Christ. It is a community that has its beginnings in God's action, not in human choice or decision. The lesson here is that the church in postmodernity must seek to demonstrate a distinctive communal form of life in our culture. The challenge of the church in postmodernity is to create a way of life that far transcends anything that Jim or Carol has ever imagined it can mean to be Christian in the name of Jesus.

19. Guroian, *Ethics After Christendom*, p. 101.

Covenant Community:
A Practical Approach to
the Renewal of the Church

PAUL C. DINOLFO

The Scriptures teach that Christians are reborn of the Holy Spirit (1 Peter 1:23), given a new nature (2 Corinthians 5:17), adopted into a new family (Galatians 4:5), made part of a new society (Ephesians 2:19), and called to live a new way of life (Ephesians 4:17). Scripture describes this reality in many different ways.

Christians are to be in the world, but not of it (John 17:14-18). They are to live as aliens in the world (1 Peter 2:11), because their true citizenship is in the kingdom of heaven (Ephesians 2:19). They are to walk in the Spirit and not in the flesh (Galatians 5:16). They are to put away the works of the flesh and put on the fruit of the Spirit (Galatians 5:19-24). In other words, Christians are to behave in accordance with their new nature. Even a casual reading of the New Testament leads one to the conclusion that becoming a Christian is supposed to result in a radical change in one's life.

This new way of life is distinctly different from that which unbelievers live in the surrounding society. The Christian's way of life is to be shaped in every aspect by Jesus Christ, the perfect image of the Father. Anything less is logically, morally, and biblically inconsistent. As a popular slogan states it: "Either Jesus is Lord of all, or He is not Lord at all."

Christians are to resist the influence of the surrounding society and avoid conforming to it (Romans 12:2). They are given specific instruction covering major areas of life, including relationships, courtship, marriage, family life, work, and finances. Often they are specifically warned not to follow the specific practices of the surrounding culture (see 1 Thessalonians 4:4-8).

One of the most serious challenges confronting the church today is the loss of a distinctly Christian way of life. Christianity is no longer the primary organizing principle that shapes the lives of most Christians. The dominant, decisive forces shaping the personal lives of most Christians are secular. Furthermore, the dominant trends within secular society have become increasingly antithetical to Christianity.

Much of the traditional Judeo-Christian understanding of right and wrong has washed out of the social moral order. By some strange logic, abortion has become a fundamental right of women. Homosexuality has been transformed from a serious developmental and behavioral problem to a perfectly acceptable lifestyle choice. Childhood temper tantrums, disobedience, and teenage rebellion, previously thought to be matters requiring parental discipline, are now viewed as natural stages of childhood development. Premarital sex has become normative. Any sexual practice is now seen as acceptable as long as it is between consenting adults. Lifelong commitment to one's spouse and children is now subordinate to the pursuit of self-fulfillment and personal happiness. Covetousness has become virtuous and necessary to a healthy economy.

Sadly, such views are held not only by secular society but also by a growing number within the church. Too often there is scant difference between the behavior of Christians and of non-Christians. The divorce rate among Christians is now within two percent of the national average.[1] Christian teenagers are as likely as their secular peers to have premarital sex.[2]

Often the church mirrors secular society, or places a Christian veneer on it, as seen in the wealth and prosperity gospel and the use of

---

1. Larry Burkett, *The Complete Financial Guide for Young Couples* (Wheaton, Ill.: Victor Books, 1993), p. 11.

2. Kevin Perotta and Kevin Springer, "A Revolution in Premarital Sex," *Pastoral Renewal* (June 1982): 92-93.

a therapeutic approach in many churches. How Christians approach their jobs, relationships, money, possessions, family, and time is usually shaped more by the values and practices of the surrounding secular culture than by Christian thought and convictions. As a result, the lives of Christians often differ little from those of unbelievers.

Perhaps the biggest loss has been the loss of Christian community. American individualism has thoroughly permeated our understanding of what it means to be a Christian. As a result, it is not uncommon for Christians to believe that regular participation and involvement in a church is an optional element of the Christian life.

The word "community" itself has been stripped of its meaning and redefined. Whereas community formerly involved the maintenance of stable, usually lifelong, committed relationships, today we "create community" by meeting and sharing as a small group for a few weeks.

The cost to the church and society has been great. The weakening of the church and family as supportive networks of relationships, values, and culture has accelerated the process of secularization. The relational networks of church and family, in addition to providing social support for their members, also serve as intervening social environments that hinder the secular state's efforts to reshape the beliefs and practices of the individual. The loss or weakening of intervening social environments like the family and the church community makes it more difficult for the individual to resist the propaganda of the secular state and culture.[3] Thus, as American Christians become increasingly individualistic and less communal, one would predict that they would also become increasingly secular in their values and practices. This is, of course, exactly was has been happening over the past fifty years.

Another consequence of the loss of community is a decline in spiritual power. The story of the Tower of Babel in Genesis illustrates the natural power of a united human community. God intervenes to weaken the human community by confusing their languages (Genesis 11:6-9). Pentecost is, among other things, a reversal of the Tower of Babel. The confusion of tongues at Babel is overturned (Acts 2:5-11). The new community is formed, accompanied by a great outpouring of spiritual power (Acts 2:41-47).

3. Jacques Ellul, *The Technological Society* (New York: Vintage Books, 1964).

Finally, the loss of community is a tragedy for the church because community is inseparable from Christianity. Thus, the loss of community presents the church with an integrity crisis. The communal nature of the church is not some peripheral quality or characteristic. It is central precisely because God, the Trinity, Three in One, presents to us a perfect community. The church is designed by God to reflect his nature, which is communal. To the extent that the church loses its communal nature, it ceases to reflect God, and thus it ceases to be the church.

Nehemiah: A Case Study in Renewal

The book of Nehemiah is very instructive in suggesting a strategy for renewing a secularized church. Nehemiah faced a situation, much like ours, in which the Old Testament people of God had neglected or rejected his ways. The people had rejected God's laws regarding courtship and marriage, keeping the Sabbath, forgiveness of debts, tithing, and worship (chapter 8 and 10:30-39).

When Ezra read the book of the law to the people and they realized their sin, their response was to repent (8:9) and to make an explicit covenant agreement to change, both before God and toward one another (9:38). All of the people made a personal commitment to this covenant. The covenant was very specific in addressing each of the areas wherein the people had been failing (chapter 10). They made a "renewal covenant": a solemn corporate commitment to rededicate themselves to living out their existing covenant relationship, specifically highlighting the areas most at issue in their contemporary situation. Other Scriptural examples of renewal covenants would include that of Joshua (Joshua 24:14-28) and the reforms under King Asa (2 Chronicles 15:12). I believe that this model of renewal covenants is applicable to renewal within the church today.

Nehemiah sought to renew the people of God in a time of nearly universal apostasy or secularization, much like our situation today. When the people received the Word of God and were convicted by the Holy Spirit, Nehemiah used the instrument of a renewal covenant to turn their good intentions into something more lasting.

Their covenant didn't simply speak in generalities. It was very specific in restoring what had been lost of their Godly way of living.

Together, the people committed themselves to obeying God in those very areas that had fallen into disrepute, or had been neglected. The renewal covenant they made reestablished them as a Godly community, a community whose identity, lifestyle, and practices were shaped by the rule of God.

It's also worth noting that Nehemiah began his reforms by working with a relatively small group of people. The Jews at this time were scattered throughout the Middle East and Eastern Europe. Only a handful were living in Jerusalem. Nevertheless, Nehemiah understood that if those in Jerusalem were renewed, gradually the renewal would spread out to other Jews. Jesus instructed his disciples to follow this same strategy by beginning in Jerusalem, moving on to Judea and Samaria, and finally going out to the ends of the earth (Acts 1:8).

Those interested in the renewal of the church today could take a lesson from Nehemiah. First, rather than working to renew the whole congregation or denomination at once, they might focus their efforts on those individuals, or groups of individuals, who are exhibiting signs of spiritual openness and renewal. Second, they would do well to look for ways to bring those who are experiencing renewal together, so that they might support and strengthen one another. Third, they should consider using some type of explicit commitment, such as a covenant, to unify the community's resolve toward living a corporate Christian lifestyle. This commitment needs to be clear and specific enough that those making it understand what they are aiming at and seeking to restore. For example, the covenant of my community, the Work of Christ, includes a commitment to daily prayer and Scripture, worship, Christian service, tithing, sharing resources, hospitality, and outreach.

What Is a Covenant Community?

A covenant community is a group of Christians who have made a stable commitment to each other and to God. The commitment that community members make to one another is not a one-year experiment or a summer experience. Christian community involves a long-term, normally lifelong, commitment among the members.

Covenant communities are concrete, practical expressions of the spiritual reality that, as children of the same Father, we are now brothers and sisters, who are members of the same family (Matthew 12:48-50 and Ephesians 2:19-22). Covenant communities are concrete, practical expressions of the New Testament communities, adapted to the circumstances of modern culture. While covenant communities vary, all share at least five characteristics:

1. They all have some form of common worship and a way of life formed by Christian teaching.
2. There is frequent interaction and relationship among the members.
3. All have instituted some form of financial and resource sharing.
4. There is a strong sense of mission and call to devote significant resources to outreach.
5. The members are interdependent with one another in practical ways.

Many people are attracted to the idea or concept of community. However, true community requires making a personal commitment to other persons and becoming accountable to them. This means being committed to Pete and Joe, or to Susan and Mary, even with all their faults and weaknesses.

Commitment is necessarily voluntary, based on a personal conviction that God has called each member to the community. For this reason several years of formation and discernment are often required before new members are allowed to make a full commitment. In most covenantal communities the initiation process often requires three to five years.

Relating Covenantal Communities to the Church

One of the first questions that usually comes up in any discussion among committed Christians is how a covenant community is related to the church. It is always a challenge to answer this question because there are so many different understandings of what the church is among Christians. To some Christians, it seems obvious that a covenant community is a model church. To others, a covenant community is obviously not a church, and they have difficulty understanding why it appears to be in competition with the church.

In spite of the challenge presented by differing ecclesiologies, I will try my best to answer this question. Over the past twenty years, I have seen three models for relating a covenant community to the local church, each with its own strengths and weaknesses.

Community Church Model

The first approach is what might be called the community church model. This is by far the most common model among Protestants, and it is actually quite simple: the members belong to the community, which is also their local church. This model has the advantage of being easy to understand and relatively straightforward to implement. Unfortunately, it normally works well only for small, independent church plants. There are some theological difficulties in equating a renewal community with the church, such as the issue of how a covenant community church can demand more of its members than the church demands. In addition, a community laying claim to be a church will find it difficult to uphold its way of life. For example, on what basis might a covenant community church justify excluding members who fail to pray daily or share their goods freely? Of course, ecumenical community is very difficult with this model.

Parachurch Model

The second approach is the parachurch model. In this model the members belong to the community, and the members also belong to one or more local churches. This model has the advantage that membership is always based on a personal choice, whereas God requires all Christians to be members of the church. Thus, it provides a rationale for upholding the community's way of life, in the same way that a missionary organization can rightly insist that its members be missionaries. Ecumenical community is possible under this model.

However, this model is not without its problems. Its members belong to two Christian bodies and relate to two separate pastoral authorities. At the minimum it makes life for the members more complex as they seek to be faithful to two sets of commitments and relationships. Still, this model has the advantage of allowing community to be formed among those who are ready and open. They might all be from one local church, or they might be from many different churches. Since finding enough interested people to begin a community is usually the greatest practical challenge, this represents a significant advantage. This model seems to work best for ecumenical community and often for church renewal.

Church Association Model

The third approach is the church association model. In this model the members belong to the community, and the community as a whole belongs to a church. Usually this means that the community exists within a local church. Reba Place Fellowship in Evanston, Illinois, is a good example of this approach. However, in some denominations, such as the Roman Catholic and Lutheran, the community could be set up as a special organization within the church akin to a religious order.[4] The advantages of this approach are numerous. Members belong to two complementary bodies and relate to two complementary pastoral authorities. The special status of the community allows a sound basis for upholding the community's way of life. There are even examples of church bodies that have approved denominational subgroupings within an ecumenical community in a variation of this model.[5] A disadvantage of this model is that it is complex, and often requires competencies beyond the pastoral capabilities of small communities. Also, it usually requires the support of denominational leaders, who may at times be reluctant to support such an approach. Nevertheless, this approach holds, I believe, much hope for the future.

4. Christ the King Association is an example within the Roman Catholic Church. See Stephen B. Clark, *Covenant Community and Church* (Ann Arbor, Mich.: Servant Publications, 1992).

5. Examples I am aware of include Arbol de Vida Community in Costa Rica, People of God Community in Lebanon, and Servant of the Lamb Community in New Zealand.

Contributions by Covenant Communities to the Church

Covenant communities can contribute in many ways to the church. Because of their small size, high level of commitment, and flexible structure, they have greater freedom to develop Christian approaches to areas of life that are most challenging in the circumstances of modern culture. For example, my community has developed a Christian approach to courtship that has proven to be very successful, and could easily be modified for use in singles groups in most church contexts.[6] The Sword of the Spirit communities have practiced a form of cooperative ecumenism for over twenty years that holds much promise for interchurch cooperation.[7] Covenant communities also can serve as a more intense or developed witness to the goodness of the Christian approach to a specific area of ministry, such as family life, service to the poor, evangelism, or ministry to the aged.

Communities can serve as models and witnesses to the essentially communal nature of the church and the gospel. They encourage other Christians to an increased level of community life. For example, Bill McCartney, the founder of Promise Keepers, first experienced accountability within a men's group that functioned as a covenant community. By their witness, communities also demonstrate the value of working together, especially in areas where there is little outside support for a Christian approach. My community's experience with courtship is an example of this.

Communities can serve other Christians and churches directly. Many members serve within their respective local church. In my community our members serve as deacons, elders, youth group leaders, Sunday school teachers, musicians, ushers, and greeters; they serve in the choir, on church councils and committees, and in the church schools.

Communities as a whole can also serve the local church directly. While each community has differing charisms and ministries, they all seek to serve the wider body of Christ in some way. Many communities offer local conferences, retreats, or seminars. Often they have so-

---

6. Several hundred couples have followed this approach over the past twenty years. The divorce rate among these couples is 2 to 3 percent.

7. *How to Be Ecumenical Today* (Dexter, Mich.: Tabor House, 1996).

cial and evangelistic outreaches to the area. For example, my community runs a food buying club and day-care center. We sponsor a 4-H chapter in the neighborhood around our community center. We have evangelistic outreaches to high school and university students and to young singles and couples. Many of those who benefit from these outreaches do not and never will belong to our community.

Communities can serve the broader church as well. Many communities sponsor regional conferences and retreats.[8] Some publish magazines, newsletters, and books. Some develop ministries that become major contributions to the body of Christ. Habitat for Humanity began as an outreach of Koinonia Partners in Americus, Georgia.

The Future of Covenant Communities

I believe that covenant communities hold much promise for the future. Those familiar with the history of covenant communities in the United States know that they have often suffered internal problems, and many have failed to survive more than a few years. Nevertheless, I am aware of scores of communities now nearing their twentieth or twenty-fifth anniversaries. Having survived a host of common difficulties, these communities are developing into maturity.

In addition, I also perceive a greater openness on the part of both communities and churches to work together. Many of the ideas that have been developed in communities can be adapted and transferred to other settings. Covenant communities are intended to be a blessing to the church. The main challenge confronting these communities in the days ahead are to remain faithful to their callings, especially the call to community, and to find ever more fruitful ways of serving and relating to the church.

8. For example, my community recently presented a seminar on "Abstinence, Dating, and Youth Groups" for church leaders and youth workers in our area.

Reaching Out without Dumbing Down: A Theology of Worship for the Church in Postmodern Times[1]

MARVA J. DAWN

A recent cartoon illustrates a problem that plagues many churches that are trying to respond to dwindling membership in postmodern times. In an effort to appeal to religious consumers, these churches become like "Saint Happy's: The Worship Place," where the slogan is "Have It Thy Way." While selecting from the overhead menu their preferences for "Liturgy Lite" or "Kiddy Kristianity," shoppers can also order "feelgood filet" or "happy homily" among other choices for sermons. They can sing "jingles for Jesus" or "boomer beat" or other happy tunes, pick their favorite kinds of bread and juice/wine from the communion bar, and sample side orders of "12-step groups" or "12-holes golf." Down on the service counter between the male and female pastors waiting to take orders is the ad, "Hey Kids! Collect: 'Pastors of the Universe Action Figures.'"

What does it take to attract the baby boomers to our churches for worship? That question, which is being asked by more and more mainline and evangelical churches, reveals a terrible confusion be-

---

1. For a fuller explication of the ideas in this article, see Marva J. Dawn, *Reaching Out without Dumbing Down: A Theology of Worship for the Turn-of-the-Century Culture* (Grand Rapids: Eerdmans, 1995).

tween evangelism and worship. It also invites many of the culture's idolatries into our sanctuaries, and leads to the "dumbing down" illustrated by the cartoon noted above. My goal is to help churches ask better questions about the meaning and purposes of worship, and to develop a theological approach to worship in postmodern times.

The Difference between Worship and Evangelism

Since my husband of seven years is an elementary school teacher, I have an 8″ x 10″ school photograph of him to carry around in my briefcase. When conducting workshops on worship, I show the participants his picture and tell them all about him — what a wonderful teacher he is, how great a gardener, how gentle and kind a person, how generously he takes care of me in the struggles of my physical handicaps. But is that how I will talk to him when I get home after being gone for several days of speaking engagements?

No! When I arrive at the Portland airport, he will be waiting with deep love in his eyes. He will take the burdens of my backpack and suitcase and will escort me to the car, help me get seated, and take me home. When I see him, I will tell him how much I love him, how terribly I miss him when we're apart, how thankful I am that he supports me in my work of teaching. He will remind me of his attributes by the ways he welcomes me home, communicates his love for me, shows me what he has done in the yard. Myron's love for me makes me a different person.

This is the difference between evangelism and worship. In the former, we talk about God to others. We tell of the Trinity's attributes and care for the world, and prayerfully invite those to whom we speak to also love our Creator, Redeemer, and Sanctifier. The focus is on those to whom we speak. Worship, in contrast, focuses on God. We worship only because God comes to us, loves us first, and enables us to worship. We respond with love and gratitude, adoration and praise. And in the worship service, we learn more about God's character and intervention in history, and we are formed by that knowledge and the Spirit's power into the likeness of Christ.

Nowhere in the Bible does any writer say, "Worship the LORD to attract the unbeliever." Rather, the Scriptures instruct us to "sing

271

to the LORD a new song, for he has done marvelous things" (Ps. 98:1). The Psalmist declares,

> The LORD is great in Zion;
>   he is exalted over all the peoples.
> Let them praise your great and awesome name.
>   Holy is he!
> Mighty King, lover of justice,
>   you have established equity;
> you have executed justice
>   and righteousness in Jacob.
> Extol the LORD our God;
>   worship at his footstool.
> Holy is he!
>
> (Ps. 99:2-5, NRSV)

The failure to understand such biblical invitations to worship was demonstrated by a speaker before me at a recent "Great Commission Convocation." He said that churches should have at least two styles of worship in order to create two points of entry for non-members into the congregation. This is a severely harmful misconception, for *worship is not the point of entry. You are!* God wants 490 points of entry, if a congregation has 490 members. Ninety-five percent of genuine conversions (and not just sheep-stealing from other congregations) happen through friendship. So worship must form believers to be the kind of friends who will introduce others to Christ and then bring them to worship the God in whom they have come to believe. If the worship service has been designed as evangelism instead of worship, it is pointed in the wrong direction.

Don't misunderstand me. Good worship will be evangelistic. When believers praise God with all their hearts, and souls, and minds, and strength, nonbelievers who are present will be moved.

Nevertheless, the difference between worship and evangelism is crucially important. Churches who confuse the two place on worship the burden of their failure to equip all the members to be evangelists in daily life. Both worship and evangelism are then reduced, and the character of the believers and of the community suffers as a result.

Idolatries That Invade the Church

The articles in this book emphasize the progression from culture to gospel by means of the church. Richard Mouw stressed that Christians must first understand the culture to find a point of contact by which we can communicate.[2] In order to discern the various aspects of our society that influence worship, we need to focus on the way certain values in the culture become idolatrous as they invade our congregations. Recognizing our own temptations not only helps us to sympathize with nonbelievers, but also reveals some of the forces that deflect our worship services from their biblical purposes. Participants who have attended my workshop sessions have often listed the following as idolatries related to worship:

materialism	spiritualism
bigger	smaller
the new	the old
traditionalism	contemporaryism
the 90s sound	favorite old hymns
organs	guitars
musical élite/classical	combos/contemporary
anonymity	the inner circle
order	chaos
haughty ritual	no ritual
quiet	no silence
homogeneity	diversity for its own sake
knowledge	feeling
lay	élite, professionalism
optimism	pessimism

musical style, particular liturgical form
entertainment, feeling good, comfort
vicarious subjectivity, performance
busyness, efficiency
a charismatic personality
expectations for what one will get
looks, show, makeup, clothes

2. Richard Mouw, "The Missionary Location of the North-American Churches," pp. 7-10.

competition, success, numbers
clericalism
choice, consumer mentality

I have refrained from imposing any order on this list. Recognition of possible idolatries by various participating groups was recorded randomly, although, obviously, sometimes one insight would touch off several others. Sometimes the way an idolatry affects worship is not immediately obvious. It is not my purpose to go into that discussion here. What is important is to consider carefully how various cultural and religious idolatries tend to infiltrate congregational worship. Many of the idolatries on the list are paired as dialectical opposites because both aspects are usually necessary in worship and both can be taken to unhealthy extremes. Many of the items on the list can be helpful attributes for shaping the character of a congregation, until they are pursued excessively or understood rigidly. All of us who plan, or lead, or participate in worship must be wary lest personal tastes or ideologies determine our choices and reactions. We must ask better questions about the meaning of worship.

This Is Not Just My Opinion

In a postmodern world, where few people believe that there is any absolute or objective truth, theologians are easily accused of foisting their own opinions on others if they suggest that some things might be normative for Christian life and behavior. Recently a young high school student asked my opinion on a moral issue. After I had carefully described some of the moral dimensions involved in the subject, she turned away saying, "I just wanted to know your opinion." "That was not my opinion," I responded. "If I had given you my opinion, I would have said the opposite."

I, too, would like to excuse some behaviors and let people choose whatever lifestyle they want. But do we really love others if we allow them to rebel against God's designs for his human creation? God's immense love and mercy for me compel me to be faithful to his Word. If the narratives of the Scriptures are to form us to be God's people, then I must use my best tools to study the Bible and be submissive to what is learned. This does not make God's Word oppressive, for the biblical narratives convince me that God commands what is good, and transforms his people into believers who want to live his best.

In a culture that deconstructs words by its prevailing philosophy and evacuates them of meaning through its "gigantesque logorrhea,"[3] I believe in a God who reveals himself, speaks to us through the Scriptures, and tells the Truth because he is the Truth. Thus, I am convinced that from God's Word we can draw some criteria by which to assess what we do in worship. Using these criteria, we can choose the best forms and materials for biblically faithful worship, and begin to defuse the worship wars between the traditionalists and the contemporaryists, between the clergy and the musicians, between the professionals and the layperson. Worship is a moral issue, for how it is conducted can form participants to be narcissistically turned inward, or form them to follow Jesus in crucifying servanthood. What questions does the Word give us to help us think more theologically, biblically, and faithfully about worship? The next three sections emphasize three fundamental criteria that I believe the biblical canon gives us for assessing what we do in worship and why.

Who Is Worship For?

Pardon my bad grammar; it is intentional. We have already noted in this article that worship is for God, in contrast to evangelism, which is for the unbeliever. Rather than ask my question with the proper construction — *"for whom* is worship?" — I want to focus here first on God as the Who, the Subject of our worship. God is the one who makes it possible for us to enter into his presence; God is the one who gives us himself in the Word, the water, and the supper. How we conduct the worship must teach all the participants that, and help enfold them into that reality. It is not the pastor who invites us into his or her living room, but God who welcomes us into a holy place set apart to honor him.

3. Jacques Ellul uses this phrase in "Notes innocentes sur la 'question hermeneutique'," *L'Evangile, hier et aujourd'hui: Mélanges offerts au professeur Franz J. Leenhardt* (Genève: Editions Labor et fides, 1968), p. 188. There he complains about "the abuse of language in advertising, propaganda, gigantesque logorrhea of information, mixing thousands of insignificant information(al bit)s with one or two significant ones. . . ."

This truth leads to many questions that we who plan worship and the worship space must ask. Does the order of worship clearly reflect that God is the Subject? Is there too much focus on the pastor or musicians that would detract from participants' awareness that God is the inviter? Does the worship space reveal God's special presence? Do the participants' attitudes, the leaders' demeanors and gestures, and the worship ambience keep God as the Subject?

Is the God portrayed by our worship the biblical God of Abraham and Sarah, of Joseph and Mary? Does our worship focus one-sidedly on comfortable aspects of God's character, such as his mercy and love, without the dialectical balancing of his holiness and wrath? Is Jesus reduced to an immanent "buddy" or "brother" without the accompanying transcendence of God's infinite majesty? Is the Trinity diminished to merely rigid doctrines without the unsettling winds of the Spirit? Indeed, the church needs more doctrine these days, not less, but not rigidly so. All these questions ask whether our worship really keeps the God of the Bible as its Subject.

God is, of course, also the Object of our worship, so indeed we do properly ask as well, "For whom is worship?" We respond to the Trinity's wooing, give thanks for the Creator's grace, praise Christ's name, ask for the Spirit's empowerment. However, unless we see God first as Subject, we cannot really answer the true adoration. Sadly, many contemporary worship leaders confuse genuine praise with happy songs, and thus cater to personal fun or comfort as the object instead of naming the attributes and actions of God. Older hymns sometimes made the same mistake (such songs as "I Come to the Garden Alone"), but such narcissism was less likely in earlier eras that were more communally directed and more theologically substantive.

Two aspects of worship contribute especially to the loss of God as both the Subject and Object. One is the architecture. Older sanctuaries, by their cross-shape and lofty height and their visual focus on the altar, could keep worship participants' gaze on God. The placement of the organist and the choir in the balcony permitted them to be servants of worship instead of performers. However, long naves looking toward elevated pulpits share modern church architecture's problem of putting the preacher (and usually now the musicians) on stage. Worship attenders in contemporary and traditional spaces must all be reminded that they are — each one — the actors in worship, that the leaders are not there to perform but to direct the action, that

God is the audience (object) of the work of the people (the Greek *leitourgia* or liturgy). Conversely, we can only be actors in worship because God acted first as Subject, and because God continues to speak to us, the audience, through texts, sermons, hymns, and liturgy.

The second aspect that especially dethrones God in worship is the reduction of the gifts of the people to merely the financial offering.[4] We have for many years failed to train believers in the meaning of worship, so that now attenders frequently say, "I didn't get much out of that service," without realizing that the problem is their failure to put much into it. Furthermore, the lack of heartfelt participation by parents is the chief contributor to their children's rejection of all that worship means.

I have asked my seventh- and eighth-grade confirmation students how many of them liked the formal liturgy that our church uses, and their answers matched one for one. Every youth who hated it was the child of a father who didn't sing it. Research confirms that the influence of fathers' worship practices on the retention of their children in faith far outweighs the influence of mothers. Most desirable, of course, is the active participation in the Christian community and worship of both parents.

I hear frequently from youth directors that the kids with whom they work reject the worship style of their parents. I think it is deeper than that. I am convinced that youth reject instead the phoniness of parents who go through the motions of worship, but whose daily lives are not transformed by it. Similarly, it is not usually the liturgy that alienates worshipers; it is the lack of Joy[5] with which it is conducted. Everywhere, as I travel throughout the world in my freelancing work, I see people who love worship because they know what it means; they know Who invites them into its holiness. By the previous paragraph I am not rejecting new styles and forms for worship. I am only rejecting the false questions. Style is not the issue. The genuine worship of GOD is.

---

4. See especially C. Welton Gaddy, *The Gift of Worship* (Nashville: Broadman Press, 1992), on the subject of offerings in worship.

5. I purposely capitalize this word, for I do not mean simple exuberance, happiness, or excitement. I use the word to signify that deep, abiding confidence and gratitude that is ours when we know God as the Subject, when our lives are transformed by the truth of the Resurrection, and when we genuinely worship God and not ourselves.

How Christian People Are Formed

Elsewhere in this volume, William R. Burrows emphasizes that the role of the church is to create people of faith.[6] Worship is one of the chief means for doing that. If we continually sing self-centered songs, we become self-centered persons. If we hear texts and sermons that show us God's concern for peace and justice in the world and encourage us to participate in his work and purposes, we are formed to be reconcilers and justice builders. If the messages in worship cater to our desire for comfort and coziness, we are abetted in our idolatries. If our hymns and songs keep God as the Subject and Object, we are nurtured in responsive faith and knowledge and love.

To ask what kind of people are formed by what we do in worship is to miss the point about worship styles. All kinds of musical and sermonic styles can contribute to cultivating godly character. Many choices of forms and worship components militate against developing genuine discipleship.

The issue of character formation by the church is critical in a declining culture of intense narcissism,[7] where young people are being molded by the escalating greed, violence, and sexual immorality with which they are constantly bombarded by the media. Christian parents and educators must seriously question how they can counteract — or eliminate — the influence of Roseanne and the Terminators if they want their children to follow Jesus.[8]

In an age of biblical illiteracy how can we teach the Scriptures in all their life-changing possibilities? One of the best gifts of contemporary music is a renewed emphasis on singing verses from the Bible. More obscure biblical images in older hymns, such as the "Ebenezer" of "Come, Thou Fount of Every Blessing," need to be explained, but are well worth the trouble for the rich biblical narratives they symbolize. Sermons must become more focused on the Scriptures themselves and the character of God and less on human speculation and opinions.

6. William R. Burrows, "Witness to the Gospel and Refounding the Church," pp. 197-200.

7. See especially Christopher Lasch, *The Culture of Narcissism: American Life in an Age of Diminishing Expectations* (New York: W. W. Norton, 1979).

8. See Neil Postman, *Amusing Ourselves to Death: Public Discourse in the Age of Show Business* (New York: Viking Penguin, 1985), on the influence of television on our thought and lives.

Most of all, if we are to be faithful, our worship must form us to be people of the cross. In a time when even some theologians are denouncing the foolishness of the cross of Jesus and the doctrine of the Atonement, we need to proclaim their truth and power and invite worship participants to respond by taking up their crosses, too. A good example of such faithfulness is found in the article by James V. Brownson on "Hearing the Gospel Again, for the First Time.[9]

Christian Community as a Parallel Society

In the epilogue of this book you will find the reflections of Mary Jo Leddy.[10] She cites Czech President Václav Havel's description that communism was defeated by the presence of the "parallel society" of those who rejected its lies and lived the truth instead whenever and wherever possible. They wrote their plays, read their poems, and believed in alternatives until they grew so strong that they could expose the inherent weaknesses of communism, and it had to fall.

In our post-Christian culture, the true church must be a similar sort of parallel society. When we gather for worship, we are formed by biblical narratives that tell a different story from that of the world around us. We have come to know the truth that sets us free and are eager to share that with the world around us, so we need worship that equips us for that mission. Rather than being a "vendor of religious goods and services," the church is called to be a "body of people sent on a mission."[11] The alternative Christian community must be an inclusive one. Our worship practices must form us to be hospitable, to welcome strangers, to provide a public space,[12] to invite newcomers, to tell others about our faith, to care for members of the community who are missing from corporate

---

9. James V. Brownson, "Hearing the Gospel Again, for the First Time," pp. 127-40.

10. Mary Jo Leddy, "The People of God as a Hermeneutic of the Gospel." pp. 303-13.

11. See George Hunsberger, "Sizing Up the Shape of the Church," Hunsberger and Van Gelder, eds., *The Church between Gospel and Culture* (Grand Rapids: Eerdmans, 1996), pp. 333-46.

12. Patrick R. Keifert, *Welcoming the Stranger: A Public Theology of Worship and Evangelism* (Minneapolis: Fortress Press, 1992).

gatherings,[13] to value each other in the great mix of ages, social classes, races, and gifts among God's people. One of my worries about congregations who create both a traditional service and a contemporary one is that the division in style almost always leads to a split by ages. The result is that the older people who usually choose the former miss the delights of fellowship with children, and the younger families who attend the latter lack the opportunity to gain from the wisdom of longtime believers.

Are our churches being formed to be inclusive of the handicapped, of various social classes and races? Do our worship services provide interpreters or earphones for the hearing impaired, large print hymnals for the partially sighted, wheelchair accessibility? I belong to a black, inner-city congregation that gives me, a white person, the opportunity to learn from my African-American sisters and brothers. It is a congregation devoted to its neighborhood and offering room in its building for scouts, African dance classes, economic development groups, and the local black history month celebrations. Worship there utilizes a wide variety of musical styles from black gospel and Lutheran hymns, to modern Bible verse choruses, to Taizé refrains.

Most of all, do our worship services make participants aware that they are members not merely of this local congregation, but of the entire Christian Church throughout space and time? When we say the Apostles' Creed, we are linked to saints in Poland and Madagascar who are saying it, too. (This tangible link of a common faith was a great delight for me when I was lecturing at seminaries in those two countries and a memoried connection to my friends there after I returned home.) When we sing the *Sanctus* ("Holy, holy, holy LORD God of power and might . . ."), no matter what style of music, we are united to God's people all the way back to Isaiah and to the angels whose version of it he recorded (Isaiah 6:3).

Congregations are not necessarily communities just because they are churches. Too many forces in our technological milieu prevent us from being genuine communities that deeply care for each other. For a model of true Christian community, we need to return to

13. There is an excellent evangelism questionnaire from St. John Lutheran Church, Northumberland, Penn., in Jim Peterson, "Join the Crowd," *The Lutheran,* October 1995, 40.

the description of the earliest church right after Pentecost in Acts 2:42-47. Our culture is characterized by a loss of skills for intimacy in inverse correlation with the rise of technicization.[14] If parishes seek to be communities of biblical faithfulness, that will require much effort and training.[15] The worship service provides the fundamental biblical narrative of community and the experience of community members being drawn closer to each other like spokes on a wheel as they draw closer to the Center, who is Christ.

Worship in the Missional Church

If the church's worship is to equip its members to be missional in their daily lives, it cannot be planned according to what will appeal to those who do not yet know the One who calls us into mission. Questions about marketing and the appeal of musical style or liturgical form usually miss the point. Rather, these three criteria establish essential foundations for worship:

1. That the biblical God be the Subject and Object of worship;
2. That worship form believers to be disciples, following Jesus and committed to God's purposes of peace, justice, and salvation in the world;
3. That worship form the congregation to be a genuine, inclusive Christian community linked to all God's people throughout time and space — in doctrine, fellowship, the breaking of bread, prayers, signs and wonders, care, and social involvement.

These criteria will raise questions of integrity, propriety, coherence, and diversity to guide our choices of worship songs and other elements. Many musical styles can be utilized, but the texts of songs will be theologically sound, and the melodies and accompaniments will offer God our best gifts. Many sermonic forms may be used, but the Word of God will be central to the dramas, and read-

14. Marva J. Dawn, *Sexual Character: Beyond Technique to Intimacy* (Grand Rapids: Eerdmans, 1993), pp. 12-19.

15. Marva J. Dawn, *Truly the Community: Romans 12 and How to Be the Church* (Grand Rapids: Eerdmans, 1992).

ings, and expositions. The grace of God will call us to be his people in response.

If the worship services of our congregations follow these guidelines, then the participants will be equipped to reach out to the culture around them in words of gospel truth and deeds of gospel faithfulness. God grant the church such worship — for his glory and for the love of the world!

Riding the Waves of Change: How to Facilitate Change toward a Missionary Identity

JON M. HUEGLI

As Kennon Callahan recently observed, "[T]he day of the churched culture is over. The day of the mission field has come."[1] In such a setting, the church's role is to bridge the gap between God's kingdom and the context of the culture in which it finds itself. In this regard, Lesslie Newbigin has called for a missionary encounter of the gospel with our own Western culture. He writes:

> Ours is not as we once imagined a secular society, it is a pagan society and its paganism having been born out of the rejection of Christianity is far more resistant to the gospel than the pre-Christian paganism with which cross-cultural missions have been familiar. Here, surely, is the most challenging missionary frontier of our time . . . how can we be missionaries to this modern world, we who are ourselves part of this modern world?[2]

---

1. Kennon L. Callahan, *Effective Church Leadership* (San Francisco: Harper & Row, 1990), p. 13.
2. Lesslie Newbigin, *Foolishness to the Greeks: The Gospel and Western Culture* (Grand Rapids: Eerdmans, 1986), p. 20.

Today we are attempting to define this "pagan" culture and our relationship as missionary churches to it.

This chapter has many purposes. The first is to develop a model of "missionary church effectiveness" for the local congregation. The second is to identify some fundamental inhibitors or blockages to that effectiveness which need to be changed. The third is to recommend some changes that could release local church ministry for missionary identity. And the last is to introduce the dynamics of change as they affect individuals and churches.

Missionary Church Effectiveness

A congregation behaves like an open system. It is porous, flexible, responsive, and self-correcting as it attempts to critique and influence its cultural setting and shape the lives of the people living within it, by utilizing the unchanging standards of the Bible. George Hunsberger noted that the gospel-culture encounter always unfolds in a Christian community as a twofold dialogue: the gospel dialogue that God has with us within our culture, and the dialogue we then have as we represent the gospel to others who share our culture.[3] John Hendrick's six characteristics of a missionary congregation provide a framework for describing today's effective missionary congregation. There are certainly other factors and criteria to use, but let us begin with these.

1. A *missionary congregation* will understand that it exists in a cross-cultural situation.
2. A *missionary congregation* will enter into dialogue with its context and culture.
3. A *missionary congregation* will provide opportunities for its members to reflect on culture from a biblical view.
4. A *missionary congregation* will pray for and seek its own transformation.
5. A *missionary congregation* will accept the marginal position in which it finds itself.

3. George R. Hunsberger, "The Newbigin Gauntlet: Developing a Domestic Missiology for North America," *Missiology: An International Review* 19, (4): 391-408.

6. A *missionary congregation* will bear witness in its social and cultural situation.[4]

An effective missionary congregation can also be looked at through a different lens. It not only seeks to fulfill its mission; it also seeks to assure its survival and growth. There is a biblical basis for thinking about missionary congregation effectiveness in these terms. It is found in Mark 4:26-29.

> And he said, "The kingdom of God is as if a man should scatter seed upon the ground, and should sleep and rise night and day, and the seed should sprout and grow, he knows not how. The earth produces of itself, first the blade, then the ear, then the full grain in the ear. But when the grain is ripe, at once he puts in the sickle, because the harvest has come."[5]

There are many levels of interpretation within this passage. At one level the passage describes the whole process for developing the kingdom of God on earth. Here the passage describes how the seed, or church, needs to adapt to its environment. At another level it lays out the elements of transforming faith. Here the passage reflects how the adaptation process occurs in an efficient way over time. At a third level it describes the fundamental processes of the missionary church. Here the passage notes how the seed goes through several stages of development and ultimately reproduces itself. The church nurtures discipleship of persons, which leads to outreach and the winning of new people, and a repetition of the process with the new converts. All of these levels look toward the church's investment in the future. Similarly, the church develops its capacities of leadership, physical facilities, and human and economic resources in anticipation of future needs.

This passage provides insight into defining more clearly the effectiveness of a missionary congregation. First, it behaves as an open system. It is porous and receptive to information from the immediate environment, its culture. It has goals for survival and growth. It adapts to information it takes in. It transforms resources into useful

4. John R. "Pete" Hendrick, "Congregations with Missions vs. Missionary Congregations," *Insights* 108 (Fall 1993): 59-68.
5. *Harper Study Bible*, Revised Standard Version, 1971.

outputs, and it undertakes this transformation in an integrative way. And finally, it builds its capacity as a living organism by continually changing and renewing itself and surviving.

Inhibitors to Effectiveness

There are at least six factors that can inhibit a missionary congregation from fulfilling effectively its mission and meeting its goals in today's culture. It is helpful to note their importance before proceeding with a more focused discussion of effectiveness.

Organizational Structure

The first inhibitor is an organization's structure. Structure in congregations today is typically a pyramid shape that places a lot of authority and responsibility in the hands of a few individuals at the top. The way that the typical hierarchical structure operates assumes that the environment or the community it operates within is static, routine, and predictable. Today's congregational structures were designed to support programmatic work, sets of activities that repeat and perpetuate themselves. The programs themselves are rather static, not necessarily changing; there's a routine about them and there's a predictability about introducing, implementing, and evaluating them.

Typically there are dual lines of reporting. The council/board receives information and gives direction to the professional staff and also to a committee structure. This committee structure usually reports directly to the council/board where its members are often leaders of each of the committees. This type of organization does not encourage collaborative and integrated work between the staff and the committee structure.

In such a structure there is inefficient vertical communication. As a command center, the council/board typically meets once a month to make decisions at an operational level. It then gives direction to the system by communicating downward to the program leaders and committee chairs. There is upward communication, but it is usually limited to reports from the committees or their chair persons. Leaders in this type of traditional hierarchy focus primarily on looking inside the congregation, paying close attention to the operations of the congregation, its government, the way it conducts itself, and its financial position. Leaders are not necessarily attuned to changes taking place in the larger context, or in modifying or adjusting the congregation's processes and ministries to stay in touch with those changes.

An alternative organization structure to the vertical pyramid is designed around an adhocracy. This consists of short-term structures such as task forces and ministry teams that have a short life that can be changed, modified, or eliminated if and when their work is determined to be over. This alternative kind of organization structure assumes a dynamic context, a culture that is in flux. Such a context is continually changing in nonpredictable ways and may create surprises for a congregation. The task forces and ministry teams provide for accountability and responsibility of the staff members. Staff typically lead the teams in their assigned work areas, and these teams report to the council/board through the staff. In this type of setting the council/board's primary purpose is to review the performance of staff within the congregation and give direction to them. On the other hand, the council/board is continuously gathering information about changes in the immediate culture and community. The council/board then directs modification or adaptation of the ministries to better fit the needs of its culture.

A second alternative structure to the vertical pyramid is the matrix, a rather new innovation in the church at large. It is designed around functional units within the organization, such as evangelism, social ministry, discipleship, education, small group ministries, and the like. Cutting across these functional units are the special ministries or projects that operate for a period of time. These structures use different people as needed, borrowing them from the functional areas. The special projects of ministries might include an evangelism drive, the implementation of a two-week crusade or the development of special worship events that attract the members of the community. These latter two designs represent alternative structures to support the missionary church in reaching the unique character of a culture in their community.

287

Jon M. Huegli

Command and Control

The second inhibitor to missionary church effectiveness is the command and control tendencies of professional and volunteer leadership. This may be called the "vision leader" method of introducing change within a congregation. Typically, a strong leader is introduced into the congregation in the form of a senior minister, someone who shapes a vision for the whole ministry. The problem with this kind of leadership is that it usually creates a dependency on the leader, who becomes the problem analyzer and the solution provider. There is a tendency with this type of leadership to focus inward rather than keeping alert to the changes in the external environment. Another problem with this type of leadership is that it tends to create bottlenecks. In one congregation, the senior minister wanted to introduce a pictorial church directory. He wanted to write the introductory text describing his vision for the church so he hung onto the directory for a four-month period figuring out just how to address his own vision. In the fifth month he left the church, and the directory was later found buried on the bottom of a file drawer.

An alternative to this sort of command-and-control type of leadership might be described as transformational leadership. The term "transformational" has taken on a particular attractiveness for today's organizations. Based on the work of Bernard Bass, the idea is that transformational leaders individually mentor and coach other leaders and members, refining the skills and developing the gifts that support the vision. This type of leader is a catalyst for change by helping lay out steps and leading the process from one change to another.[6] With individuals and in small groups, the transformational leader encourages and builds the confidence of leaders and followers to step out into the future in faith to fulfill the vision that God has for that congregation. Finally, the transformational leader expresses a resilience in the change process.

6. Bernard Bass, "From Transactional to Transformational Leadership: Learning to Share the Vision," *Organizational Dynamics* 18 (Winter 1990): 19-31.

Decision Making

A third inhibitor to the missionary congregation's effectiveness is that decision making tends to be operational and short term. There is a tendency for leaders to be inward-focused both at the professional level and at the volunteer leader level. A fair amount of attention is given to budgets, committee activities, concerns about maintenance, burned-out light bulbs, worn carpeting that needs replacing, and the boiler that needs attention. The decision makers in these environments tend to be out of touch with the spiritual development of the members. They tend not to ask spiritual questions. They tend to ask questions about how to maintain the church and keep it running.

As an alternative to this, the missionary congregation needs to be outward in its focus — leaders need to be involved in gathering information from outside the church. On a regular basis they should assess what is going on in the community in order to modify and adjust the ministries and the focus of the congregation. At the same time there needs to be an inward gathering of information. Leaders can form focus groups or undertake comprehensive or focused surveys of the congregation's spiritual health and well-being. During informal contacts with members, such as before and after services and events, leaders can center conversation on members' spiritual lives and how they are being nurtured. There can also be formal feedback on a regular basis with the staff, who provide reports on performance against goals and strategies. Effective missionary congregations regularly revisit their strategic or master plans, and challenge the assumptions or strategic issues that may need to be reconsidered for the future.

Member Commitment

A fourth area that inhibits the missionary congregation from fulfilling its mission is the ever-growing problem of low member commitment and deployment in the congregation. The primary reason for today's missionary congregation's ineffectiveness to minister in its context lies at the feet of its members and their unwillingness to sacrifice lifestyle commitments in lieu of investing in the ministry of the congregation. In today's culture, most church members are strapped for time due to 55+ hour workweeks and dual-income families that stretch the capacity of the family to nurture their young and develop wholesome lives with one another. Parents come home burned out and are not looking at their congregation as a place to do ministry, but rather as a place to be ministered to. They expect to be consumers of the services provided by the congregation. This places members in an entirely different role from that of sharing in the ministry and expanding the missionary congregation's capacity.

Member Deployment

A fifth inhibitor lies in how we go about deploying our volunteers in ministry in the church. Members are often deployed through persuasion and availability rather than through spiritual giftedness. In this process, people are not placed in ministries for which they have a passion. Often members are not trained for the positions they hold and feel frustrated about the time wasted in meetings, or in undertaking tasks that no longer have relevancy.

How can we more effectively gain member commitment and their deployment in a way that fulfills the congregation's mission? We need to understand members' passions, temperaments, and spiritual gifts. We also need to catalog the positions that are needed in a congregation to determine what gifts are required, and then proceed to match people to positions by their giftedness and their passion. It is possible to attract individuals to take part in the ministry of a congregation if such a process is developed.

This introduces an entirely different focus in understanding human resources. It is easy to access the untapped reservoir of energy and satisfaction that is available when individuals find a ministry that is valued and which they see as integral to the life of their congregation. Individuals will recommit themselves and will carve out time to give to the congregation when they feel that they are conducting ministry that uses their gifts and also provides them with satisfaction and fulfillment.

Communication

The sixth and final inhibitor to the effectiveness of missionary congregations today is their antiquated forms of communication, both internal and external. What are some indicators of the problem? First, most church leaders do not recognize that different constituents use different media and channels for specific kinds of information. For instance, in terms of looking at the events going on in a congregation, some readers will look to the bulletin for information. Others may look in the newsletter for information about events. Or for some, the prayer chain may function, not only to transmit prayer requests, but also to provide a channel for gaining information about members' personal lives.

The most frequent media used in churches today are written. This presents somewhat of a problem at a time when individual reading abilities are dropping into the fourth grade level. The reading ability of Generation X is lower than prior generations. Many of these persons have been used to receiving messages both visually and aurally rather than through the written word. Frequently the media we use are mostly one way; they focus on telling, rather than soliciting, information and needs. External communications are antiquated as well. Typically they consist of yellow page advertisements, brochures, and leaflets, which can hardly compete with other, more stimulating messages — the sound bites of today's mass media blitzes. Potential constituents have difficulty taking the time to read documents when it is much easier to tune in and turn on.

The alternative to the antiquated ways of communicating internally and externally is for congregational leaders to find out how their members go about obtaining information, and then putting information into the channels of media that are relevant for their congregation. Church leaders need to recognize that messages need to be redundant. For instance, the same message about coming events needs to appear in the bulletin as well as in the newsletter and possibly on a hotline. And finally, it is important for today's congregations to get online and in tune with the kind of media that people are using to receive information. These might include hotlines, TV monitor banks in church lobbies, e-mail, oral briefings, and kiosks.

These six areas are significant inhibitors to the life and well-being of missionary congregations. Substantive changes are going to be needed in many congregations in order for these problems to be overcome. This requires an understanding of the change process and what it will take to initiate such changes for a missionary congregation to be more effective.

Change Process

Organizational change processes will need to be employed to eliminate the inhibitors noted above. To understand and use a complex organizational change process, we first need to know how change affects individuals.

The human person and the missionary congregation are very similar when it comes to change. In order for us to survive and grow, we must take in information, interpret it, and then change and adapt to the demands placed on us by the external environmental. You and I do not have a choice about making many personal changes. Similarly, a congregation that does not take into account the changing demographics of its constituency — say, a replacing of the seniors with young marrieds in the community — and does not change ministries to appeal to those young marrieds may die of old age.

It is not a question of whether we will make changes, but rather of how we will make changes that can lead to a positive outcome with the least amount of pain. This raises another interesting dilemma — it seems that humans will not initiate change unless they experience enough pain to drive them out of the status quo. In addition, we will not seek an alternative way of doing things unless we estimate that the benefits outweigh the pain of remaining in the status quo.

A way of concretizing these concepts is to examine a formula for change as exhibited in the formula below:

$$(C = D + G + P + S > R)$$

- C represents change.
- D represents dissatisfaction with the status quo.
- G represents a clear and appealing goal or vision for the future.
- P reflects the presence of practical first steps that people can take toward the goal or toward the vision.
- S represents a supporting system that brings some level of new stability to the rest of the church while certain changes are made. And finally, all these must be greater than
- R — the resistance to the change itself.

To understand how change affects a missionary congregation, we first must recognize how it affects an individual, particularly when change is occurring at lightning speed in short cycles and rapid intervals. Think of a recent situation in which you were confronted with a change that brought on distress or "future shock," that is, a feeling that the demands were greater than your capacity to control. What were your feelings? What were the physical symptoms of distress? What were some of your dysfunctional thoughts and behaviors, which actually got in the way of or blocked the achievement of your change goal?

Daryl Conner, in *Managing at the Speed of Change,* suggests that individuals really pass through eight different phases as they attempt to deal with future-shock change.

1. Stability — precedes the announcement of the change; it represents the status quo.
2. Immobilization — shock, temporary confusion to complete disorientation; unable to relate to what is actually happening.
3. Denial — an inability to assimilate new information into the current frame of reference; change-related information is often rejected or ignored; "It won't happen to me" statements.
4. Anger — frustration, hurt, exhibited by irrational, indiscriminate lashing out, directed to those in close proximity who are willing to be supportive.
5. Bargaining — people begin to negotiate to avoid the negative impact of change; i.e., requests for deadline extensions, reassignments; this marks the beginning of acceptance.
6. Depression — resignation to failure, feeling victimized, lack of emotional and physical energy, disengagement from one's work; can indicate a positive step in the acceptance process; full weight of the negative change is finally acknowledged.
7. Testing — regaining a sense of control helps people free themselves from feelings of victimization and depression; acknowledging the new limitations while exploring ways to redefine goals.
8. Acceptance — responding to the change realistically; acceptance is not synonymous with liking it; the person is more grounded and productive within a new context.[7]

7. Daryl Conner, *Managing at the Speed of Change* (New York: Villard Books, 1992), pp. 132-35.

Initiating changes in the missionary congregation must take this understanding of personal change into account. Making a change in the congregation is a function of multiple individual decisions to make that change. When individuals feel that change or changes are outside their capacity to control, their responses are often dysfunctional. They may comply without internalizing the change, they may actively resist and disrupt the change, or they might passively resist and quietly undermine the change.[8]

Church members resist change and behave dysfunctionally when they feel a loss of control in the following: first, in social status and relationships with others; secondly, in skills and abilities they need in applying a new technology; thirdly, in the way the change takes place itself; and finally, in the future state to which the change will lead.

An individual works through three phases when he or she experiences personal change. These three phases are ending, transition, and a new beginning.[9] An example of ending might be where a church member is one of a group that is asked to serve as the core to start a second, contemporary service. This service is considerably different from the traditional one. The member must first experience an ending — a letting go of the old service. The change is both inward and outward, and there will be endings to the relationships with the people in the other service which have served as definitions of who that person is. The member experiences the pain of disengagement, dis-identification, disenchantment, and disorientation.

The second phase a member experiences is described as transition. It is a period of confusion and distress. The member brings to the transition phase a set of coping feelings and behaviors that allow him or her to deal with the loss or the ending and to adapt to the new. The member is learning new things, such as music and worship form and flow, and usually wants to appear confident and capable of adapting to new experiences. But there may also be a yearning for the old and familiar ways of doing things, even while surrendering to the new way. The member may experience dissonance, which is a degree of distress and a longing for the familiar while trying to accept the new. At this

8. Conner, *Managing at the Speed of Change,* pp. 136-37.
9. William Bridges, *Transitions: Making Sense of Life's Changes* (Reading, Mass.: Addison-Wesley, 1980).

point, the member feels most vulnerable and uncertain about the change, and disillusionment might set in with a retreat to the familiar.

The third phase is described as a new beginning. It represents an internalization and commitment to the change process. As new skills are learned, a distancing from old patterns and relationships occurs; a realignment of thinking and feeling begins; and there is an internal shift and identification with the new contemporary service. There is positive reinforcement to participate, and even more, to invite others and thereby legitimize the service as a part of the church growth process.

Implementing Change

In managing and implementing changes in the missionary congregation, the leader needs to apply a process, a strategy, and a plan. A change activity, such as introducing a new organization structure, can be thought of as a six-step process as represented in *Figure 1*.

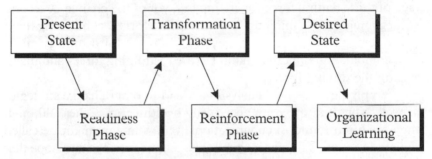

Figure 1: Stages of Change Process

The first stage might be described as defining the *present state* of affairs. We might say that the church is frozen into the status quo. The second phase — *readiness* — is an activity in which the change agent is preparing the church and making it ready for what is coming. In this phase, the change agent is developing enough pain in order to stimulate people in the church to search for alternatives and therefore look to make changes from the status quo. The third stage is described as *transformation,* which is similar to the kind of transition stage talked about in the personal change model. In transformation, the pain causes the status quo to heat up and flow into a transitional stage. The fourth stage is described as *reinforcement*. Once the change has been initiated, the change agent needs to provide enough reward and recognition to encourage application and use of the new skills or practices that have been introduced. The fifth stage is the *desired state*. Here the change refreezes and solidifies into an institutional form much like the status quo. This final stage would be called *organizational learning*. Here the church leaders look back on the change process and ask, "What can we learn from this? How effective were we? How efficient? How positive was the change? What might we do differently?"

A strategy for change can be developed around an assessment of the natural "restraining" and "driving" forces associated with change. Kurt Lewin developed the principle of what he called a force-field analysis. It identified those natural forces that drive a change forward in positive ways. He described those forces that were creating a level of resistance as "restraining forces."[10] A change strategy might be developed around an understanding of those two kinds of forces. One strategy might be to maximize the driving forces to take full advantage of those natural forces operating in favor of the change. A second strategy might be to minimize the restraining forces, eliminating them or reducing the negative effect they might have. A third strategy might be a combination of both minimizing the restraining forces and maximizing the driving forces.

Applying force-field analysis can lead to other change strategies as well. Not all of these are necessarily healthy approaches, although they are often found in congregations. One strategy might be called unilateral action. The leaders announce a major change and hope that it will take hold. This strategy emphasizes leadership, authority, and power. Action is directed downward through levels of staff, committee structures, and finally individuals of the congregation. A shift in a Sunday morning schedule may be an example of a downward and unilateral action where no opportunity is provided for members to voice their concerns or even challenge the assumptions about the new schedule.

10. Kurt Lewin, "Group Decision and Social Change," in T. M. Newcomb and E. L. Hartley, eds., *Reading in Social Psychology* (New York: Holt, Rinehart and Winston, 1947), pp. 330-44.

A second strategy could be described as replacement. Another way of describing it would be the modular strategy. Key staff and volunteer leaders are removed from positions as a means of reducing or eliminating resistance. If people do not comply with what the system requires they are extricated and replaced. For instance, a council may want to stimulate evangelism of the unchurched of the local community. A senior minister may resist this effort and may want to retain the status quo. If the senior minister does not cooperate, he may be replaced.

A third strategy is restructuring. People who resist or fail to adopt the intended change are sidelined. For instance, a senior minister who may not conform to the change demands of a council/board may be placed under the close scrutiny of an administrative or personnel committee. The committee then takes away his or her autonomy and scrutinizes performance.

A fourth form of strategy may be called manipulation and co-optation. In this strategy those who register disagreement are co-opted; that is to say, people who are opposed to the change are encouraged to publicly make statements in favor of it. Throughout the change process they are held to their word.

Another form of change strategy might be described as shared power. In this strategy, the leaders involve the people in planning, implementing, and evaluating the change process. A shared power strategy will probably be the most effective strategy for addressing resistance and for helping individuals positively make change.

The transformational leader also needs to articulate a plan, a clear goal or vision for the future; he or she needs to show how the vision supports cultural values, beliefs, and behavior of the church. Second, the leader needs to orchestrate pain messages in the church by involving people in analyzing the problems of the status quo in order to pull them away from the present way of doing things. He or she needs to involve people in researching steps for moving toward the vision or goal, and, in so doing, build a dominant coalition of people in support of the change.

Fourth, a leader needs to sober-sell the change; help people realize that adopting a change involves a learning curve in which there is a steep climb to learn new skills and methods and practices and that there may be loss in terms of effectiveness and efficiency in the way the church manages itself for a while.[11] In addition, the leader needs

11. Conner, *Managing at the Speed of Change*, pp. 140-41.

to initiate the first few steps of a change process. For instance, a church leader may obtain information from a focus group meeting with the congregation and introduce a pilot change in the Sunday schedule. Secondly, the leader may communicate the upcoming change, and indicate that the pilot is temporary and will be evaluated and reassessed after its initiation. Another task for the leader is to train people in the use of practices, processes, and methods which provide messages of confidence and self-esteem. In addition, the leader needs to reward and celebrate full accomplishment of the goal. This might come in the form of a tea or fellowship event, following a period of time when individuals who have taken risks are recognized and affirmed. And finally, the leader needs to follow up on feedback from members regarding the impact of the initiative of a change effort.

Research into the strategies and methods used to manage resistance has uncovered a number of reasons in how resistance is reduced and under what conditions this takes place.

Resistance is reduced when:

1. Key people are involved in the development of a plan of change.
2. Change is introduced in a way consistent with the church culture.
3. Participants see the change as reducing rather than increasing their current burdens.
4. The change offers the kind of new experience that interests church members.
5. Church members feel their autonomy and security are not threatened.
6. Participants have joined in on diagnostic actions leading them to agree on what the basic problem is and to feel its importance and impact on them.
7. The change is adopted by consensus following group discussion.
8. All members can see both sides of the question and recognize valid objections and take steps to relieve unnecessary fears.
9. It is recognized that innovations are likely to be misunderstood and misinterpreted, and if provision is made for feedback of views on the project.
10. Members of the church can begin to develop acceptance of each

other when there was disagreement and so experience support, trust, and confidence in their relationships with one another. Finally,

11. The change is kept open to revision and reconsideration if experience indicates a change in direction or emphasis.

In conclusion, in order for the missionary congregation to be effective today, it must engage its culture, both within its organizational life and at its contextual boundaries. That is to say, its boundaries need to be porous, capable of taking in information from the external culture and adapting to those changes. For the missionary congregation to accomplish its goals, to survive and grow into the future, it needs to consistently and continuously accept change as a way of life. And its leaders must have the capacity to lead and move the church from one change cycle to another. We've looked at how important it is for that change process to take place. We've offered some suggestions about how individuals and the church as a whole experience change, and the phases and stages that both must experience as they work through the change. We've suggested a number of different strategies that would be effective in managing and handling resistance to change, which is a natural part of the change process. And we have focused on how to improve change processes by including individuals in the planning, implementation, and evaluation of the change as a fundamental way of succeeding in leading the church through change.

Today's church leaders need to take on transformational leadership qualities. First, they need to articulate the shared vision through imagery, and continuously attract people toward that vision. Second, they need to help lay out the necessary steps to initiate the change. Third, they need to develop the competencies and skills in the individuals who will make the change happen. Fourth, they need to build the confidence of these individuals so that they can envision themselves fulfilling the actual vision. The effective missionary congregation anticipates and proactively engages in continuous cycles of change.

Epilogue

Many of the articles in this book point out the changed location of the church within the postmodern condition. Terms that are used to convey this shift include: marginalized church, alternative church, and counter-culture church. One of the more helpful ways of conceiving this shift was introduced in the closing address of the conference by Mary Jo Leddy. She drew on the experiences of the Czechs who were seeking reform of the communist regime that controlled their country, and of their leader Miroslav Václav Havel. These people conceived of themselves as a "parallel community," one that did not capitulate to the dominant culture it lived within, but learned to live by a different set of values. Applying this image to the church summed up for many participants the primary message of the entire conference. Because it serves as a helpful summary of the articles in this book, her message is included here as an epilogue.

The People of God as a Hermeneutic of the Gospel

MARY JO LEDDY

I note with interest that it is 8:30 on Saturday morning. This is quite early for so many people to be gathered together. Most people don't do this on a Saturday morning. It makes me mindful of a true story that I heard about a young rabbinical student in New York City who was doing his field education in a mental hospital. One of his first responsibilities was to give a homily for the high holy days. He worked diligently on this homily and polished it. It was his intent to culminate this homily with the question, "Why are we here?" On the particular night he was to give it, all the people — the old people and the mental patients — came into the little synagogue. He got up and proceeded to get going in the rolling cadence of his sermon. He talked about what had happened 4,000 years ago, 2,000 years, 1,000 years ago, in Spain, and at the time of the Holocaust. Finally, he boldly introduced his question: "Now I ask you, 'Why are we here?'" From the very back of the little synagogue an old man got up and said, "Well rabbi, maybe because we're not all there."

So here we are on Saturday morning at 8:30 talking about the gospel and culture. On a more serious note, another story. I work with refugees and live in a community with them at the Romero House in Toronto. One day a young refugee girl came to our doorstep. Her English wasn't too bad, because she had spent some time in the United States on her way to Canada. So after we had gotten some information clear, I invited her to the back of the house, to the kitchen, for a cup of tea. In the kitchen, there is a window that looks out over the backyard. We were sitting having tea, and she turned to me after she had looked out the window and asked, "Who lives out there?" I said, "Nobody lives out there." She said, "But someone must live out there?" I said, "Nobody lives there, it's a backyard." She said, "But, house out there, person out there." I looked out the window and I couldn't see, and she said, "House out there." I looked again and the only thing I could say, and the words dropped like stones from my mouth, "It's a house for a car." She looked at me and asked, "A house for a car?" And I said, "Yes, it's a garage. It's a house for a car." She quietly reflected, "A house for a car."

In the days that followed, I drank a lot of tea and looked out the window staring at my garage. Finally, I shared the story with our ministry team, and we concluded, "Let's turn the house for a car into a room for a person, because in our city there is a great housing shortage." So we drew up the plans. Of course, we had to go to City Hall to get a building permit. I don't know what such departments are like in your city, but ours is circular in every way. I went from office to office to office, to turn a house for a car into a room for a person. Of course the conversation — and I am summarizing by about two feet of paper here — went like this. "Well, you can't do that." And I would ask, "Why?" The standard response was, "Well because, because then everybody would do it." And I would say, "RIGHT!" And they would say, "But then there wouldn't be room for the cars." And the conversation went around and around.

So we couldn't turn the house for a car into a room for a person. We sat and looked at the garage some more, and finally we concluded, "We will turn it into a house for God! We will make it into a meditation room." This time, however, we were not going to go to City Hall, because we were quite sure there would be some code that would prevent us from turning the house for a car into a house for God.

So there the garage sits — you wouldn't know it from the outside — but from the inside, it's a very simple Meditation Room where refugees from all nations come. It is a place where those of us who live with them share a space where we acknowledge that we are of God, and that we are for God. It is in the garage that we are reminded that there is space in our hearts for people, because God has made room in his heart for all of us.

Our garage is only one small space in a culture that seems to have endless houses and cars. In general, I don't question the usefulness of cars, but I do question the mythology that surrounds the car in this culture. There is a myth that the car will make you happy — that Buick saves and sets you free. The myth is that a car will give you meaning and purpose, that if you just drive fast enough you will think that you are going somewhere. This myth is so strong that you can even hear some people say at times, "I will die if I don't have it." The car of course does not bring happiness. It does not bring satisfaction. Even if I buy the Buick, there is the Ultima, and once again I am dissatisfied and unhappy. The car, of course, and the house for the car, are merely symbols for the culture we live in. It is what I call the "culture of money."

Although we come from many and diverse cultures on this continent, we all live in the culture of money. Ours is a profoundly materialistic culture. It is soul destroying, and it is dispiriting. I think that all of us at this conference, at conferences such as this, are quite conscious of how debilitating, how dissipating are the more conspicuous forms of consumerism. But I think we have yet to probe how our economic system, how capitalism, transforms us at the deeper levels of our spiritual being. Let me briefly evoke the soul-destroying dynamics of capitalism. First, capitalism is driven by consumption. Second, there can't be production unless there is consumption. And third, we become consumers to the extent that we listen to the words of advertising which we see in images.

We get the message that we must have more to be more: that we must have more things, that we must have more experiences, that we must have more relationships, even perhaps, that we must have more spirituality. We come to believe that we have to have all these things to be happy. What first seems like a luxury soon becomes a basic need such that we feel, "I will die without it. I won't be happy without it." We get the message that it is never enough. We desire more, we need more, it is never enough. This unsatisfied need was pointed out by Richard Mouw, who quoted the Rolling Stones, "I can't get no satisfaction."[1] We get the message that it is never enough, and slowly but surely that message transforms us at the deeper levels of our being. "I

1. Richard J. Mouw, "The Missionary Location of the North American Churches," p. 14.

don't have enough," becomes "I am not enough," becomes "I am not good enough," until finally we conclude, *"I am not enough."* There is a feeling of powerlessness. It is common for this feeling to begin to translate into a vague feeling of guilt — not specific guilt, but vague guilt.

This becomes a very perplexing situation. In the most powerful nation, the richest culture on earth, most people generally feel powerless and vaguely guilty. The self-help gurus tell us that the vast majority of our families today are dysfunctional. How can this be, that there is such an ideology of powerlessness in the most powerful culture on earth? It is because the culture of money has its own psychology and spirituality. Pastorally speaking, I think that in our churches we often treat vague powerlessness, vague feelings of guilt, and general feelings of unhappiness as if these were personal problems requiring psychological treatment. Please note that all of this leaves the culture of money intact, a culture based on the myth that if we only have more, we will be happy. It is a myth that gets stronger, especially when we begin to doubt that things will get better and better. We want more and more because then things will get better.

Our culture, of course — and all of the speakers at this conference have addressed this — has been profoundly shaped by modernity. The myths of progress and technology are quite something, like if we just work hard enough, if we just think smart enough, things will be better tomorrow. We believe that things will be better for our kids, if we just think hard enough and work hard enough. However, this secular confidence is now being shattered. We now need to reckon with the possibility that tomorrow might not be better. But even more critical than that, we need to face up to the question, "What if there won't be more for us or for our kids?"

To the extent that the church has buttressed this secular confidence, calling it hope, the confidence of the church is also beginning to shatter. The church shares in the crisis of meaning within this culture, even though we've worked hard at trying to resolve it. We've had a lot of conferences on the "how-to's." We've designed strategies, developed visions, and devised programs to shore up the culture. But confidence is now eluding the churches as much as it is the culture within which the churches live. A crisis of meaning is now beginning to be internalized by churches in both the United States and Canada. A "crisis of meaning" is an abstract term, but it becomes more concrete when we pose it as a question. "Does it matter, does anything I do matter, does my existence make any difference?" There are many symptoms today that people are asking such a question. Some people feel paralyzed in the church, in the face of the huge crisis confronting us. Other people keep very busy, and are exhausted, or burned out, because they have tried so hard to find meaning.

The gospel tells us, however, that we do matter and that the choices we make are important. Within the church today, liberals and conservatives cope with this crisis of meaning in different ways. In our present time of decline, liberals are retreating into forms of personal development, personal rights and projects. Freedom is their renewed word. On the other hand, conservatives, as they see the social fragmentation and moral chaos, are seeking to reimpose some kind of order on society. These are really just two ways of trying to cope. There is a lot of time and energy being wasted in the churches as these two groups fight it out. These positions, however, are more alike than they know. In reality, they are just mirror images of one another.

Beyond coping or beyond mere survival, what is the call of the church at this hour? Can we go beyond that temptation which Jim Brownson called the temptation to manage risks?[2] Can we enter into what Doug Hall called redemptive self-doubt?[3] Can we, as Bill Burrows asked, realize that we are in over our heads, that we cannot save ourselves?[4] By God's grace, the answer is "Yes." Here and there, at conferences such a this, I hear people say, "I don't know what to do anymore. I've tried everything and it's not working." This is the moment of ultimate defeat, of a humiliation for those of us who were raised with the modern mind-set, which told us that we are supposed to know. We are supposed to be in control. We deeply believe that if we just think hard enough, and work smart enough, it will work out. The admission that, "We don't know, it's not working," that admission may just be the beginning of faith.

This beginning of faith may be the time when we really begin to become Christians, and really begin to experience Christian commu-

2. James V. Brownson, "Hearing the Gospel Again, for the First Time," p. 136.

3. Douglas John Hall, "Metamorphosis: From Christendom to Diaspora," p. 76.

4. William R. Burrows, "Witness to the Gospel and Refounding the Church," p. 202.

nity. It may just be the time when, together as communities of faith who don't know, we finally are ready to inquire, "To whom shall we go? Show us the way." When we feel the burden of our times, and bring its weight to the foot of the cross, only then will we know the blessing of the cross. Only then will the privilege of being called disciples, of being missionaries in this context, take on meaning in this time and place. Ours is a time of a call to live in real discipleship. Ours is a time of a real captivity where we are subject to our own Babylonian empire. We are in captivity, and here I think we can hear anew the words of Daniel when he spoke to those who lived in a time of captivity: "We have no leader. We have no prophet. We have no priest. Still, we follow you unreservedly. We do not even know how to celebrate your name. We no longer have the words. We no longer have the images, and yet we follow you unreservedly."

Many of us have not yet acknowledged, however, that it is not working. We need to turn again to the Scriptures to read as for the first time the words that always mean more than we can say. We need to hear Jesus say to us that, "We will not be happy if we crave many things. We will only be happy when we come to desire God above all things." This desire is who we really are. Do we trust this, do we trust it in ourselves, do we trust it in others? As Richard Mouw observed, such a desire for God does exist in this culture.[5] We must never doubt that. We can spend a lot of time talking about the "hows" of awakening the desire for God. But we must ask ourselves at a level deeper than words, "Do we really believe that people in this time and in this place desire God?" It is a desire, of course, that will never be filled completely, but it can be paradoxically satisfying in a way that nothing in this culture can be.

We come to really know this when our lives are grounded in gratitude. In Jesus, we see a person whose life was grounded in gratitude. To live gratefully is to move outside the vicious circle of cravings that the culture sets up within us. To live gratefully is to say, "Enough, what has been given is enough. We don't need more." Most of us in a capitalistic culture, I think, have a rather ledger view of life. Life consists of a series of pluses and minuses, and we add them up periodically to see where we stand. Sometimes it comes out more positive, and sometimes more negative. In the process, we miss the amazing

5. Mouw, p. 4.

thing that we even have a life to add up. We miss that we have been given this chance — this one chance — not a perfect chance, but a real chance to live, to know God, to love one another.

To live gratefully is to begin to understand the economy of grace, that God's love is offered to each of us for free, and is offered to all of us forever. How different this is from the economy of capitalism which works for only a few, rather than for the many. The message of Jesus, indeed of the Bible, is that God loves us for nothing — not for what we do, not for what we produce, not for how we look, and not for what we earn. God's love is for no reason. It is unearned. This is good news for this culture.

To live in this awareness is to begin to ask the foundational religious question. I think that question is, at the most basic level, "Can we love God for nothing?" When we know God loves us for nothing, only then do we begin to contemplate, "Can we love God for nothing, for no reason? Not for what we will get out of it. Not for how God shores up the church and helps us increase and multiply. But rather, can we love God because God is God?" That is the beginning of worship. Worship services are not yet worship when we ask what we are going to get out of it. Our questions betray us, "Is it meaningful? Is it relevant? Was it a good sermon?" I'm sure that you have had this experience, when coming back from a service on Sunday a person will ask, "How was it?" You know what they are asking, "Was it a good sermon? Was the music good? Who was there? How many were there?" All these are questions that think in terms of loving God for *something*. Now, when people inquire of me," How was it?", I have my little act of resistance and I say, "Valid."

To our profoundly unhappy and dissatisfied culture, Jesus tells us that we are unhappy because we have allowed others to define happiness for us. He says you will be happy if you are grateful, if you are poor in spirit. You will be happy if you are pure in heart. You will be happy if you do not crave many things, but desire only God. You will be happy if you choose to make real in this world the economy of grace. You will be happy if you hunger and thirst for justice, even if you suffer and die for it. To those who have lost a sense of meaning and purpose, as our culture drifts and disintegrates, Jesus tells us that our lives have meaning. We are exhorted to: "Love one another. Do good. Become salt, yeast, light." These exhortations, however, are not a blueprint. What they represent is a vision of faith. It's not about how, its about why.

We will only know it is true if we try to live it. You see, it is not possible for us to solve questions of meaning. We can't really figure them out, but we can live them out. In this regard, I live with a number of young people who are volunteers at the Romero House. They come and work there for nothing for a long time. I believe it is in their patient service that they often discover the love of God. I think the disciples had often heard the words of Jesus, but it was when they saw his life, when they saw how he lived, and more importantly how he died, that they could say to themselves and to the early church, "We know he meant what he said."

We who live as the church between gospel and culture must say what we mean, what Jesus means, with the testimony of our lives. There is really no shortcut. There is no program, no meeting, no study, that can take the place of saying what we mean with our lives. Only our lives give weight to our words. Still a question remains. How can we sustain a gospel sense of happiness, of meaning, and of purpose in this culture? It's not good enough just to make these assertions.

Doug Hall mentioned his experience with the Christians of Eastern Europe.[6] I have found the writings of Miroslav Václav Havel extremely helpful as indicating a way, not an answer, but a way for us to live in the situation we now find ourselves within in North America. Havel, as you may know, was a dissident playwright under the communist rule. Under that regime, he was jailed. Now he is the president of the Czech republic. He has written a book called *Living in Truth,* in which there is a wonderful essay called "Power in the Powerless."[7] He analyzes how the people in his country learned to live in the dominant materialistic culture of communism before it fell.

He says that during the 70s and 80s it seemed to them, the dissidents, that the system would never change. It seemed impermeable and immutable, an iron curtain, a system that dominated every aspect of people's lives. It wasn't just "out there," it was also "within" — within their heads, within their hearts, within their spirits. It looked like it would never change, even though it was a system based on a lie. The lie was quite simply, "You'll be happy if you have enough things."

6. Hall, p. 70.
7. Miroslav Václav Havel, *Living in Truth,* ed. Jon Vladislav (London and Boston: Faber and Faber, 1989).

So Havel and other dissidents began to ask, "How can we live the truth in a culture based on a fundamental lie, especially since the lie is in our heads? How can we begin to live into the truth? We desire so much more than just things. We want something to hope in, a reason to believe."

So in his country, as in other iron-curtain countries, people began to set up what he called "parallel cultures." They had underground study groups. They studied Plato. They had drama. They had music groups. They wrote novels and poetry, and published them underground. He called this a "parallel culture." It was not a counter-culture because, he said, it was impossible for us to live totally outside the system. You cannot live outside a culture. But you can create within it zones and spaces, where you can become who you really are. It is in such places that one can speak the truth, where one can gather with others who share that truth. This went on for years, not without difficulties, but for years. Over time, the truth became stronger and stronger, and at a certain point people began to walk in the streets and to say to the system, "We don't believe you anymore." And the system fell. It fell, not because of the power of Western nuclear equipment, but because the people said within the system, "We don't believe you anymore." It was a vision that had been nourished within those parallel cultures.

Of course, the story doesn't end there, and that's another thing to reflect on. But it does seem to me that Havel's notion of a "parallel culture" is what Bill Burrows meant when he said the church could be the "zone" that connects us with home truth.[8] It could be what Doug Hall meant by a "diaspora existence."[9] I think each one of us needs to reflect on what this might mean concretely in our local situations. I can't do that reflection for you. I simply want to point out that I find the notion of "parallel culture" helpful because it's not the same as saying the church is a counter-culture. It is far more than saying we're building a counter-culture to say that we are looking for the enemy within. I think that the sense of a parallel culture, one in which we become grounded in truth, is a much more powerful notion. It is in such a culture that we can be nourished in thought, poetry, imagination, and religious practices. It is in such a culture that we can truly seek to become God's people.

8. Burrows, p. 192.
9. Hall, pp. 67-68.

Another person who has reflected on this very helpfully is the Appalachian poet and philosopher Wendell Berry. He is very critical of the U.S. government. But he notes that if all he did was criticize his government, he would become just like what he was fighting against. He is also critical of those who say very thoughtlessly, "I love my nation — America right or wrong." He says that both those who critique and those who declare unblinking affirmation hold such views as abstractions. He says it is important that we become grounded in some specific place. This place for him is a piece of land in a certain county in Kentucky where he is grounded in the life of a rural community. But this plot of land could also be a set of streets, a community, a region, a stretch of beach, a river, or a town. It is whatever becomes for us, as he says, "the beloved country." It is when we are located in a smaller space, a beloved country, that we are able either to critique our government and not be overwhelmed by it, or are able to say, "Yes, we love this country."

So also within the church, we cannot just criticize it or just blindly say we're loyal to it. We must first find somewhere, some local church, that we call "a beloved community." It needs to be somewhere, a specific place where we have come to know the gospel as good news, as the saving and redeeming grace of God. It is from such a beloved community that we can then critique both the culture and the church, and where we can also affirm both of them in a real way.

In closing, I want to say that small communities, beloved communities, and parallel cultures are not necessarily powerless. At this conference we have heard the critique of Christendom, and I think most of us share the very convincing critique of the problems it had with power and control. I believe in this critique, but I also believe that at times we deny it. Christendom was a model in which the church exercised power in a worldly way, where power was manifested as both domination and control. We do well to reject this model of power. But many of us have often taken on the Enlightenment model of power as our alternative, where power is knowledge and to know is to control. We need experts, we need people who can tell us how to do things, how to work things out. We will also do well to reject this worldly form of power. But are these the only models of power?

We need to redefine power, not to become powerless, but to think about what power really means. I don't think that the only power is a power of domination, nor is it a power of predictability and control. As Christians, we know a different power, the power of the Spirit. Here, I think, we should carefully consider that the Spirit's power is not a thing that some people have a lot of, and others have a little of. It's not a quantity in that sense. It is not a piece of pie that is divisible, and therefore there always have to be power conflicts. We might do well to think of spiritual power as an energy. Spiritual power is the energy that happens when people are in-relation to one another. It is what happens in-between people. This is a power that happens when people gather in Jesus' name. When they interact, there is energy, there is power. This is why significant change has often happened when small groups come together.

This is what happens when Christians function as a parallel culture. Power has nothing to do with numbers, it has to do with the quality of relationships, what happens in-between. It is important for us to remember that the power of God arises when we are in-relation to God. This is how power was experienced in the upper room. People gathered, they talked, and they prayed. They were there in a sustained interaction. And then there was power between them. It was not a power that any one person possessed. They were possessed by the power of God, because they were in-relation to God as a community. And then they went forth with great power as missionaries. Today, just as 2,000 years ago, may we too come together in-relation and experience power, the power of the Spirit of God.